Sacramental Theological Thinking in the African Symbolic Universe
Affinities with John Henry Newman

European University Studies

Europäische Hochschulschriften
Publications Universitaires Européennes

Series XXIII
Theology

Reihe XXIII Série XXIII
Theologie
Théologie

Vol./Bd. 525

PETER LANG
Frankfurt am Main · Berlin · Bern · New York · Paris · Wien

Isidore Okwudili O. Igwegbe

Sacramental Theological Thinking in the African Symbolic Universe

Affinities with John Henry Newman

PETER LANG
Europäischer Verlag der Wissenschaften

Die Deutsche Bibliothek - CIP-Einheitsaufnahme

Igwegbe, Isidore Okwudili O.:

Sacramental theological thinking in the African symbolic
universe : affinities with John Henry Newman / Isidore
Okwudili O. Igwegbe. - Frankfurt am Main ; Berlin ; Bern ; New
York ; Paris ; Wien : Lang, 1995
    (European university studies : Ser. 23, Theology ; Vol. 525)
    Zugl.: Rom, Pontificia Univ., Urbaniana, Diss., 1994
    ISBN 3-631-48130-6

NE: Europäische Hochschulschriften / 23

BX
2203
.I48
1995

ISSN 0 721-3409
ISBN 3-631-48130-6
US-ISBN 0-8204-2942-2
© Peter Lang GmbH
Europäischer Verlag der Wissenschaften
Frankfurt am Main 1995
All rights reserved.

Satz: Unitext, Frankfurt am Main

Printed in Germany 1 2 3 5 6 7

Dedication

To my sisters Gerardine, Clementina and Chibuzo

ACKNOWLEDGEMENT

My gratitude to my parents, Sylvester and Josephine Igwegbe. From them I learnt the virtue of hope, the sense of wonder and the ability to discover the hand of God in all things. I am grateful to my brothers, sisters and relations for their love and support.

I sincerely thank my bishop, Most Rev G.O. Ochiagha for permitting me to study dogmatic theology. To my moderator, Prof. J.O. Egbulefu my deep thanks for accepting to moderate this work and constructively guiding me. My correlators, Profs. R. Lavatori and J. Stern helped me through their erudition and scholarly criticisms. Prof. Stern's thorough knowledge of Newman's thought was a valuable enrichment for this study. To them I remain deeply grateful.

My indebtedness goes to the Sacred Congregation for the Evangelization of Peoples for the bursary award. I wish to express my debt to d. Luigi Toffolo and the Spresiano Christian community, d. Battista Barbaresco, d. Andrea Pierdonà, Pastor Dalsing, Pastor Gellner, Fr Maurice Jiwike, the families of Mr and Mrs D.N.Nwoke, Fidelis Muo, Baldo, Barbon, Cremonese, Salvadori, Bader, Payr, Henneken, Frau Bröcker, for their love and solidarity.

I thank Fr Folley and Mrs Gael Ayers for correcting my scripts; and to Conferenza San Vicenzo (Spresiano), the families of Wechelmann, Bockholt, Ute Winkelkötter, the staff of Peter Lang Verlag and to all others I say a big thank you.

ABBREVIATIONS

I. JOHN HENRY NEWMAN

Apo.	Apologia pro Vita Sua
Ari.	The Arians of the Fourth Century
Ath.	Select Treatises of St. Athanasius vol.i, ii.
AW	John Henry Newman: Writings, ed. Henry Tristram
Call.	Callista: a Tale of the third Century
Cons.	On Consulting the Faithful in Matters of Doctrine
DA	Discussions and Arguments on Various Subjects
Dev.	An Essay on the Development Christian Doctrine
Diff.	Certain Difficulties felt by Anglicans in Catholic Teachings vol.i,ii.
Ess.	Essays Critical and Historical, vol.i, ii.
GA	An Essay in Aid of a Grammar of Assent
HS	Historical Sketches, vol.i, ii, iii.
Jfc.	Lectures on the Doctrine of Justification
LD	Letters and diaries of John Henry Newman, ed. Dessain
LG	Loss and Gain: the story of a Convert
Mix.	Discourses addressed to Mixed Congregations
Moz	Letters and Correspondence of John Henry Newman, ed. Anne Mozley, vol.i, ii.
OS	Sermons Preached on Various Occasions
OUS	Fifteen Sermons preached before the University of Oxford
Prepos	Present Position of Catholics in England.
PPS	Parochial and Plain Sermons, vol.i-viii.
SSD	Sermons bearing on Subjects of the Day
VM	The Via Media, vol.i, ii.

II. OTHERS

AAS	Acta Apostolicae sedis
AFER	African Ecclesiastical Review

CCL	Corpus Christianorum, Series Latina
CSEL	Corpus Scriptorum Ecclesiasticorum Latinorum
DS	H.Denzinger and A.Schönmetzer, Enchiridion symbolorum, definitionum et declarationum de rebus fidei et morum, (Barcelona, 1973)
ITQ	Irish Theological Quarterly
PG	J.Migne, Patrologia Graeca
PL	J.Migne, Patrologia Latina
ST	Summa Theologica

GENERAL INTRODUCTION

PREAMBLE

The Creator of the world left his seal on creation. By means of this seal God can be known to a certain extent even where the biblical revelation is not known. In fact natural man is not insulated from or aloof to religious sentiment. Men have the idea of God from God Himself.

Man desires his creator. This is manifested in man through spontaneous and conscious acts and gestures. It in turn may be abused, suppressed, or denied but the light in the conscience of man cannot be put out.[1] God, on the other hand, leaves Himself to be found. He reveals himself while man discovers him through religious experience. Thus there is a kind of exchange between God and man.

In this divine-human contact, man does not encounter God as naked and pure. No one can withstand the face of the triple holy God or directly encounter He "... whose home is in inaccessible light ... (I Tim 6,15-16;Exod 33,22-23). God's self revelation to human beings is usually realized symbolically: as a burning bush, a glorious court and sanctuary, a dazzling light, the voice of a child, etc. (Exod 3,2-6;Acts 9,3;). Such a symbolic way of manifesting makes God accessible to man since the complete disparity between God and his human interlocutor makes an unmediated presence and communication impossible.

CHOICE OF THEME AND SCOPE OF STUDY

Religious man knows no other God than the clothed God. Symbolic clothing means that God, in order to communicate with human beings, clothes Himself in a created medium that retains a creature-like quality but is transparent to an interpretative recognition of God. The history of

---

1 Cf. Newman, *Callista: a Tale of the third Century*, 314; see *also D. Martin Luthers Werke, Kritische Gesamtausgabe* (Weimar, 1883ff), 19,206. Henceforth cited as WA.

salvation is weaved in sacramental signs and symbols. God "accomoda-tes" Himself to man's capacity to understand and approach him.

Such "accomodations" which make the material world sign and instru-ment of the Sacred constitute the basis of the Sacramental Principle. God's relationship to human beings, then, is necessarily sacramental. He comes to men through mediation. History, events, persons, while retain-ing their uniqueness, contain and relay God's message. Thus by the will of God, created things have a potential for "sacramental vocation". As long as human beings have existed sacramental structures, gestures, events characterize the history of God with them.[2]

In the whole history of God and humanity, God communicates with human beings sacramentally and human beings in turn respond through a sacramental complex: persons, gestures, words, things, etc. Man's ten-dency to "symbolise" or to express himself through the language of signs and symbols is neither owed to the creativity of the human spirit nor to a simple fact of imitatio Dei[3].

Man's tendency to symbolise is rather owed above all to the fact that through signs and symbols religious man reassures himself of the reality of God and of God's steady presence[4]. In order to act or think sacramen-tally as befits the religious precincts, religious minds need symbols as stepping stones. Thus religion and its expression are realized through sacramental symbolism. Religion is therefore, a universe of sacramental signs and symbols.

Signs have no intrinsic but rather mere conventional relationship with what what they signify (for example: red traffick light means 'stop' while a red sanctuary lamp means divine presence and indicates the blood of the Lamb of God poured out for the remission of sins).

Symbols rather have permanent intrinsic relationship with what they symbolise though they are not always capable of communicating a sa-cred person and salvific reality. For instance bread is always for the sat-isfaction of hunger. But while a kitchen bread satisfies natural hunger, an altar bread satisfies supernatural hunger. The relationship between a symbol and the symbolised is a priori and as such comes from God.

---

2 Cf. Herbert Vorgrimler, *Sacramental Theology*, Collegeville, 1987, 3.
3 This would mean that man as the image of God, expresses himself through signs and symbols in the same way as God does when he reveals himself.
4 The yearning of the elected people for "... a god to go at the head of us ..." and the casting of a golden calf can also be explained from this perspective (Exod 32,1-6).

Symbols, whether objects (e.g Temple), institutions (e.g. monarchy), or words, generally refer to secular or sacred reality. As such they *only* indicate another but not always another's thought. Sometimes, symbols can indicate the presence or name of another, but not another's mind.

The symbols which go beyond mere "indication"; and contain, represent, communicate and effect what they indicate, be it a sacred person (God, Holy Spirit), be it a sacred thing (grace, eternal life), are sacraments. Sacraments are more than symbols. Sacramental thinking is therefore, more than symbolic thinking.

In this work, the word "Sacramental" is used to express the *experience of faith*, by which a religious mind, through the Son of God and in the Spirit perceives "more than" and "real and efficacious presence" in certain sensible objects or symbols.

From this premise, two conclusions can be drawn: i) Sacrament or Sacramental is proper to Christian faith. ii) whatever is sacramental must be necessarily symbolic, but not everything symbolic is necessarily sacramental.

As the Church is so she thinks. Being Sacrament of Christ, she does things sacramentally. If the Church by her nature as Sacrament of Christ thinks sacramentally, then the work of Evangelization of the peoples which seeks to build up the Church out of them into one people of God, includes the project of making the peoples think sacramentally.

But can the African people cultivate such a sacramental thinking? Responding affirmatively to this question, the thesis presents the African symbolic thinking as a point of departure for the Evangelization of the African people. Since a major reason of contemporary African Protestant intelligentsia for rejecting conversion to the Catholic Church and culture, is not so much the prevailing offuscation of the link between symbolic and sacramental thinking but also the fear of losing their intellectual liberty to the Magisterium, the dissertation seeks to clarify the need for a passage from the mere symbolic to more perfect sacramental reasoning and there upon deploys the example of Newman, the erstwhile Protestant theologian who later converted to the Catholic Church.

Such an example dispels fear and renders superfluous the prejudices against the magisterium which hinder self transcendence into a more Catholic (all embracing) pattern of thought and life on the side of the contemporary Protestant intelligentsia. The motivations therefore for choosing Newman as the object of this research are three fold.

In Newman's mental framework one can notice some affinity with the typical African manner of thought and African Traditional Religion which are replete with symbolic categories and signs of a "semi-sacramental-character". It is through the "symbolic path" that African religious minds reach to God.

It therefore cogent to inquire into the relevance a thinker like Newman can have for the African in his passage from symbols to sacraments, from symbolic to sacramental mode of thought, from semi to real sacraments.

The work is a kind of "dialogue" with the African Protestant intelligentsia who may be convinced of the veracity of Catholic Church and its doctrines but who are scared of embracing her for fear of losing their liberty to the Authority of the Catholic Church.[5]

By entering into dialogue with the Protestant intellectuals, the dissertation proposes Newman as a prototype of an intellectual who perceived the "stumbling block", doubted and refuted it; but whose intelligence of the Christian faith brought to such heights from where he became convinced of the veracity of the Catholic Church and her sacramental system. It can be argued that the more insight one has into the mystery of faith, the more one is in a position to see beyond the human fabric of the Church.

Newman's decision to enter the Catholic Church was not casual. His step belonged to the tradition of conversion. Many intellectuals: St. Paul, St. Augustine, etc. took similar steps before him. This is why Newman has got a validity beyond British boundaries.

If Newman's road was hazardous, it is all the more easier for the African Protestant intelligentsia today. It can be easier for the African intelligentsia because the Catholic Church has all this while made an improvement: shifting from monologue to dialogue, from being exclusive to inclusive.

---

5   In fact the question of the number of the sacraments and the problems it arouses have been softened in many hearts. Many Protestants have realised that accepting more than two sacraments means the recognition of the operation of God and the presence of grace in many other aspects of the life of the Christian. Many have realised that multiple sacraments represents the multiplicity of grace. And nobody refuses grace. For many, then, the doctrine of more than two sacraments is appealing. The stumbling block however, is often the so-called "monster", the "usurper of individual religious freedom and the place of Christ", that is to say, Authority, as they see it represented in the Catholic Church.

The Protestant intellectuals have purposely been chosen as interlocutors because in the Protestant confession, the theologians are almost or constitute the magisterium. They are the "spokesmen" of the masses, the interpreters of Scripture and doctrine. In a way the thesis addresses itself to the intellectuals in order to reach the protestant masses.

Thirdly, this work also addresses other Africans: Christians, non Christians and cultural Revivalists. To these Africans, the thesis attempts to put across the message that those things which constitute the fulchrum of African traditional society and Religion, were "figures" or "shadows" of a higher reality definitively manifested in Jesus of Nazareth. And being as they were providential but provisional, they have been overtaken by the presence and claim of Him whose "images" they are.

To this group of Africans this study proposes a "simbolic reinterpretation" of the fulchrum of African traditional religious society in the light of Christ in the manner as the Jewish Christians reinterpreted their Scripture in the light of Christ. The average African's itinerary to the triune God has to pass from natural symbols, through the God-man, Jesus of Nazareth to the Trinity. This is to say that the African believer has to pass from symbol to sacrament.

In trying to identify the relevance of Newman's Sacramental thought pattern to Africans, an attempt is made to consider Newman totus, that is, a global overview of his life and sacramental theology that puts his meaning for African believers in a better light.

Consequently, the point of departure is a "relevant survey" of Newman's life in order to pinpoint what influence his experiences in life had on his theologising. The reader should bear in mind that this investigation is not concerned with a biography of Newman as such, rather what has been indicated is a relevant biographical sketch of what helps to highlight Newman's sacramental theology.

With the mention of Sacramental theology, it is common to immediately think of the seven classical sacraments. With work on the sacraments, it is also commonly expected that such a work will deal with one of the seven sacraments if not all. This is not the case with this work.

The reader can be sure that "Newman's Sacramental theological thought" does not mean Newman's tracts on the individual sacraments, but his theology as based on sacramental reasoning. For from a particular frame of mind or a pattern of thought flows a particular theological system.

Above all, sacrament and sacramentality are wider than the seven classical sacraments in Newman's theology. He understands that the sacraments strictly called are the realization of the Sacramental Principle.

The investigation endeavours to show how the Incarnation is the fundamental realization of the Sacramental Principle, and how the Incarnation is the foundation of what may be called a "catena sacramentorum". The "catena sacramentorum" is a complex of realities in the New Dispensation which serve as "channels" the for prolongation of the meaning of the Incarnation. Such realities are the Church as the sacrament of Christ and the Sacraments in the strict sense of the term, and Tradition and Authority which have sacramental characters.

One can now begin to understand why sacraments and sacramentality are wide, and why in handling the theme under examination, all the component parts of the "catena sacramentorum" have been taken into consideration.

There is a system underlying Newman's sacramental theology. Without Christ there is no Church, no Tradition, no Authority, no Sacraments. Analogously, without the Church there is no Tradition. And without Tradition there is no Authority or Sacraments. Yet Incarnation, Church, Tradition, Authority are closely related to each other.

Hence, sacramental theology in Newman refers here to this catena, and the Relevance of his Sacramental theological thought for African believers, means the relevance of this catena or at least its principles.

The consequences of Newman's Sacramental theology for believers in search of God in the African Context should be seen in the right perspective. In this work, "African context" does not merely refer to the "piece of geography" or "geographical location" (though this is also included), the primitive and dark continent, in short a part of the third world, as it is commonly thought by some. Africa is more than this.

Our "African context" embraces the subsaharan Africa. This means that we are dealing with a vast area with important differences between many ethnic groups. Subsaharan Africa is not a static entity. It has seen continuous mutations. Yet underlying these changes, there are elements or essentials which resist change and endure through time and which characterize Africa.

Such "enduring essentials"[6] are African cultural heritage made up of profound religious beliefs and practice, a peculiar philosophy of life and behavioural patterns such as the "joy of living", sense of mystery and wonder, communal spirit, and above all that rhythm of heart beat called "sacramental" or symbolic mentality, by which «creation is a language of God, a legible signification of His idea, and by which the sense of unity of nature is seen as a book of signs, to be read, ad manifestandam invisibilium Dei sapientiam».[7] Together these features or traits constitute the African genius.

These common African features in the midst of diversity and huge differences permit one to speak of Africa in general terms. When therefore the African genius is under discussion, making generalizations about Africa and Africans is difficult to avoid.[8]

While it is true that most of the visible structures of the traditional society on which the African genius was formally based may have disappeared, the African genius is still alive. Africa or African genius will not perish as long as Africans do not perish, since Africa is not just represented by the geographical subsaharan zone and its visible characteristics, but is present in the souls of its people. The soul is the true dwelling of the identity of an individual or a people. It is there that African genius is located.

African religion is clustered with sacred symbols, which provide Africans with a vision of reality in its positive and negative aspects. And African Traditional Religion asserts that the good life for man is to live realistically and religiously. Among such a cluster of sacred symbols, the ancestors, tradition, community, wielders of authority, ritual ceremonies, on which African value-systems lean, are particularly conspicuous.

In daily life, the values and attitudes which people hold and aspire to are the direct expressions of their dominant beliefs. Scholars, such as Shorter, have underscored the importance of these values and symbols in

---

6 see Frank A. Salamone, "Continuity of Igbo Values After Conversion: A Study in Purity and Prestige', in *Missiology*, vol.3, no.1, 1975, 35; also K.C.Anyanwu and E.A.Ruch, African Philosophy, Rome, 1984, 79.

7 Robert M.Stein, 'Signs and Things: The Vita Heinrici IV Imperatoris And the Crisis of Interpretation in Twelfth-Century History, *in Traditio. Studies in Ancient and Medieval History, Thought, and Religion*, vol.xlii, New York, 1987, 106.

8 see Jan Heijke, 'Belief in Reincarnation in Africa', in *Concilium*, 5, October 1993, 46.

evaluating the impact of change on traditional African socio-cultural and religious life:

> Such values are the most important and lasting elements in African traditional religion. Long after the visible aspects of African religion have disappeared and some cults and practices have ceased to be performed, the values and even many of the themes, survive in the minds and hearts of men who have adopted one of the immigrant religions.[9]

The ancestors, tradition, community, ritual ceremonies, etc. form the African catena sacramentorum. In considering the relevance of Newman's sacramental theological thinking for African believers, the reader can then intuit that African catena sacramentorum is the central focus.

METHOD AND STRUCTURE

In the first part, effort is made to dispose the reader by concentrating on who Newman was, what he was, which helps to understand why his Sacramental theology is the way it is.

The second half of the first part deals with the Search for God in Africa with special emphasis on the complex African symbolic universe, which is central to the whole thesis.

The second part is an exposition of Newman's sacramental theology. The approach here is systematic. The point of departure is the Incarnation, which is the chief sacrament, outside of which there is no sacrament or sacramentality. Newman's sacramental spirituality and hierarchical understanding of sacramental dispensation are highlighted as well.

Where necessary, Newman has been allowed to speak for himself through his works. In some cases, attempts have been made in this study to interpret his thoughts in order to bring out what was considered latent.

In the third part, an attempt is made at the examination of African catena sacramentorum in the light of Newman's sacramental theological thought. Generally the method adopted is expository, analytical, interpretative and dialectical, which in theological research is known as oratio obliqua.

---

9   Aylward Shorter, *African Christian Theology*, London, 1975, 111.

I am aware of the limits of every theology as a human reflexion on God and divine things. This in itself is a limit of this study. Added to this is the fact that Newman left no systematic work on sacramental thinking. Like in the works of other Newman scholars before, it was necessary to scan through his writings and collect relevant fragments. The experience of such a work has been like working to create something approaching a mosaic.

To use the words of Roderick Strange, «such a disparate material required careful handling. At times it was like a detective mystery, at times like working on a jigsaw».[10] It is hoped that the evidence has not been forced in a way incompatible to Newman's way of thinking.

There has been no study of Newman in an African Context. This is therefore a pioneering work and as such has its shortcomings. The eccentric positions adopted in this work should not be imputed to none but author. These and other mistakes found herein remain his full responsibility.

SOURCES

The sources of information used in this work are principally five. The first is the writings of Newman. And the second, the British writings of the 17th-19th centuries. The third group concerns the works on Newman. The fourth, works on Africa and African Religion. The fifth group is general.

Concerning the works by and on Newman, the staff and libraries of the International Centres of Newman Friends in Rome, England, Austria, and Israel were helpful and prompt in supplying information requested. Rich and useful information and materials were obtained from different libraries of the following universities: in Rome, La Sapienza, Gregoriana, St. Thomas Aquinas, and Urbaniana; and in Germany, Osnabrück, Münster, Tübingen, and Maternushaus, Köln.

During the elaboration of this thesis, it became apparent that Sacramental theology is a field where abstractions and conceptualizations yield scarce dividend. Sacramental theology is more of life than "logia".

---

10 Roderick Strange, *Newman and the Gospel of Christ*, New York, 1981, vii.

It is a question of being involved: Tua res agitur. Sacramental thinking is therefore, that pattern of thought of the sons of the Church; it is that mental framework of those who "know" and follow the ways of Jesus Christ.

PART ONE:

HISTORICAL SETTING
DISPOSITION

1.1 PRELIMINARY REMARKS

This part begins by situating Newman in his historical context. His background is relevant to his reflection on the sacraments, since nobody speaks from nowhere.

Those stages of his life that helped to shape his thought will be examined. Afterwards, there will be a brief examination of the African religious world, its deep symbolic characteristic, its encounter with Christianity, the outcome of the encounter, and the future prospects.

1.2   JOHN HENRY NEWMAN

1.2.1   RELEVANT BIOGRAPHICAL SKETCH

1.2.1.1   EARLY BEGINNINGS

John Henry Newman was born in Victorian England on February 21, 1801, a period profoundly disturbed by the repercussions of the French Revolution and the beginnings of industrialism. Newman's England saw religion sink to a low ebb. The "great age of progress", rather like our own, did not see religion as something as important as technical science. His was a world that thought many of religious values to be "useful", but not imperative or binding.

The other factor which contributed to the steady deterioration of the state of religion in the nation was the Protestant tradition of individual judgment and the splintering of Protestantism into numerous sects. Newman once noted that «All over the world the Church is breaking up».[1]

His family enviroment and school were not touched by the blowing wind of Evangelical revival. His parents were affluent, simple believers

---

1   SSD, 432 (14.4.1833).

and belonged to what Newman later called the "national religion of England" or "Bible Religion" which "consists not in rites or creeds, but mainly in having the Bible read in Church, in the family, and in private".[2] Thus, he was "brought up from a child to take great delight in reading the Bible".[3]

At home, he learned high moral standards, and a sense of providence but no direct devotion or personal religion. Newman was also taught the Anglican catechism, but had not yet formed religious convictions.

By the age of fourteen he was toying with ideas of unbelief and of his own self-sufficiency, reading atheistical books and objections to Christianity such as Tom Paine's tracts against the Old Testament and some of Voltaire's and Hume's essays. At this period, his general frame of mind was the classical ideal, namely, to be virtuous, but not religious since he "did not see the meaning of loving God".

To confound matters further, many intellectuals regarded the articles of the Christian faith as either very elastic indeed, or else of no importance. Christian teaching was being eroded by liberal rationalism which, at best, was indifferent to religion.

His was the century of evolutionary theories which shattered mankind's ideas of a static earth just as the astronomical theories of the sixteenth century had. Newman often compared these two revolutions of thought which radically altered the human perspective and seemed at first destructive of all traditional beliefs and values. No wonder they were greeted coldly in some quarters. However, historical changes are irresistible.

The world of the nineteenth century was opening its mind to new discoveries in science or history and new investigations in philosophy. The fresh air of the intellect was very exacting. The Roman Catholic Church was wary of this new current and suspiciously shrank from this new knowledge. It felt horror at evolution.[4]

Newman was courageous enough to take the bull by the horns, to take the theories of evolution seriously. He was brilliant enough to discern from the wisdom of the world what was valuable to read and to interprete the Christian faith, a feat which distinguished him from his peers and contemporaries.

---

2   GA 43.
3   Apo 15.
4   Cf. Owen Chadwick, Newman, Oxford, 1983, 1.

One can say that to some extent, the theory of evolution influenced but did not determine his theory of development of doctrine. Owen Chadwick has called Newman the first theorist of Christian doctrine to face the challenge of modern historical enquiry.[5]

1.2.1.2 THE WAYS OF PROVIDENCE

The happy and affluent life of Newman's family was seriously shaken when, in March 1816, as a result of the depression after the Napoleonic Wars, ruin hit the world of business and the bank of John Henry Newman's father was not spared. Newman was summoned home to be told the sad news. In the summer when Newman's school vacated, he could not go on holidays and remained alone at school. As Newman brooded over this fate he fell sick.

Newman interpreted this sickness as the "heavy hand of God" which brought about "a great change of thought" in his life. The sickroom at school became a symbol of horror and desolation, and its memory was later to reoccur during another serious illness in Sicily in 1833. These experiences of 1816 marked his first conversion, an experience so crucial that he always considered that it had caused him to undergo a fundamental change.[6]

Newman did admit that the incident of his sickness at Ealing in 1816, "allowed 'room' for particular 'influences' to be brought to bear - those of 'an excellent man, the Reverend Walter Mayers ..., from whom he received deep religious impressions ... Calvinist in character, which were to him the beginning of a new life'".[7]

The great change occasioned by this conversion led him to accept the dogmas of Christianity, viz, Incarnation, Redemption, the Gift of the Spirit, Heaven and Hell and the Catholic doctrine of the war between the City of God and the powers of evil, etc. Newman's own very words are indicative of what he went through,

When I was fifteen, ... a great change of thought took place in me. I fell under the influences of a definite creed, and received into my intellect impressions of dogma, which, through God's mercy, have never been effaced or obscured. I have changed in many things: in this I have not. From the age of fifteen, dogma has been the funda-

---

5 Cf. Ibid.
6 see LD XXXI 31 (19.2.1885).
7 Apo 17; also AW 29 (13.6.1874).

mental principle of my religion: I know no other religion, I cannot enter into the idea of any other sort of religion; religion, as mere sentiment, is to me a dream and a mockery. What I held in 1816, I held in 1833, and I hold in 1864. Please God, I shall hold it to the end.[8]

The incident of 1816 led Newman to the conviction that Christianity was founded on the objective nature of dogma.[9]

In fact, early notebooks betray his intellectual justification of his new certitudes. It was a conversion of the whole man, the turning point of his life. For the famous Newman scholar Charles Dessain, «his unfolding mind was captured by the Christian Revelation, his heart by the Scriptural ideal of holiness».[10] When later he found himself in the throes of another crisis in 1859, he recalled the event of 1816 as he scribbled an address to his Creator in his private diary:

Thy wonderful grace turned me right round when I was more like a devil than a wicked boy...He saw in Himself the sin of intellectual pride, the demon of self-sufficiency. But God "mercifully touched his heart," and his whole being was changed, an event to him more certain than he had hands or feet.[11]

In the divine-human encounter the initiative comes from God. God's grace has touched the lad Newman and had changed his being. No one remains the same again after encountering God. Abram became Abraham after encountering God, Saul of Tarsus became Paul after encountering Christ. The encounter with God is a transforming one. For Newman this encounter was a conversion, one that made him a new man.

It may be pertinent here to point out that in 1816 Newman was converted to a Evangelicalism of a Calvinist brand.[12] Newman was converted to a "reactionary type" of Evangelicalsm within the bosom of the

---

8   Ibid., 4; also 49.
9   Cf. Josef Cardinal Ratzinger, 'Newman gehört zu den grossen Lehrern der Kirche' in *John Henry Newman. Lover of Truth*, (Edited by Maria Katharina Strolz & Margarete Binder), Roma, 1991, 143.
10 Charles Stephen Dessain, 'John Henry Newman. A Short Biographical Sketch', in *Newman Studien*, vol.10, 1978, 21.
11 AW 250 (15.12.1859).
12 Newman was not wholly and entirely converted to Calvinism. Sheridan has cautioned that «The term Calvinist as used by Newman and others in connection with English Evangelicalism has none of the precise doctrinal content it has when used with reference to continental Calvinism» (Thomas L. Sheridan, *Newman On Justification*, New York, 1967, 16).

then Anglican Church against the prevailing religious atmosphere of the time in which, for reasons well articulated by Sheridan, very little but the outward forms of Christianity had been preserved.[13]

Against this background, the Evangelicals posited a subjective religion or a spiritual Church as the right relation of the individual soul to God, which was brought about, not so much through the aid of worship and system an ordered society might provide, as through the free, interior action of the Spirit of God upon the spirit of the individual man.[14]

The result of this religious tendency was that external forms of worship, ordinances of grace were contestedly emarginalised as empty formulae. In fact «By the time ... Newman joined these ranks, the denial of the doctrine of baptismal regeneration had come to be the touchstone of Evangelical orthodoxy».[15]

Coming from such a background as he did, for a religious person like Newman, the meaning of the discovery of a visible Church and sacraments, especially baptism as a means of grace, cannot be over-emphasised.

It was when struggling with the problem of baptismal regeneration in 1825 that he wrote: «It seems to me that the great stand is to be made,[16] not against those who connect a spiritual change with baptism, but those who deny a spiritual change altogether».[17]

From 1828 onwards, Newman discovered the sacraments as efficacious means of grace. Froude was very helpful to Newman in this regard. This discovery of the sacraments as the means of grace is a matter of great importance to Newman's sacramentology as it later developed. Newman ridiculed as "fighting God's battle in their own" those who have little regard for outward signs of grace. According to him such people,

For outward signs of grace ... substituted inward. It is surely too bold an attempt to take from our hearts the power, the fulness, the mysterious presence of Christ's most holy death and resurrection, and to soothe us for the loss with the name of having it.[18]

---

13 Cf. Thomas L.Sheridan, Ibid.
14 See Vernon Storr, *The Development of English Theology in the Nineteenth Century*, London, 1913, 67, quoted in Sheridan, Ibid., 23.
15 Vernon Storr, Ibid.
16 The second part of this work echoes some of Newman's stand.
17 AW 78 (13.1.1825); also 208 (29.5.1825).
18 Jfc. 57.

When they discovered the sacraments as means of grace, some other Tractarians had similar reactions against the Evangelical "tendency".[19]

1.2.1.3 THE FLAME OF THE KINDLY LIGHT

At the time of his conversion Newman became convinced that God willed him to lead a single life,[20] an element of what he felt to be a total dedication to God's service, a radical following of Christ as a eunuch.

This choice was later to facilitate his entry into the Catholic Church's hierarchy. This intuition, even at this prime stage of his life, is an indication of the secret "Kindly Light" at work in his life.

After this "great change of thought", he discarded Tom Paine and the modern sceptics and began to live an intense spiritual life.

In 1822 he was elected a Fellow of Oriel, then at the peak of its fame and, «at that time the object of ambition of all rising men in Oxford».[21] This election raised him "from obscurity ... to competency and reputation". He felt at the apex of his life and "never wished anything better or higher than ... to live and die a fellow of Oriel".[22]

In 1824 he was ordained a deacon in the Church of England and on 29 May 1825 ordained as a priest. For some time he worked as a curate at St. Clement's. In 1828 Newman was appointed vicar of St. Mary's Oxford. He then became a tutor at Oriel, a position he soon lost as a result of skirmishes with the Provost Hawkins; much to his great regret.[23]

As he wrote desperately to Froude in 1830 "all my plans fail", a frustration understandable if one considers Newman's love for teaching and education: «from first to last, education ... has been my line»,[24] and the possibility of pursuing that line appeared now very remote.

---

19 F.W.Faber, for example, after entering the Tractarian circles in 1836 admitted the fact of his conversion and gave the reason thus in a letter to Roundell Palmer: «I have departed from the evangelical doctrine of faith; and it is because I have departed from their sad notions of sacramental grace» (J.E.Bowden, *Life and Letters of Frederick William Faber*, 5th ed.. London, n.d., 47; see also R.Chapman, Father Faber, London, 1961, 33). This is almost the best expression of the sentiment of those who are convinced of 'having escaped from darkness to light'.

20 Cf. Apo 19-20.

21 AW 49 (3.12.1820).

22 Ibid. 63. (12.4.1822).

23 see LDXXII 218 (20.4.1866).

24 AW 259 (21.1.1863).

1.2.1.4 FROM DISAPPOINTMENT TO DISCOVERY

As a consequence, Newman invested his teaching energy into his sermons at St. Mary's Church. As well as pouring his teaching acumen into sermons, Newman wrote his first book during these years.

Hugh Rose and Lyall, editors of the New Theological Library, invited him to write a volume on the Councils of the Church[25] but the vastness of the material led him to concentrate on the preliminaries of the Nicene Council.

He became so interested in the development of the Arian party, that the Council itself was relegated to a summary in the end. The fruit of this labour was published in 1832 as *The Arians of the Fourth Century*.

His immersion in the world of Christian antiquity and the discovery it led to shook his conception of the Church of England. Newman considered the Anglican Church to be a branch of the Catholic Church. But about 1839 he began to doubt his conviction: «For the first time a doubt came upon me of the tenableness of Anglicanism».[26]

As he reflected on the theological controversies of the early Christian Antiquity and their consequences, he was struck by St. Augustine's phrase "securus judicat orbis terrarum". He was stunned by the resemblance he saw between the fourth and fifth century crisis and the sixteenth century Reformation.

Using this Augustinian principle to read these events, Newman entertained the idea that if "Rome" was right in the fourth century, she was right as well in the sixteenth century.[27]

According to his discoveries the Roman Church was the Church of the Fathers, and the Anglican Church was in schism for actions taken in the sixteenth century. Those who left the Church were necessarily wrong: "securus judicat orbis terrarum".

Given that it was so, Newman had another hurdle to jump, namely, the additions and corruptions which he believed the Roman Church had made to the teachings of the primitive Church. Serious consideration of this question led him to believe that the so-called additions or corruptions were new formulations of old truths, progress of the human intel-

---

25 Cf. Apo 25-6.
26 Ibid., 108.
27 Ibid.; see also Ess.II.101 (Note on Essay X).

lect as it reflects on divine mysteries. In short, there is development of doctrine.

Consequently Newman was led to take a decision, that of joining the Roman Church which he did on 9 October 1845. Later he documented the burning question which prompted him to decide crossing the carpet:

> This I am sure of, that nothing but a simple call of duty is a warrant for any one leaving our Church; no preference of another Church, no delight in its service, no hope of greater religious advancement in it, no indignation, no disgust, at the persons and things, among which we may find ourselves in the Church of England. The simple question is can I (it is personal, not whether another person, but I) be saved in the English Church? am I in safety, were I to die tonight? Is it a mortal sin in me joining another communion?.[28]

On Newman's step to abandon the Anglican Communion, one can say that truth resists dissection. Unity, integrity and totality are its intrinsic characteristics. And if it is inflicted dissection it yearns for completion.

If the voice of conscience which warns of the missing link is obeyed, a search for the whole is embarked upon. Such was the case with Newman. In leaving the Church of England and joining the Church of Rome, Newman looked for the one and true Church (of the Fathers) with whose faith he had tried to live:

> I looked at her (the Catholic Church); at her rites, her ceremonial, and her precepts; and I said 'This is a religion'...[29]

Newman's decision to join the Church of Rome cannot be put down to instability of youth. He was fortyfour when he took this step. His spirituality and theological outlook were largely formed: men rarely change drastically at such an age.[30]

The process of a true conversion is not often without something of the shadow of the cross upon it, some renunciation of what one is or has, indeed a risk. Yet in the case of Newman it was a veritable birth-pang.

It was this that made him in the most true sense of the word the "father" of many souls - he had passed through most of their difficulties

---

28 Ibid., 231.
29 Ibid., 340. Newman realised that his former idea of the Anglican Church as a branch of the Catholic Church has been a dream.
30 see Geoffrey Powell, 'The Roots of Newman's "Scriptural Holiness". Some Formative Influences on Newman's Spirituality', in *Newman Studien*, vol. 10, 13.

beforehand for them, so that they could courageously make the leap, confident that they would not hit their feet against a stone.[31]

Pope John Paul II has described Newman's journey in the following terms:

> Newman's itinerary speaks to us of deep intellectual honesty, fidelity to conscience and grace, piety and priestly zeal, devotion to Christ's Church and love of her doctrine, unconditional trust in divine providence and absolute obedience to the will of God wherever it might lead.[32]

1.2.1.5 THE CATHOLIC NEWMAN - A BRIEF SURVEY

After being received into the Catholic Church, Newman's next step was to decide what to do with his life since he was no longer in the service of the Anglican Church. Newman's bishop, Wiseman, knowing the stuff Newman was made of, suggested he should enter the Catholic priesthood, a suggestion which Newman accepted gladly.

The following year Newman proceeded to the College of 'Propaganda Fide' in Rome in order to prepare for ordination to the priesthood, which he received on May 30th, 1847.[33]

Once in Rome, Newman felt that if he were to join a religious order, he could no longer quite be himself or continue the work he had begun. Attracted to the life of the Oratory founded by St. Filippo Neri, Newman decided to join and introduce it into England.

Intellectually speaking, the option for the Church of Rome did not entail much change for Newman. His ideas and principles were the same. As he wrote, «I was not conscious to myself on my conversion of any change intellectual or moral ... I was not conscious of firmer faith in the truths of Revelation».[34]

Nor did his submission to the Church of Rome blunt his sharp and constructive critical spirit. As he once told a fellow convert, J.H.Polen, «we must throw ourselves into the system. But a firm unruffled faith in

---

31 Cf. Henry James Coleridge, 'A Father of Souls' in The Month, No 70, 1890, 161.
32 John Paul II, *Letter to the Archbishop of Birmingham, His Grace George Patrick Dwyer*, AAS 71 (1979) 657-658.
33 Cf. LD XI 269-273 (6.11.1846).
34 LD XIX 10-11 (6.1.59); see also Apo 317.

the Catholic Church should not preclude giving a strong expression to our common conviction of the miserable deficiencies which exist».[35]

Newman was a "big catch" for the Catholic world. This is evidenced by what followed his conversion to the Roman Catholic Church. Anxious to make use of so eminent a convert, the authorities, namely the Irish bishops, invited him to establish a Catholic University in Dublin for the English speaking world.

1.2.1.6 NEWMAN'S DESERT EXPERIENCE

Like Saul of Tarsus, Newman was hunted by "Jews" and dreaded by "Christians"; tagged apostate and straggler by Anglicans and called hypocrite and half-Protestant by Catholics, thought a crypto-Romanist while in the Church of England, and a crypto-Protestant when he was in the Roman Catholic Communion. Throughout his life many of his critics "spotted" him out as bearing the "mark of Cain".

For many years he lived in continuous tension. He once noted that his life, actions, words or silence were so monitored and interpreted so that he had to be cautious in everything. In the face of growing antagonisms and misunderstandings he groaned on January 21 1863:

O how forlorn and dreary has been my course since I became a Catholic! Here has been the contrast - as a Protestant I felt my religion dreary, but not my life - but, as a Catholic, my life dreary, not my religion!.[36]

This situation and sensation, this state of mind, this cry from the depths I call the desert experience of John Henry Newman. Cuthbert Butler rightly pointed out that but for the Cardinalate at the end, Newman's Catholic life was from the human point of view a sad one:

The trials were real, and beyond the lot of most of us ... His life was, from the standpoint of this world, a long drawn tragedy ... it was indeed the way of the Obscure Night. The explanation of it all is to be found in the spiritual diaries and intimate letters reproduced by Ward: not insensibility but acceptance, resignation, faith, trust, are the dominant notes.[37]

---

35 Ibid.
36 AW 254; see also LD XVIII, 488 and 521. He documented similar sentiments again in 1865, 1868 and 1874 consecutively.
37 Cuthbert Butler, The Life and Times of Bishop Ullathorne, vol.II, London, 1962, 313.

Newman's elevation to the Cardinalate vindicated him against "the cloud" with which extremists had surrounded and labelled him as unsound, half-Protestant, half-Catholic and sealed approval by the Church of his labours and plight. His elevation to the Cardinalate was a clear indication that he did not topple by following the "Kindly Light" to where it had led him.[38]

Having briefly seen the panorama of Newman's eventful life, let us now explore the factors that helped to make him what he was and still is today, since men are to some extent formed by their enviroment, what they see and hear, and the company they keep

1.2.2 FORMATIVE ELEMENTS AND SOURCES OF NEWMAN'S THEOLOGICAL THOUGHT

1.2.2.1 SACRED SCRIPTURE

Regarding his attitude to Scripture, Newman was to a certain extent faithful to the principle of the Reformers and Anglican tradition. In one of the Thirty-Nine articles of the Church of England, the comprehensive character of the scriptural principle is amply applied and illustrated:

Holy Scripture containeth all things necessary to salvation; so that whatsoever is not read therein, nor may be proved thereby, is not to be required of any man, that it should be believed as an article of the faith, or be thought requisite or necessary to salvation.[39]

Newman was faithful to the Anglican tradition in that he accepted the normative role of Scripture and drew his inspirations from its fundamental teachings. We have already seen him describing his parents as following the "Bible Religion", of which Sandys said: «the foundation of our religion is the Written Word, the Scriptures of God, the undoubted records of the Holy Ghost. We require no credit to be given to any part ... of our doctrine, further than the same may be clearly and manifestly

---

38 see LD XXIX 63 (6.3.1879), 72 (11.3.79).

39 *The Book of Common Prayer and Administration of the Sacraments and Other Rites and Celebrations of the Church According to the use of the Church of England*, Article VI, Cambridge, n.d.; see also Philip Edgcumbe Hughes, *Theology of the English Reformers*, London, 1965, 19.

proved[40] by the plain words of the law of God, which remaineth in writing, to be seen, read, and examined of all men».[41]

Stern, like all Newman scholars would admit, notes that «first from his parents and later from his Evangelical teachers he had learnt to consider the Scriptures as the locus of God's conversation with man».[42]

Thanks to his parents and the Anglican Church's heritage, Newman was groomed in the habit of scriptural thinking. He was brought up from childhood like Timothy to take great delight in the knowledge of the Bible. Attention to the Scriptures punctuates his whole life and thought. Even after he had joined the Catholic Church as a preacher he thought in constant conversation with the Scripture.

According to Blehl, Newman's theology and preaching are characteristically scriptural:

He often displayed a profound understanding of the spirit of the Bible and perceived inner connections between its parts particularly between the Old and the New Testaments. He likewise could project himself imaginatively into the events related in Scriptural truths and realities to his overriding purpose of expounding Scripture in a way that it will be relevant and applicable to the spiritual needs of his congregation to lead them to holiness.[43]

1.2.2.2 TEACHERS, CONTEMPORARIES AND FRIENDS

Newman's roots as we have so far seen reveal that he took Revelation very seriously.[44] Fundamental to Newman's formation was his Evangelical teacher Walter Mayers, who, by force of character, conversations and sermons, and with the aid of several useful books, all of the school of

---

40 As we shall see in subsequent pages, proof in Newman is to be understood in the light of testimony of the Tradition and the witness of the Fathers of the Church and not to be understood in the modern sense of the term.

41 Sandys, *Works*, London, 1844, 221.

42 Jean Stern, 'The Institutional Church in Newman's Spirituality', in *Newman Studien*, vol.10, 30.

43 Vincent Ferrer Blehl, 'The Spiritual Roots of Newman's Theology' in Stolz and Binder (edts.), John Henry Newman. Theologian and Cardinal, Rome, 28 1981.

44 see Archbishop Robert Runcie, 'Newman's Journey and His Intellectual Example Should Encourage Us Never To Rest Complacently', in *John Henry Newman. Lover of Truth*, 157.

Calvin put into Newman's hands brought about "the great change"[45] in Newman's life.

Newman tells us what he had read: From Romaine he learned the doctrine of final perseverance, namely that the regenerate cannot fall away, a doctrine which he came subsequently to abandon at about the age of twenty-one.

Thence he passed to Thomas Scott's *The Force Of Truth*, the famous Evangelical commentator on the Bible, «who made a deeper impression on my mind than any other, and to whom I almost owe my soul.

It was he who first planted deep in my mind that fundamental truth of religion»,[46] namely, the trinitarian root and grounding of the Christian faith, the deeper understanding of which was Newman's personal effort. Hence he took these proverbs from Scott: "Growth the only evidence of life" and "Holiness rather than peace".[47]

It was from Butler's *The Analogy of Religion Natural and Revealed to the Constitution and Course of Nature* (1736), that Newman learned that the very idea of an analogy between the separate works of God leads to the conclusion that the system which is of less importance is economically or sacramentally connected with the more momentous system.

On this book of Butler, Newman asserts that "its inculcation of a visible Church, the oracle of truth and a pattern of sanctity, of the duties of external religion, and of the historical character of Revelation, are characterisitcs ... which strike the reader at once".[48]

A voracious reader, Newman read Newton's *On the Prophecies*, and as a result he became convinced like most Anglicans of his day that the Pope was the Antichrist predicted by Daniel, St.Paul, and St.John. As he remarked, "my imagination was stained by the effects of this doctrine up to the year 1843".[49]

It was the Vicar of St. Mary's and later on a Fellow of Oriel of name Hawkins who led Newman out from his world of biblical unilateralism

---

45 Cf. David Newsome, 'The Evangelical Sources of Newman's Power' in Allchin and Coulson (ed.), The Rediscovery of Newman, London, 1967, 12.

46 Apo 108.

47 Cf. Ibid. 109.

48 Ibid. 10; see also K.Dick, 'Das Analogieprinzip bei John Henry Newman und seine Quelle in Joseph Butlers Analogy' in *Newman Studien* vol.5, 1962, 9-228; Seynaeve, J., *Cardinal Newman's Doctrine on Holy Scripture*, Dissertatio, Universitas Catholica Lovaniensis, 1953, 221-228.

49 Ibid. 6-7.

to the understanding of the importance of Tradition in the life of the Church.[50]

Henceforth the fact was brought home to his consciousness that Christian faith was handed on down the generations as a recognizable body of teaching by a necessary "living guide",[51] and that the Word of God is intelligible in the light of the Living Tradition.[52]

Newman acknowledged that "... as to doctrine, he [Hawkins] was a means of great additions to my belief; ... he gave me the *Treatise on Apostolical Preaching*, by Summer, from which I was led to give up my remaining Calvinism, and to receive the doctrine of Baptismal Regeneration".[53]

Richard Whately drew the shy young Newman out from his shell and developed his capacity for vigorous thought. Under the influence of Whately Newman recognized the Church as a divine appointment with institutional laws and structures, independent of the state.[54] It was Whately «... more than anyone else» who, «broke me from the remnants of Evangelical influence»,[55] said Newman.

The personal influence of John Keble and Froude deepened the truths he learned from Butler and the Fathers. In the end Newman found it difficult to analyse Keble's precise influence upon him, because it was the total influence of a person rather than a number of ideas.

Yet one can suspect that «one aspect of that personal influence which was significant, was what Keble showed Newman, by his own practice as much as by his teaching, of the ways in which intellectual pride, to which Newman's private journal shows him to have been prone, could be countered».[56]

Richard Hurrell Froude taught him devotion to the Mother of God, belief in the Real Presence and the full doctrine of sacraments. In a new way Newman learnt,

---

50 Cf. Ibid. 112.
51 Cf. Dev. 97.
52 Cf. Stern, J., *Bible et Tradition chez Newman*, Ambier-Montaigne, Lyon, 1967, 62-65.
53 Apo 21.
54 See AW 66 and 69, (14.11.1826)
55 LD XV, 175 and 179 (10.10.1852).
56 Geoffrey Powell, 'The Roots of Newman's Scriptural Holiness ..., 17.

...that there was a visible Church, with Sacraments and rites which are the channels of invisible grace ... after reading Anglican divines on the one hand, and after prosecuting the study of the Fathers on the other ...[57]

Walter Mayers gave Newman a copy of the *Private Thoughts upon Religion* by William Beveridge. In thanking Mayers for his gift, Newman spoke of his need of "some monitor" to direct his life, and prayed that the Holy Spirit «by whom Beveridge was enabled to establish his article of faith, to form resolutions upon them, and to put the resolutions in practice might also be his guide».[58] Newman confessed that no book was more dear to him, or exercised a more powerful influence over his devotion and habitual thoughts and that in his private memoranda he wrote in its style.[59]

However, Newman specifically states that he did not consider Beveridge's works shaped his doctrinal development, but Beveridge'e *Private Thoughts* drove home to him the close connection between Christian faith and Christian living, the practical and experimental character - as it was frequently put at that time.[60]

Newman read William Law's *Serious Call to a Devout and Holy Life*. Through reading Law, he says, the "Catholic doctrine of the warfare between the city of God and the powers of darkness was ... deeply impressed upon my mind".[61]

Newman's approach and devotion to the Eucharist, was to some extent shaped by Haweis' *The Communicant's Spiritual Companion: or an Evangelical preparation for the Lord's Supper.*

He acknowledged his debt to these devotional books the most of which were by Evangelical writers. Yet, it is important to note what he found particularly important and what influenced him most.

In his autobiographical memoirs he writes that "the evangelical teaching, considered as a system, and in what was peculiar to itself, had from the first failed to find a response in his own religious experience ....

---

57 Apo 49.
58 AW 152 (18.9.1850).
59 see Apo 54 and 59.
60 Cf. G.Powell, 'The Roots of Newman's "Scriptural Holiness". Some Formative Influences on Newman's Spirituality', 15.
61 Apo 19.

He had indeed been converted by it to a spiritual life and so far his experience bore witness to its truth".[62]

These books had made him fully aware of the divine truths about our Lord and His Person and Offices, His grace, the supreme duty of living, not only morally, but in His faith, fear and love.

And as to the origin of Newman's wonderful style which so enchanted his hearers and readers, that nervous lucidity which keeps them alert but never wholly satisfied, he admits that as a youth he «copied Addison« and «wrote in the style of Johnson», that his ears «rang with the cadence» of Gibbon's sentences, but that «the only master of style he ever had ... was Cicero».[63]

Newman tells in the Apologia how in the year 1823 he learned the doctrine of the apostolic succesion from the Rev. William James, then a Fellow of Oriel.[64] Unfortunately, Newman does not give precise information on what the content and meaning of this doctrine were to Willaim James.[65]

Last but not the least, one should not forget the contribution of the Church of England and the English religious tradition in the moulding of Newman's theological thought. He paid tribute to individual Anglicans and the Anglican Communion for what they taught him:

O my, brethren, my Anglican friends! I easily give you credit for what I have experienced myself.[66]

As a man who had deep faith in Providence and saw it at work in all things, Newman acknowledged that it was the Church of England which prepared the ground for his conversion to Catholicism:

The Church of England was the instrument of divine Providence in conferring on me many benefits; - if I were a Presbyterian, I may not have known the divinity of Christ; if I had not passed through Oxford, I may not have heard of the visible Church, Tradition and other Catholic truths. It was Oxford, who until now is the seat of those traditions which constitute all that is Catholic in doctrine and in Anglican

---

62   AW 79 (13.1.1825).
63   LD XXIV, 242 (13.4.1869).
64   Cf. Apo 10.
65   see Alf Härdelin, *The Tractarian Understanding of the Eucharist*, Uppsala, 1965, 115-6.
66   Diff. I, 82 (Lect.III. The Life of the Movement of 1833 Not Derived from the National Church).

principles who was the pedagogue that brought us to the true Church. It was not Catholics who made us Catholics; Oxford made us Catholics. The Established Church has always remained a defence against unitarism, fanaticism and misbelief.[67]

1.2.2.3 THE FATHERS OF THE CHURCH

After Newman underwent conversion in 1816, one of the books he read was Joseph Milner's *Church History*. Milner's History had an equally profound effect, for here Newman first discovered the Fathers of the Church, the religion of the primitive Christians, the great Greek and Roman thinkers of the fourth and fifth centuries.

He was immediately attracted by this paradise of delight[68] as he significantly called it, and compared their thought to music, his favorite art. Greek clarity of reasoning met the concrete symbolism of the Hebrews in a fusion of intellect and imagination which instantly appealed to a mind where these forces were held in unusual balance.[69] He says that he was quite enamoured of the long extracts from St. Augustine, St. Ambrose, and other Fathers which he found there.[70]

From 1828 onwards, Newman made a systematic study of ancient Christian records. He tells us in the Apologia how his study of Athanasius - "the champion of truth", introduced him to the philosophy of Clement and Origen and how he found in them the confirmation of ideas he had for so long lived with:

the broad philosophy of Clement and Origen carried me away; the philosophy, not the theological doctrine.[71]

The Anglican Church, from its inception and throughout its history, has always revered the tradition of the Fathers in which her different generations of theologians have seen evidences of authentic Apostolicity.[72]

---

67 LD XIX, 352 (2.6.1860).
68 see VM I, 126 (Doctrine of Infallibility Politically Considered).
69 see Meriol Trevor, *Newman's Journey*, 17.
70 Cf. Apo 23; also 7 and 20; LD XI, 252 (24.9.1846): "St. Ambrose in Milner's History was one of the first objects of my veneration".
71 Ibid., 36-7.
72 Cf. Jean Honoré, *Itinerario spirituale di Newman...*, 59.

Faithful to his Anglican background, Newman had come to recognize in the true exponent of orthodox Christianity, namely Christian Antiquity, the support and bastion of the Anglican Church. In his efforts to gain further knowledge of the truths contained in the Scriptures and to grasp more fully the revealed truths he learned from teachers, friends and contemporaries, Newman turned to the Fathers. In turn they were true to him in name as *Fathers of the Church*; through them he was reborn from a Protestant frame of mind to a Catholic one.

His reading of the Fathers and their exposition of the revealed truth removed his objections to the Catholic Church. In them Newman found both «an authority and a guide»,[73] however, an authority and a guide which Newman understands as always relevant. Thus in the famous "Letter addressed to Rev. E.B. Pusey on the Occasion of his Eirenicon" in 1867, Newman wrote:

> ... I am not ashamed still to take my stand upon the Fathers and do not mean to budge. The Fathers made me a Catholic, and I am not going to kick down the ladder by which I ascended into the Church.[74]

And for the rest of his life, Newman did not cease to laud the good fortune he had through the introduction to the world and mind of these exponents of Christian wisdom:

> ... these principles, which I now set forth under the sanction of the Catholic Church, were my profession at that early period of my life, when religion was to me more a matter of feeling and experience than of faith. They did but take greater hold upon me, as I was introduced to the records of Chrisitan Antiquity ...[75]

It is remarkable that these elements which influenced his formation also constitute the sources of his theological thought. And to the aforementioned elements, the following can be added.

1.2.2.4 PERSONAL EXPERIENCE OF GOD

To be qualified to talk about God and divine things, one has to encounter God, experience Him, and strive to live in His presence. Newman had this good fortune.

---

73   Jfc. 123.
74   Diff, II,24.
75   The Idea of a University, 4.

May I underline here that what is peculiar about the experience of God is the *decisive change it causes* and the *indelible impression it leaves behind* so that he or she who experiences this can always recall and refer to it as *illo tempore.*[76]

For Newman it was the experience of 1816, when "the heavy hand of God came upon me", when God "mercifully touched his heart" which turned him right round, and brought "a great change of thought" of which he was more certain "than that I have hands and feet" which constitutes his own *illo tempore.*

This was an experience which prepared and qualified him to speak like the prophets, Apostles and Saints who announce what they saw, heard, touched and contemplated.[77] They (including Newman) spoke like men who in a qualified sense were there,[78] as participants and not as on-lookers to the Word in whose service they are.

Like St. Augustine before him, Newman wrote and preached and reflected on the faith as one who had been reborn due to his conversion. And this conversion was to a God who had communicated knowledge of himself in terms of a "definite Creed".

Newman's religion mostly rests on this personal encounter with God.[79] We catch echoes of Newman's strong sense of Providential guidance, and particularly of his interpretation of his three illnesses (1816, 1827, 1833) as significant interventions of God which represented turning points in his religious development. The first illness made him a Christian. The second Newman interpreted as a curb for his intellectual sin, namely, pride. The third created the conditions that made Newman to compose the "Pillar of Clouds", commonly known by the first words of the first stanza: "Lead, Kindly Light".

---

76 In John 1,35-39, the Apostle records for the edification of believers the circumstances of the call of the first disciples of Jesus, the time of their call, and the change that it inflicted on them *there and then*. Every authentic disciple remembers *when* and *how* he or she encountered the Lord, and the experience that makes a change in his or her life.

77 Cf. 1 Jn.1,1-2.

78 see Karl Barth, *Evangelical Theology. An Introduction*, London, 1963, 216.

79 Solus cum solo, «Myself and my Creator» (Apo 127). The words of Job summarise well this point: formerly I knew you only by hearsay; but now, having seen you, with my own eyes, I retract all have said; for you are different from what I previously heard (Job 42,5-6).

The great role of experience in his life is reflected in his prayer: «Enable me to believe as if I saw; let me have Thee always bodily and sensibly present».[80]

Referring to the experience "when God in his mercy created me anew", and which brought a total and lasting change in him, the conclusions he drew he expressed metaphorically thus: «I know and am sure that before I was blind, but now I see».[81] It is a bonus for Newman that in spite of his personal involvement in divine mystery, he was able to live and function beyond the dangers of religious subjectivism.

Newman lived in full conviction of the presence of God in his life, the unfailing flame of the "Kindly light": «God's hand is ever over his own and he leads them forward by ways they know not of»[82] he was to say in 1838.

Having surveyed briefly above the history of Newman's search for God - how it began, how it grew, the factors that influenced his search, where they led him, the sadnesses and joys it entailed for him, let us now examine the African soul's search for God, always bearing in mind where Newman's pilgrimage and ours meet in order to draw the necessary conclusions.

1.3   THE SEARCH FOR GOD IN THE AFRICAN CONTEXT

1.3.1   THE AFRICAN WORLD AND RELIGIOUS BELIEF BEFORE THE ADVENT OF CHRISTIANITY

1.3.1.1   AFRICAN COSMOLOGY

Deep within his being, the African feels an irresistible religious imperative. It is religion which makes the first and most absolute claim in the life, hopes, aspirations, fears and joys of the average African person.

African religion is at the very heart of traditional society. This religion, its beliefs and practices and how these affect the African community is the key to understanding the Africans and their world, which they strongly believe is permeated by the presence of the Sacred. The words

---

80   *Meditations and Devotions*, 51-52.
81   AW 165 (29.9.1820).
82   PPS IV, 261 (25.12.1838).

of an eminent scholar of African religion comes to mind immediately
here:

> It is religion, more than anything else, which colours their (the African) empirical
> participation in that universe, making life a profoundly religious phenomenon. To be
> is to be religious in a religious universe. That is the philosophical understanding
> behind African myths, customs, traditions, beliefs, morals, actions and social relati-
> onships. Up to a point in history this traditional religious attitude maintained an
> almost absolute monopoly over African concepts and experiences of life.[83]

The central point is that there is an absolutely integral relationship
between religion and culture. African tradition was inherently holistic.
Here less than anywhere could you discern the secular from the sacred.

Religion permeates almost everything, particularly the crucial aspects
of life, namely, marriage, birth, naming ceremony, initiation, illness,
healing, and death. At one with culture, religion is inextricably linked to
the whole of life whose personal and communal activities it animates.
The feeling of wholeness is an important aspect of African life.[84]

It is to religion that the Africans turned in the face of the existential
questions about human life: who is man?, where does he come from?,
where is he going?, how must he live?; the source and meaning of pain
and joy, suffering and disease, health and life after life. At this juncture,
what Major Arthur G. Leonard said of the Igbos of Nigeria can be applied to traditional Africa as a whole. These people (Igbos),

> ... are, in the strict and natural sense of the word, a truly and a deeply religious
> people, of whom it can be said, as it has been said of the Hindus, that 'they eat reli-
> giously, drink religiously, bathe religiously, dress religiously, and sin religiously'. In
> a few words, the religion of these natives, ... is their existence, and their existence is
> their religion.[85]

At all times they are religious; at every crisis, personal or collective,
religion is called upon to provide a solution, prevent disintegration, and
strengthen the bond of human cohesion and sanctity. It was religion that

---

83   Mbiti, J.S., *African Religions and Philosophy*, London, 1975, 262.
84   Cf. Kofi Appiah-Kubi, 'Jesus Christ - Some Christological Aspects from African
     Perspectives', in Mbiti J.S. (ed.), *African and Asian Contributions to Contempo-
     rary Theology*, Celigny/Bossey, Switzerland, 1977, 204-8.
85   Arthur G. Leonard, *The Lower Niger and Its Tribes*, London, 1966, 429.

provided a system of values relevant to the fundamental requirements of individual society.

1.3.1.2 GENESIS OF AFRICAN RELIGION

No one knows when African religion began and by whom it was founded. What is certain, however, is that African religion is as old as the first African, and if the word "founder" may be used, then the first African is the founder of African religion.

In the African context, authority and antiquity are highly valued.[86] The elderly persons and ancestors are greatly revered, so Africans follow the traditional religion precisely because it was practised and handed down by the ancestors.[87]

The origin of African religion is simple to explain. Judging from the very *nature* of the Africans, one can say that African Traditional Religion originated from the Africans' experience *in* the world and *of* the world. Africans are very observant lovers of *nature*, and are imbued with the sense of mystery and wonder.

Their attentive observation of nature and natural phenomena: different cycles, birth, growth, death, transience of being and man's limits before sickness and death, led them to the conclude that a Creator and Provident-Being must exist. Overwhelmingly struck by the hills, mountains, thick forests, big trees, rivers, rocks, deserts, and terrible beasts, they concluded that there is someone Greater and at the origin of all.

It was their reflection on their experience that led them to reverence and fear, and therefore to religion. For Africans, as for Newman, the existence of creatures implies a Creator, of order an Orderer, and of harmony a Harmonizer.[88] Thus, among the channels through which Af-

---

86 "What my parents and ancestors were, so I intend to be", is essentially the African spirit. African traditional culture is very conservative.

87 Ancestors are not just the forefathers as the term is understood in its first nuance. Nor are they ghosts or simple past heroes or patriots like Patrice Lumumba, Jomo Kenyata, etc. Ancestors are those past Africans (men and women) who are believed to have lived well, who feared God, obeyed his laws, and loved their community of brothers and sisters, thus leaving behind examples of a good life, and for whom, above, all proper burial and funeral rites have been made.

88 Cf. Newman, *Callista*, 314: «... order implies an orderer, an echo a voice; a voice a speaker ...»; see also J., Keble, The Christian Year, Lyra Innocentium and other Poems, Oxford, 1914, 489f.

ricans acquired the knowledge of God and the duties to Him, is the course of the world, the witness of their own minds or consciences[89] and the collective voice of the human community.[90]

On the same note, the idea of a Supreme Being implied a religion; and a sense of mystery and wonder implied adoration as a spontaneous reaction to Mystery. As such, religion can be described as the response of man to the actions of God; it can be defined as «... the knowledge of God, of His Will, and of our duties towards Him ...».[91] For the purpose of clarity, let us take religion in both subjective and objective dimensions:

> Subjectively, religion is the consciousness of one's dependence on a transcendent Being and the tendency to worship Him. Objectively, religion is the body of truths, laws and rites by which man is subordinated to the transcendent.[92]

African religion comprises both though not in a systematic manner.

1.3.1.3 CHARACTERISTICS OF AFRICAN RELIGION

African religion is purely monotheistic. It recognizes the existence of one supreme, transcendent Being with myriads of hierarchically structured beings who act as his ministers and mediators with humanfolk, namely, the spirits and the ancestors. He is not of the rank and file of the deities; He is not one of the deities but One among them. The uniqueness of the supreme Being is manifested in the the names peculiar to Him:

> The principal name of the Supreme Being may be the generic name for deity in general, in which case there is a qualifying suffix or qualifying word to distinguish between the Supreme Being or the deities; and the generic name plus the suffix or qualifying word belong uniquely to the Supreme Being. There are cases where the name for the Supreme Being is uniquely his, and no part of it is shared by any other being. It should also be noted that where the deities share the basic generic name

---

89 Neweman calls conscience the voice of God in the nature and heart of man as distinct from the voice of Revelation; a principle implanted within us (see A Letter Addressed to his Grace the Duke of Norfolk on occasion of Mr Gladstone's Recent Expostulation of 1874, Diff.II,247-8).
90 see GA 303.
91 Ibid.
92 Parente, P., *Theologia Fundamentalis*, Torino, 1954, 9.

with the Supreme Being, it only serves to emphasize the fact the deities, derive their being from him.[93]

And when worship to the Supreme Being is clouded by attention to the spirits, the impression of polytheism is created.

African religion thrives in a cultural context which is based on an oral tradition. It is fundamentally an oral religion preserved in myths, philosophy, songs and sayings handed down from generation to generation.

Priests, diviners, parents, elders teach this religion to the young through discussion, etc. It is also learnt through participating in religious activities such as ceremonies, festivals, rituals, and so on.[94]

African religion has no Scriptures or Sacred writings. This also explains why it has been greatly affected by the wave of cultural changes and other great religions. In the absence of written codes, those entrusted with the custody of African religion can freely add or subtract from its teachings and practices.

It has no formal dogma, theology or theologians. Then again, it has no formally condemned heresies, neither has it given rise to schisms or sects, controversies[95] or reformation. However, inter-tribal contacts through marriage, trades, wars, migration sometimes brought about adaptation, with certain religious acts being assumed and others being dropped.

African Religion has no missionaries and proselytes to convert others. This accounts for why it is for Africans only and remains with them wherever they are found: people are born into it, not converted to it.

---

93 J.O.Kayode, & Adelowo E. Dada, 'Religions in Nigeria' in Richard Olaniyan (ed.), *Nigerian History and Culture*, Ikeja, 1985, 235; see also Idowu, E.B., *African Traditional Religion*, London, 1973, 149.

94 Cf. Mbiti, J.S., *An Introduction to African Religion*, London, 1975, 13.

95 For us, Religion and the religious sphere are sacred precints where devotion but not rivalry has the final say. We quarrelled and disagreed over injustices suffered in the community. We never imagined that people could disagree or even fiercely quarrel on religious issues. The different Christian denominations which flocked to the African continent in the 18th and 19th centuries in search of followers, Africans initially saw to be believers in different gods. Of course these Christian denominations with their differences succeded in delivering a devastating blow to the natural ties that existed in our traditional society. Until then we never dreamt of people who claim to believe in the same God fighting one another over their different understanding of this God and how to worship Him.

This religion is obligatory in character. To the average African, religious cult is an imperative. Religious worship, rituals and ceremonies, involves the whole community.

1.3.1.4 DOCUMENTATION OF AFRICAN RELIGION

Given that African traditional society is essentially orally based, African traditional religion has no sacred writings. However, this does not mean that its tenets and practices are not documented. Documentation goes beyond material writings.

African religion, its doctrine, liturgy and values are documented in multifarious ways: symbols and signs, music and dances, prayers and ejaculations, proverbs and riddles, customs and beliefs, names of persons and places, rituals and festivals, shrines, sacred places and works of art.

It forms the themes of songs, provides topics for minstrels, finds vehicles in myths, folk-lores, proverbs and sayings, and is the basis of African philosophy. All these are very easy to remember and pass on to other people.

The oral traditions are, in fact, the source of what we may call the Scripture of African traditional religion wherein is contained the history of their religious awareness.[96]

As elsewhere, in Africa religion has inspired art, though Africans do not make images of God. Symbols and works of art however, constitute vital documentation of African religious experience.

Proverbs and wise sayings are common ways of expressing religious experience and philosophical wisdom among Africans. They crystallize the accumulated experience and wisdom handed down by the elders. The spiritual heritage of the Africans is to a large extent preserved and transmitted through the language, and is intimately bound up with it.[97]

1.3.1.5 STRUCTURE OF AFRICAN TRADITIONAL RELIGION

What now follows is a synthesis of African religion. This is divided into three parts, reflecting the fact that every religion comprises Object of belief, Cult to the object, and the way of life of the believers: dogma, cult, and value sytstem or morality.

---

96 Cf. Kayode, J.O. & Adelowo E.Dada, Op.cit., 233-4.
97 Cf. Westermann, D., *The African Today and Tomorrow*, London, 1949, 121.

1.3.1.6 OBJECTS OF BELIEF

The direct object of African religious belief is essentially God, the Supreme Being. The spirits and ancestors are indirect *objects* of worship, in as much as they act as go-betweens through which prayers, oblations and sacrifice are rendered to God. The structure of the objects of worship is triangular. At the apex is the supreme God, on one side of the triangle are the nature gods or spirits and on the other side, the ancestors.

1.3.1.6.1. GOD

That Africans firmly believe in the existence of a supreme Being is as certain as the reality of the world itself: it is as clear to every African as his own existence, the existence of his clan or community; it is as obvious as day and night.

In the traditional life there are no atheists. Only a doubly foolish person would doubt or negate the existence of God and refuse to worship Him.[98] And if the existence of such a "strange fellow" is ascertained, it is a matter of urgent and serious concern for the entire community.

The community is disturbed about having given birth to an "abnormal person", without a conscience and religious heart and consequently incapable of participating in the fundamental obligation of the community, namely, the acknowledgement of a supreme Being.

Numerous sayings underline this point. An Ashanti proverb in Ghana says: "No one shows a child the supreme Being".[99] This means that knowledge about God's reality is so fundamental that it is acquired at a very early stage[100]. Even a child learns to know, to accept, to consent to the reality of God.[101]

---

98 Such a profound conviction tallies with with the position of the biblical world. The Scriptures attribute the "doctrine" of atheism to an idiot. "The foolish man says in his heart that there is no God" (Psalm 14(13),1). Yes, the Bible says that there is no God! But a careful look at the context of this statement indicates that it was made by a fool. Yet in the traditional society, not even fools and hooligans doubted the existence of God.

99 Cf. Rattray, R.S., *Ashanti Proverbs*, Oxford, 1923, 50.

100 The Knowledge of God comes by intuition; it is the first act of the human conscience.

101 Cf. Mbiti, J.S., *Bible and Theology in African Christianity*, Nairobi, 1986, 101.

To the Supreme Being, Africans ascribe the attributes of the Almighty and omnipresent. They believe He created the universe, and so is held before all other idol-gods though they do not pray directly to Him, or offer any sacrifices to Him.[102] The concept of God's transcendence is summarised well in a Bacongo saying, that, "He is made by no other, no one beyond Him is".[103]

This supreme God is thought to have withdrawn to the skies and left the government of the earth in the hands of the spirits who act as His representatives in the theocratic government of the world. Yet He is immanent so that men can and do in fact establish contact with Him.

It is, in acts of worship however, that men acknowledge God to be near and approachable. "Of all the wide earth the supreme Being is the elder", say the Ashanti. Only He possesses the fullness of life, which he generously dispenses to all in creation and providence.

On this providential attribute, the Bambuti say that if God were to die, the world would collapse.[104] He averts calamities, supplies rain, provides fertility, and assures rich harvest and security from evil forces.

On God's mercy, the proverb: 'God drives away flies from the tail-less cow' is widely known all over Africa. Some, like the Akamba, Bacongo, Herero, Igbo, Ila and others say categorically that God only does good, so that they have no reason to complain. The Ewe firmly hold that "He is good, for He has never withdrawn from us the good things which He gave us".[105]

God alone is most wise and powerful. "No one but God can put a crown on a lion", says the Yoruba[106] while the Zulu conceive of God's power in political terms. They describe Him as 'He who roars so that all nations be struck with terror'.[107]

Praxis rather than words, confirm the holiness of God. Holiness like faith, is not a common word in traditional religious vocabulary though they feature prominently in daily life. On the holiness of the supreme Being,

---

102 Cf. William Bosman, A New and Accurate Description of the Coasts of Guinea, Divided into the Gold, the Slave, and the Ivory Coasts, 1705, 348 cited in Geoffrey Parrinder, West African Religion, London, 1969, 14.

103 Claridge, G.C., *Wildbush Tribes of Tropical Africa*, London, 1922, 269.

104 Cf. Schebesta, P., *Revisting my Pygmy Hosts*, London, 1936, 171.

105 Cf. Westermann, D., *The African Today and Tomorrow*, 197.

106 Cf. Idowu, E.B., *Olòdùmarè - God In Yoruba Belief*, London, 1962, 30.

107 Cf. Smith, E.W., *African Ideas of God, Edingburgh*, 1926, 167.

The Ila hold that God cannot be charged with an offence, since he is above the level of fault, failure, wrong, and unrighteousness. And in the eyes of the Yoruba God is the pure king ... who is without blemish.[108]

The concept of God's holiness is also manifested in the fact that many African peoples have strict rules that guide the performance of rituals for God[109].

Sacrificial animals, for instance, have to be of a sacred colour (usually black or white as the epitome of all colours), of a particular sacred number (usually four to indicate totality or in pairs, to indicate completeness), and priests or officiating elders must refrain from sexual intercourse and from certain foods or activities for some time before and after the ritual.

1.3.1.6.2 THE LESSER GODS OR SPIRITS

Originally, says a popular African myth, earth and sky formed a unified spherical whole. God lived quite near the earth, and the sky could be touched, and men could visit, see and speak with God. But this familiarity was abused.[110] God severed the link between the earth and the sky and moved away to the distant heights in the sky.

He permits normal life to continue without intervention. If God comes too near, sickness, madness, or death is likely to come. God has delegated powers to his spirits, and has retired from any direct involvement in the petty affairs of earth-folk. He has therefore made and appointed the lower spirits, who are nearer to men, as overseers and middlemen between Him and the earth.

They are often personifications of natural forces since the universe is thought to be peopled with spirits. There is no part of the world, no ob-

---

108 Idowu, E.B., *African Traditional Religion*, 47.
109 see Mbiti, J.S., *African Religions and Philosophy*, 38.
110 What this abuse consisted of varies according to tribes or localities. Some say men abused their familiarity with God by committing abomination in God's presence; some say men were wearing away the sky by breaking off parts to use as firewood, some say one day a woman, pounding yam in a mortar with a long wooden pestle, hit the sky and when God called out to her to stop, she paid no heed. Whatever case, this myth of the "retreat of God" can form the basis for discussion of the Judeo-Christian doctrine of original or first sin. African traditional religion has no clear notion of original sin; consequently it knows nothing of the Incarnation, passion, death on the cross and resurrection.

ect or creature, which does not have a spirit of its own or which is not
nhabited by the apparitional entity known as spirit, whose good will
nen seek by appropriate offerings.[111]

The average African pagan does not investigate the nature, number
und origin of these entities. He only tries to cultivate their friendship and
o avoid their wrath. Talbot writes that:

> The nature of these spirits is a question into which the African pagan does not ge-
> nerally probe. He is more interested in what they can do: they have superhuman
> power to help or to hinder. From African religious life, cult, prayers, sacrifice, etc.,
> his short synthesis can be made: The spirits are invisible. They are above man but
> below God.[112]

Whether the Africans pray to the spirits or offer sacrifices to them, it
s with the intention and understanding that these spirits will ultimately
relay the sacrifice to God who is the final recipient of all sacrifice, expressly stated or not.

1.3.1.6.3. THE ANCESTORS

The ancestors have always been a part of the human family. There is a
general belief that communion and communication are possible between
hose who are alive and the deceased, and that the latter have the power
o influence the former.

Of course, not all the African dead are ancestors. African ancestorship
has some criteria; for instance: i) It is based on natural relationship
which can be consanguinous or non consanguinous, ii) The ancestor is a
model of behaviour, not only because his earthly conduct was good, but
because it is the conduct of one who is endowed with a supernatural
condition and power.[113] This last point is fundamental as Africans are
very meticulous about what concerns virtue and conduct. Nyamiti con-
inues that,

> ... in African teaching a dead parent who was totally bad is no ancestor and has no
> itle to any regular sacred relationship with his offspring. This title is based on the
> fact that the parent was morally good and is - thanks to his death - in a supernatural
> state. An ancestor whose conduct on earth was totally reproachful cannot be a proto-

---

111 Cf. Geoffrey Parrinder, *West African Religion*, 26.

112 Talbot, P.A., *The Tribes of the Niger Delta*, London, 1932, 63.

113 Cf. Charles Nyamiti, *Christ as our Ancestor*, Gweru, Zimbabwe, 1984, 15-17.

type of behaviour for his or her descendants and has no basis to the title of mystical communion with them.[114]

It is to be noted here that the ancestors have ceased to be in the ordinary world. They are spirits and are approached accordingly, even though they are spirits with a difference given their family connections with their earthly folk.[115]

Not only are ancestors revered, but they are felt to be still present, watching over the household, directly concerned in all the affairs of the family and property. They are the guardians of the tribal traditions, morality and history. Dr. Busia describes well the general African attitude towards the ancestors:

> ... stories are always circulating about the ancestors ...The ancestors are believed to be the custodians of the laws and customs of the tribe. They punish with sickness or misfortune those who infringe them ... Constantly before the Ashanti, and serving to regulate his conduct, is the thought that his ancestors are watching him, and one day, when he rejoins them in the world of spirits, they will ask him to give an account of his conduct, especially of his conduct towards his kinsmen. This thought is a very potent sanction of morality.[116]

Old men and women, and parents are treated with great respect for it is believed that due to their age and experience they are nearer to the ancestors and will soon join them.

Africans believe that their dead are constantly near, even when they are not seen. And one of the most important duties, therefore, is to see that the burial and mourning ceremonies for the dead are duly carried out. Sickness and misfortune are often believed to be due to some neglect in fulfilling the last rites with due care".[117] The International Theological Commission has recently acknowledged this communion and constant exchange between the living and the living dead[118] in African religion. The Commission says:

---

114 Charles Nyamiti, 'African Tradition and the Christian God', in Spearhead, no.49, 48.

115 Cf. Kayode, J.O., & Adelowo E.Dada, 'Religions in Nigeria', 239-40.

116 Busia, A.K., *The Position of the Chief in the Modern Political System of Ashanti*, Oxford, 1951, 24-5.

117 Cf. Geoffrey Parrinder, *West African Religion*, 116.

118 This term, living dead, was aptly coined by J.S.Mbiti to express the fact that the deceased members are not totally dead. Rather they are alive in the spirit world

The idea of a family union of souls through death is not foreign to many African religions and offers the opportunity for interreligious dialogue with them.[119]

It can not be over-stressed that a typical African family comprises of both the living and the living dead.

Belief in reincarnation is wide spread, but only good ancestors come back to life again. This is possible in African traditional logic because the ancestors are the patrons of the community, which they never abandon. It seems that only a part of the ancestor's spirit is believed to be reincarnated.

Temples holds that "it is explicable by the philosophy of forces: the ancestor does not create the child. Africans do not hold that, for they know that God does this. It is not strictly the ancestral spirit that is reborn, but the child is supposed to come under his particular influence and to receive part of his vitality and qualities. Thus the ancestral name is renewed in the family and the clan has an added advantage".[120]

1.3.1.7 CULT

Genuine reverence for a supreme Being is part of almost all African religions, despite considerable variations even within the same culture in how this reverence is expressed.

African peoples respond in many ways to their spiritual world of which they are keenly aware. Religious rites mark marriage, birth, the seasons, and related factors such as planting, harvesting, rain-making, hunting, etc. This response generally takes on the form of worship which is externalised in different acts. These acts may be formal or informal, regular or extempore, communal or individual, ritual or unceremonial, through word or deed.

Worship generally takes the form of prayers, offerings, sacrifice, observance of certain customs and participation in certain ceremonies. The goal of worship is not personal salvation or sanctity. It is generally to

---

from where they exercise a strong influence on their living kin and community. Cf. Mbiti, J.S., African Religions and Philosophy, 107.

119 'Some Current Questions in Eschatology' published in The Irish Theological Quarterly, vol.58, no.3, 1992, 209-243, esp. 222.

120 Temples, P. *Bantu Philosophy*, Paris, Presence Africaine, 1948, 18.

gain favour or to thank God for a favour obtained or to ward off a disaster, and to be looked upon favourably by the spirits and the ancestors.[121]

One of the frequently encountered justifications for lack of direct worship of God is that God is so good he would never inflict misfortune or illness on anyone, so that one must appeal directly to lesser spirits who, when honoured in worship, desist from harming mankind, and even aid the devotee.

Arinze suggested that a second and important reason why the cult of God is not frequent in African religious culture in comparison to the cult of the spirits and ancestors, is an atmosphere of mystery about the supreme God:

> The more pious pagans are confounded with perplexity as to how to worship God. They are not sure how exactly to worship Him. His awe and majesty perplex them. He is entirely transcendent. Hence they think it more courteous and more within man's range to appeal to the spirits to obtain requests from God.[122]

Being dazzled by the majesty of God, the pious Africans rely solely on and follow the instructions of the priests and diviners whom they believe to be the interpreters of the will of the supreme Being.

Generally wielders of sacred power, spirits and ancestors are to God what servants are to kings. And "even if sacrifice to God is rare yet all offerings to lesser gods are regarded as efficacious only with the approval of the Great God; and ultimately destined to him".[123]

1.3.1.8 VALUE SYSTEM

Having seen what the pious African pagans believe and how they worship, let us now examine how they live their religion since "in all things they are religious and religion forms the foundation, the all-governing principle and the keynote of their life".[124]

Man is believed to be in the hands of the supreme Being whose dictate is law, and who is waiting on the other side of this life to render to man that which he deserves. African traditional morality can be articulated under four fundamental values dear to the African soul: 1) Respect for

---

121 Cf. Kayode, J.O & Adelowo E.Dada, 'Religions in Nigeria', 234.
122 Francis Arinze, *Sacrifice in Ibo Religion*, Ibadan, 1970, 10-11.
123 Geoffrey Parrinder, *African Traditional Religion*, London, 1954, 39.
124 Idowu, E.B., *Olòdùmare, God in Yoruba Belief*, London, 1962, 5.

life, 2) sense of community life, 3) hospitality, 4) sense of the sacred and love for proverbial sayings.

1.3.1.8.1 RESPECT FOR LIFE

Africans believe life is the most precious gift man receives from God, the source and fullness of life. The spirits, ancestors and human beings and all creation partake of this life in a web of spiritual interchange. This pragmatic orientation of African religion expresses a profound spiritual assurance of the goodness of life as the Africans understand it.

It is this that accounts for why life for Africans is a feast. No wonder they celebrate the institution of the beginning of life (marriage), the in-auguration of new life (birth, in which there is rejoicing at the addition of another life to the community), and death (when it is believed that the deceased joins the happy group of the ancestors).

Community members learn to refrain from evil conduct which threat-ens the quality of life or diminishes the life force of the community. On the other hand, good acts and humane relationships are considered to enhance the life of the community.

Life is taken in its entirety to include the life of the unborn, the living and the dead. The presence of old or elderly persons in the family or community is considered a blessing. Hence it is normal that the «elderly remain at home as long as possible, rather than being sent to special nursing homes or hospitals. Sickness and dying are not usually faced in hospitals but in homes and villages with the conforting presence of rela-tives and neighbours».[125]

1.3.1.8.2 SENSE OF COMMUNITY

In the African world social relationships are essential to spiritual equili-brium. One must therefore be loyal and generous with the living family and community members, and be in loving and harmonious solidarity with one's community in order to be inwardly at peace and flourish out-wardly. One of the ways of demonstrating one's committment to one's community is by doing something concrete for it[126].

---

125 Peter Schineller, *A Handbook on Inculturation*, New York, 1990, 79.
126 A similar sentiment is present in the synoptic tradition. Luke reports the story of a delegation of elders of Capernaum to Jesus with the request that he cures the ter-

To be without or to be cut off from a community is to be alienated. To be is to be with others. Outside the community, there is no life, nothing.[127] Maimela has brought this point out well in the following words:

African anthropology is human-centred and socially oriented. Accordingly, individuals were continually reminded that a fulfilling life cannot be lived in isolation from their human fellows. Rather life is possible only in communal relationships in which individuals try to strike balance between the private life and the social life, thus maintaining the network of relationships with their fellows so that every person is provided with a space to breathe and live a meaningful life. A human being is human only because of others, with others and for others. Hence it was important to teach people to avoid dehumanizing and bad relationships, by refraining from activities that are injurious to our human fellows or threaten to undermine the social fibre and the stability.[128]

Solitude or ostracism to Africans is a dreadful plight. In this light, it is interesting to reflect on the relationship between the mentality of the African community and the ecclesiology of Cyprian. Cyprian gave a spontaneous vent to the African in him when he incorporated in his ecclesiological theology the maxim: "extra Ecclesiam nulla salus", no salvation outside the Church.

Just as it is only in the community that "life" is found in the African context, so Cyprian maintains that it is in the community of the Church and in it alone that one finds eternal life or salvation and the means to it, namely, Word and sacraments. For Cyprian, it is only in the bosom of the community that the Word of Salvation is proclaimed and salvificly heard. And just as outside the community, there is no life but solitude and dangerous risks, so is the Word outside the Church, according to the Ecclesiology of Cyprian nothing but a mere human theorizing, a dead letter, surmise or rumour.

Just as the communal heritage is valued and significant only within and among community members in the African world, so Cyprian maintains that the sacraments are efficacious only in the Church community,

---

minally ill servant of the centurion. The elders went to Jesus because they were convinced that the centurion deserved such a favour. He so loved the people of Capernaum that he built a synagogue for them (Lk 7,1-9).

127 see Zuese, E.M., 'African Traditional Religion', in Abingdon Dictionary of Living Religions, 7.

128 Simon S. Maimela, 'Religion and Culture: Blessings or Curses?' in Journal of Black Theology in South Africa, vol.5, no.1, May 1991, 1-12, esp. 5 and 6.

and are mere empty, formal amd magical formulas outside the Church.[129]

It may even be continued that those who cut themselves off from the community are no longer entitled in the full sense of the word to the patrimony of the community as long as they are outside it.

We can notice again here another Africanness in Tertullian who in his days argued that heretics had no right to the Sacred Scriptures, which belong to the community[130] of believers.

In the African world-view, all things hang together, each depends on the other and on the whole. This particularly applies to human beings who are closely connected with each other and with God.[131] Just an example: while I am here in Rome, my link with my community in Orlu-Nigeria is as real to me as my identity as a man, as certain as the fact that now I am in a room, as a fact to me as the presence of the table in front of me. I live with this consciousness daily.

The community as the custodian of the individual encourages all to follow the ordinances of God by following the foot-steps of the ancestors. A Lozi proverb confirms this: "Go the way that many people go; if you go it alone you will have reason to lament".[132]

At the origin of the African community spirit is the extended family system. Every African person has a network of relations, many brothers and sisters. This network of relations participate in our joy and sadness, wealth and poverty; with them and for them we live.

To a large extent, it is true that if the West stands for truth,[133] Asia for contemplation, Latin America for liberation, Africa for stands fraternity. God in the fullness of life, must be fullness of sharing.[134]

---

129 see Cyprian, *De Unitate Ecclesiae* 6; CSEL 3/1, 214.
130 Cf. Tertullian, *De Praescriptione Haereticorum*, III,2, PL 7, 966.
131 Bénézet Bujo, *African Theology in Its Social Context*, Nairobi, 1992, 23; see for example St.Thomas Aquinas in Summa Contra Gentiles, III,122: 'Non enim Deus a nobis offenditur nisi ex eo quod nostrum bonum agimus'.
132 Davidson, B., *The African Genius, An Atlantic Monthly Press Book*, 1969, 31.
133 It is logical truth that is referred to.
134 see Joseph Healey, *A Fifth Gospel: In Search of Black African Values*, London, 1981, 178. This affirmation is a hypothesis. Cultures are not so radically different. These elements: truth, contemplation or prayer, and fraternity are present in different degrees in all cultures.

1.3.1.8.3 SENSE OF HOSPITALITY

The value of respect and kindness to strangers is treasured in the African world. The reason for this demeanor is very religious. It is generally believed that spirits and ancestors may sometimes appear in the form of visitors or strangers.

Hence, a religious halo surrounds visitors whether they are known or unknown[135]. Hospitality is expressed in symbolic ways: supply of necessary information and assistance to the visitor, presentation of kola nuts, traditional wine, and even food. Failure to comply with this is always considered a grave misdeed. F.C.Okafor has argued that,

> In traditional African culture, whenever there is food to be taken, everyone present is invited to participate even if the food was prepared for a less number of people without anticipating the arrival of visitors. It would be a height of incredible bad manners for one to eat anything however small, without sharing it with anyone else present, or at least expressing the intention to do so.[136]

The host is obliged to make the visitor feel safe and at home throughout his or her stay, and unless the visitor goes safe and sound the hospitality is not pure.

1.3.1.8.4 SENSE OF THE SACRED AND LOVE FOR PROVERBIAL SAYINGS

We have already seen that religion and religiousity is part and parcel of the African cultural heritage. To be is to be religious, to be religious is to be in the full sense of the word. The African recognizes that he is not master of the world.

The full responsibility for all the affairs of this life and the one beyond belongs to the supreme Being, who through all the circumstances of life, through all its changing scenes is in complete control.

Every African believes that an invisible universe was in action all around him or her, and that his or her life principle and that of the entire community is diminished if he or she happened to contravene the established order. He or she felt it was right and just to propitiate them, and to

---

135 Abraham and his wife warmly received the visitors before allowing them to proceed with their mission to Sodom (Gen 18,1-33).

136 Okafor, F.C., *Africa At Crossroads*, New York, 1974, 21.

conquer their goodwill. That was the fundamental reason why he had such a penchant for sacrifice in all its many forms.[137]

The ordinary life of the African is conducted in relation to the sacred. Africans take their religion wherever they go: in their families, at work, in the market, in the village square, they are conscious of their religious imperatives. Life and morality are considered direct fruits of religion. They do not make any attempt to separate the two, and it is impossible for them to do so without disastrous consequences.[138]

Local wisdom is highly appraised in the African world. Wisdom is weaved in proverbs and wise sayings, which constitute common vehicles for expressing and conveying religious ideas and feelings. Proverbs embody wisdom and wisdom in turn causes joy. One of the reasons behind African penchance for proverbs is the conviction that certain truths are so sublime and sacred that they may not be directly expressed. Such truths need to be "economised" in order to be expressed. This is in a partial sense similar to God's own way of acting through his Son, Jesus of Nazareth. Jesus is the Wisdom and Word of the Father. Always faithful to the Father's ways of acting, Jesus, taught most of the truths of the kingdom of God in wise sayings and parables.

Elders, considered as fountains of local wisdom are revered, among other things, for their proficiency in using the proverbial diction. To be a real African includes the ability to draw from this corporate depositum of the community. "Proverbs crystallize the accumulated wisdom handed down by the ancients, They reveal profound thoughts, the real soul of the people. This field is often closed to strangers".[139]

Thus was our world, a holistic universe which knew no distinction between the sacred and the profane. Thus we lived and worshipped before the arrival of Christianity. This is the African background to which the Christian faith has come.

Wherever Jesus of Nazareth passes, there He leaves his trace. Just as Elijah with a touch of his mantle made Elisa restless, so has Jesus' mantle touched us, and restless we have become, desirous to follow Him wherever He goes, wanting to possess Him and Him alone.

Since His entrance into our culture, things are no longer the same. We have realized that encounter with Jesus the Lord is one that "hits" and

---

137 Cf. Jordan, J.P., *Bishop Shanahan of Southern Nigeria*, Dublin, 1949, 126.
138 Cf. Idowu, E.B., *Olodumare - God In Yoruba Belief*, London, 1962, 146.
139 Francis Arinze, *Sacrifice in Ibo Religion*, 3.

remains. No individual or culture can encounter God and remain the same again.[140] Encounter with Him transforms, it elevates, it purifies, it sieves, it creates a crisis which, if it is well harnessed, leads to self-fulfilment and true realization. The details of this encounter between the African religious culture and Christianity is what now follows.

1.3.2 RELIGION IN AFRICA SINCE CHRISTIANITY

1.3.2.1 EVANGELIZATION OF AFRICA

As early as the first two decades after the death and resurrection of Jesus, the Good news had reached the African continent. It is popularly believed that St.Mark evangelized Egypt in the year 42 AD.

In these early and important days, the Christian message was so acclaimed that in the first seven centuries, a great part of North Africa, as well as Ethiopia and much of the Sudan witnessed a flourishing Church. By AD 180, North African Christianity had already produced its Martyrs of Scilli.

In fact, the first seven centuries witnessed a vibrant Christianity known for its theological and pastoral contribution to the whole Church:

> It was a dynamic form of Christianity, producing great scholars and theologians like Tertullian, Origen, Clement of Alexandria, Cyprian, and Augustine. African Christianity made great contribution to Christendom through scholarship, participation in Church Councils, defence of the faith, movements like Monasticism, the famous Catechetical School of Alexandria, and even heresies and controversies.[141]

This religious boom did not last. At the first "jolt" from the "wind of trial" from the Muslims and some Arab warriors, nearly the whole edifice crumbled, probably because of divisions in the Church, but above all due to its lack of contextualization or incarnation in the local cultures. It was built on sand with some false rocks in it.

---

140 I dwelt much on this point elsewhere. See my Dissertation ad Licentiam entitled *The Understanding of Sacrament In Contemporary Catholic and Protestant Theologies...*, Pontificia Università Urbaniana, Rome, 1992, 64-68.
141 Mbiti, J.S., *African Religions and Philosophy*, 229-30.

However, in Egypt and Ethiopia where attempts at indigenization were made, and where the local cultures were to some extent taken seriously, Christianity has, though battered and bruised, survived to this day.[142]

The second phase of Evangelization between the 15th and 18th centuries did not make much impact because of political manouvres and conflictual trivial interests between the Portuguese and the Papacy.

A more effective evangelization was embarked upon during the late 18th and early 19th centuries. This is directly or indirectly the consequence of the modern missionary movements which began in Europe and later in America at the end of the 18th century.

The reaction of the African to the advent of this new religion was a mixed one: from suspicion to antagonism, from indifference or rejection to neutrality, and from admiration to collaboration, and then to conversion.[143]

The initial reservations of the Africans towards Christianity is understandable if we consider that African religion had for centuries supplied them with direction and answers to many of the problems of this life even if not the right answers in every case.

And people are not willing to abandon easily what has always sustained them when they are not yet sure of what the new entails and where it leads.

1.3.2.2 REASONS FOR CONVERSION TO CHRISTIANITY

One of the reasons for conversion to the new faith was the curiosity of the African[144] populace in the face of the white missionaries whom they received according to the canons of traditional hospitality.

---

142 Cf. Ikenga R. Ozigbo, *Igbo Catholicism*. The Onitsha Connection 1967-1984, Onitsha, 1985, 115.

143 see Francis A. Arinze, *Answering God's Call*, London, 1983, 4.

144 Curiosity before divine Mystery and its manifestation is at the origin of many vocations. It was Moses' curiosity at Horeb that brought him nearer to God and led to his call to collaborate with God in liberating the people of God from bondage (Ex.3). It was their curious desire to see where Jesus lived that brought about the vocation of the first two disciples of Jesus, curiosity brought about their following Jesus and "remaining" with him (Jn.1.35-42). One can say that curiosity "implicated" these biblical personalities.

First and foremost the white missionaries were strange creatures to the natives, a spectacle for a people who hitherto had no contact with them. Curious, Africans drew closer to see, and from seeing they heard what these visitors had to say, and from hearing the good news of salvation proclaimed by the visitors, many Africans were converted to Christianity. In other words curiosity "implicated" the Africans.

The claim of the missionaries, namely, that they had a message from the supreme God, who came down from the sky, and was born like us, was seen, heard, touched by men with whom he grew, was maltreated, killed, resurrected, returned to the sky, and has «despatched us to announce these things to you»[145] provoked unprecedented attention.

Above all the missionaries proffered a holy book where, with the authorization of the supreme God, these things were written down. Africans could not resist the news of God's direct, definitive, and unique intervention in human history.

That the invisible, inaccessible, God is now accessible to the African ear, was indeed good news, a real cause of joy[146]. Africans imbued with the sense of mystery and wonder gave in to this announcement.

Africans were also deeply touched to hear that this Son of the supreme God was innocently murdered as He came to save all men from their sins and from the oppression of evil. The expression «for us and for our salvation He was crucified and died» provoked in many Africans a feeling of guilt for having contributed to the death of the Son of God. This feeling of responsibility ignited a spontaneous desire to express solidarity with him and with his cause. Blood for the Africans is highly significant. Anything that entails the spilling of blood for us strikes a note of great concern. That this Jesus came to give his life for others for, Africans implied something serious was at stake.

That His blood was spilled by those for whom he came and innocently too provoked feelings of unrestrained sympathy and led to conversions. "Something great must be behind all this". With this understanding many more joined the new faith.

---

145 St. Clement of Rome, 1 Cor. 42. 1-2; PG 2,57.
146 It was curious for Africans to hear that God who had withdrawn had once more pitched his tent among men. On this very point inumerable moving songs have been composed. I limit myself to documenting one in Igbo: 'O bu ihe oñu n'ezie, O bu ihe oñu n'ezie, Jisus Nwa Chukwu biara n'uwa a, O bu ihe oñu n'ezie; literally rendered: 'It is indeed a cause of joy, it is a cause of joy, that Jesus the Son of God came to the world, is a cause of joy'.

Many, however, remained adamant and suspicious of the foreign intruders. It may be recalled that the missionary evangelizing activities went hand in hand with the colonization of Africa by Western countries. Many Africans were overpowered, oppressed, and even carried away to slavery.

In order to send away these foreigners for good, in some places they were given lands belonging to the most sinister spirit-gods to clear and inhabit. The intention was to lure them into the rancour of these gods who would inflict untold woes on the unwelcome visitors. In many other places sacrifices were offered in abundance to the spirits so that people could be liberated from the foreigners.

Yet the results were drammatic. Instead of meeting with untold harm, the missionaries grew stronger daily in winning converts. "A God is at work among gods", many pious pagans admitted. And that God is the Christian God! Practically the failure of the traditional gods to assure protection and security of their followers at the moment of their desperate trial had put the credibility and repute of these gods into question.

Since they had proved powerless in the "contest" with the New God and his followers in spite of their having the advantage of being on home ground, they now merited being abandoned. Facts have proven the superiority of the Christian God and his followers. A missionary reporting of the frustration of some Ibo group who had asked him to dismantle the shrine of a now impotent god writes:

> I inquired of them why, if this was their firm conviction, they did not destroy such a spiteful god? They were anxious to do so, they replied but declared that the task was beyond their powers;....When I rounded upon them...and told them that I had no wish to be eaten by the 'spirit', or be overwhelmed with disaster, they were emphatic in their declaration that Ngenne could not exercise power over one who prayed to Chukwu (The Supreme being). These people were pure heathen, wholly untouched by christian teaching and influence.[147]

They proved to be impotent before "the God whose will is supreme". They failed the test of potency. The words of the psalmist had been verified: "they have mouths, but never speak, eyes, but never see, ears, but never hear, noses, but never smell, hands, but never touch, feet, but never walk ..." (Psalm 115,3-8). Those who relied on these gods ended up like them weak, defenceless, conquered, and disarrayed.

---

147 Basden, G.T., *Among the Ibos of Nigeria*, London, 1966, 214.

The ritual wealth which characterize the Chrisitan religion was an important factor. The fact that through some rituals or sacraments believers enter into communion with the Redeemer of mankind and share in his life was appealing to many Africans for whom ritual celebrations signify a great deal. The desire to partake of the life of the Saviour in the rituals of his Church led to some conversions.

The sight of the white missionaries and their "squad" with superior ships, guns and bullets, mirrors, cigarettes, different hot drinks, and other "goodies" of civilization, and the impression that these people were able to acquire these things because of the power and knowledge of their God, is another factor.

Desire to learn the "key" to the white people's secrets, and the thought of having these advantages by joining this new religion cannot be ruled out as one the reasons for some conversions to Christianity.

The evangelizing strategy of the missionaries was a vital factor. The provision of missionary schools and education for the young later served as a bait to attract the parents. Many pagans encouraged their children to follow the missionaries so as not to lose whatever advantage the new movement might bring.

And as the young drifted en masse some old people, for the sake of solidarity with their children, joined the queue. It cannot be ruled out that some pagans became Christians for fear of loneliness. They prefered to be where their children were, in this world and in the next. We have already seen that for the Africans to be is to be with others in life and in death.

Another important reason is the dedicated work of the missionaries themselves, their noble deeds, perseverance, endurance, determination, sometimes with heavy costs of life, material welfare, health and career, for the sake of the gospel.[148] Now, sincere sacrifices are rewarding, and the blood of martyrs ever fruitful. Just as from the blood of Jesus was born the Church, so after Him has the blood of all who die for His cause kept the Church fertile and sustained. In the same way, from the labours of the missionaries and over their bones the new African Church sprung forth.

The "live and let live" attitude or the tolerant nature of the traditional religion was another reason for conversion. Hardly was anyone persecuted for professing a particular faith as long as he did not disrupt nor-

---

148 Cf. Mbiti, J.S., *Bible and Theology in African Chrisitanity*, 8.

mal life in the community. Added to this factor is what C.N.Ubah called "the structural and organizational weaknesses of the traditional religion". He writes:

> It had no common leadership or common authority structure .... There was no common deity symbolising a common identity of the followers of this religion and which would have served as a rallying point for collective action on a large scale. The village groups' deities had a very limited territorial appeal, ...[149]

These are the circumstances from which God has called us. This is a picture of our own history of salvation. And saving the best for last, I add here the grace of the Holy Spirit which stands behind every experience of conversion and which works through different circumstances.

Jesus was referring to this when he said: "No one can come to me unless the Father draws him" (Jn.6,44). Africans have been drawn to the Son by the Father from the above situations. This is how and why we became Christians.

Using the strong words of Jürgen Moltmann, one can say that we are Christians for Christ's sake.[150] And following Newman, one can say God's mercy did for us, what the system in which we were in failed to do.[151] What may be enough for us may be totally insufficient for other people.

The novelty of Christianity for Africans did not consist in its proclamation of one God, but rather in the more complete and definite proclamation of that one God whom Africa already knew, and who is also the God of Jesus Christ.

According to Newman, Christianity tells us what its Author is by telling us what he has done.[152] More clearly than the African Traditional Religion, it showed how this one God is and wishes to be, and can be better known, loved and worshipped.[153]

In the light of the role of grace, Africans have reason to say that our supreme Master has definitively imparted truths to us which nature

---

149 C.N.Ubah, 'Religious Change Among the Igbo During the Colonial Period', in *Journal of Religion in Africa*, vol.xviii - Fasc.1, February 1988, 87.
150 see J. Moltmann, *Experiences of God*, London, 1980, 9, 17.
151 see LD XX, 340 (5.11.62).
152 see GA 73.
153 see Bujo, B., 'Der afrikanische Ahnenkult und die christliche Verkündigung', in *Zeitschrift für Missions und Religionswissenschaft* 64, 1980, 293-306, esp. 298; see also Bujo, B., *African Theology in Its Social Context*, 18.

taught only in part to us. Christian Revelation is unique for in it nature and grace work harmoniously together; Christianity is the completion and supplement of Natural Religion, and of previous revelation.[154]

1.3.2.3   FRIENDS OF GOD BUT NOT WORSHIPPERS IN "SPIRIT AND TRUTH"[155]

In order to facilitate our encounter with His Son, Jesus the Christ, God prepared us from the beginning of our history. The Christian message is therefore not strange to the African religious world.

Just as Judaism and Greek philosophy prepared their adherents for the final truth of Christianity, so did African religion and culture prepare the Africans. "There is but one river of truth", Clement wrote, "but many streams pour into it. The Law is for the Jew what philosophy is for the Greek, a school master to bring them to God".[156]

In some sense, what the Law and philosophy were to the Jew and the Greek, traditional religion and culture were to the African. Yet, despite its important preparatory role for the Gospel, African religion and culture cannot be totally equated to Judaism or Hellenism. Judaism constitutes a religious tradition expressly chosen by God for revealing himself. Thus the Old Testament has a definitive place and role in salvation history. It is the word of God, Sacred Scripture.

Hellenism on the other hand constitutes an instrument for explicating the revealed data and definition of dogma. It was an instrument in the hand of the Church for the explanation and formulation of her understanding of divine revelation. Certain concepts of Greek philosophy were adopted, transformed and incorporated into the Church's vocabulary. Once incorporated such concepts as 'prosopon' (persona) assumed a new meaning. One can say that while the Old Testament constitutes Verbum Dei, Hellenism constitutes Verbum Ecclesiae. And both Verbum Dei and Verbum Ecclesiae have a universal validity.

---

154 see GA 250.
155 Of course this is the tag name for the new cult inaugurated by the Son of God himself who has revealed to all the way henceforth God wants all true worshippers to go. Africans worshipped God meticulously but not in this way.
156 Stromateis, 1.5.28; PG 8,685; see also W.H.C. Frend, 'The Christian Period in Mediterranean Africa, c. AD 200 to 700' in *The Cambridge History of Africa*, vol.2 From c. 500 BC to AD 1050, Cambridge, 1978, 400.

African religious culture for its own part is a place for the actualization of the revealed data. The revelation made to the Jews, and through them to all men; this revelation formulated in categories of Greek philosophy, is addressed to African culture.

In making the intellectus fidei, African Christians can adopt and transform some African categories and symbols for the clarification of their faith and in doing so, arrive at a particular verbum Ecclesiae. Even when this is done, it may not claim as much universal validity as the other two.

In a sermon on Whit Sunday in 1841, Newman noted that religious minds embrace the Gospel mainly on the great antecedent probability of a revelation, and the suitableness of the gospel to their needs.[157] Thus all men have been capacitated in different ways to live in friendship with God, pending the definitive disclosure of the new cult:

pagan literature, philosophy and mythology, properly understood, were but a preparation for the Gospel. The Greek poets and sages were in a certain sense prophets.... There had been a directly divine dispensation granted to the Jews, but there had been in some sense a dispensation carried on in favour of the Gentiles. He who had taken the seed of Jacob for His elect people had not therefore cast the rest of mankind out of His sight.[158]

Belief in revealed truths of Christianity presupposes belief in natural revelation, while acceptance of the arguments for Christianity rests on acceptance of certain general religious truths.[159]

The definitive divine eschatology in Jesus of Nazareth also implied a purification of the Word of God (which has been addressed to men in different ways) from those corruptions and additions to which it has been subjected by men, and the perfection of the same. Newman is therefore categorical in affirming not only that Christianity fulfils natural religion, but it is the continuation of a revelation that goes back to the beginnings of time,[160] what he calls elsewhere,

... a primeval tradition which is universal and which must exist if there was an Adam, a father of men, in direct communication with his Creator ...[161]

---

157 see OUS, 279.
158 Apo 36.
159 see GA 250.
160 Ibid.
161 LD XXVIII, 257 (23.10.1877).

The work of the Church becomes then like that of a good choirmaster who makes melodies from simple voices by training and fitting in discordant voices in order to produce a harmonized chorus. Newman expresses this idea beautifully:

... from the beginning the Moral Governor of the world has scattered the seeds of truth far and wide, over its extent and those have variously taken root, and grown up as in the wilderness, wild plants indeed but living; and hence that, as the inferior animals have tokens of an immaterial principle in them, yet have not souls, so the philosophies and religions of men have their life in certain true ideas .... What man is amid brute creation, such is the Church among the schools of the world; and as Adam gave names to the animals about him so has the Church from the first looked round upon the earth, noting and visiting the doctrines and wisdom she found there. And wherever she went ... still she was a living spirit, the mind of the Most High "sitting in the midst of the doctors, both hearing them and asking them questions", claiming to herself what they said rightly, correcting their errors, supplying their defects, completing their beginnings, expanding their surmises, and thus gradually by means of them enlarging the range and refining the sense of her own teaching ....[162]

It is clear then, that true Christianity does not subtract but recognizes and adds to the wealth of values of peoples, knowing full well that it can easily prove its claims by an appeal to what men already have,[163] and so that under the Gospel, men do not lose any good part of nature, but rather they gain something more.

1.3.3 FEATURES OF AFRICAN CHRISTIANITY

Christianity has come to stay in Africa. Its encounter with the African religious culture has left the latter in crisis. Since the encounter, the "edges" of the traditional religion are no longer as sharp as they were before the advent of Christianity.

Much of the old faith has crumbled because some of the traditional structures that upheld it are no longer the same. However, much of the old religion remains under the surface and continues to influence men's thinking. One has therefore, to be cautious against two tendencies: talk-

---

162 Ess. II, 231-232 (Milman's View of Christianity).
163 see GA 388; also 413.

66

ing of African religion in the past tense and speaking of it as if it were still in the golden age:

> It is a mistake either to look at the religion as if nothing happened, or to treat it as vanished without a trace. Neither the isolationist nor the archaelogical attitudes are adequate to modern times.[164]

Generally the features of African Christianity are mixed: positive and negative, joy and concern, growth and threat, hope and fear, deep and superficial faith, vibrant and threatened. To borrow the wording of Newman, what our Church is now living can be called its spring, an uncertain, anxious time of hope and fear, of joy and suffering, of bright promises and budding hopes, and certain set-backs.[165] So far, the picture of the African Church is one of double-image, coincidentia oppositorum.

1.3.3.1 VIBRANT DYNAMISM

Young as it may be in comparison with the Christianity of other continents, African Christianity is already a religion of tradition - a genuinely African traditional religion. Its ministry and sacraments are in daily high demand and in a Christian sense traditional enough already.

In many parts of Africa, Christianity is almost as indigenous as maize-meal, foofoo, or banana beer. Biblical verses are the themes or objects of popular songs and greetings. The Bible is the only large book to be published in the vernacular of most African people.[166]

Africans have carried over their religiousity and gaiety to the new cult, and this religious instinct has been increased by the very quality of Christianity, as a religion of sursum corda.[167] It is a religion which separates and elevates man from the state of "fallenness"

Christianity is a religion which raises man up and puts him at a "noble" distance from sin and evil. Jesus promised to draw all men to himself. Christianity is therefore able to elevate man because it came from heaven.

---

164 Geoffery Parrinder, West African Religion, 187.
165 Cf. OUS, 179-80 (6.1.1839); see also Pre.Pos., 225.
166 Cf. Adrian Hastings, *African Catholicism. Essays in Discovery*, London, 1989, xi.
167 Newman says: «Christianity raises men from earth, for it comes from heaven ...» (DA 272-75).

Many African Christians have realised this, and do not make private or secret of their faith. They carry and manifest it everywhere.[168] In Nigeria, for instance, even commercial and private buses, transport lorries, houses, business centres have religious phrases, biblical slogans and verses, and short epithets: Kyrie Eleison, In the Name of the Father, One with God is majority, Ave Maria, The Lord is my Shepherd, Jesus is Lord, Jesus is Power, Glory be to God, etc., written on them.[169]

Innumerable songs composed from biblical passages, and from Christian creeds and prayers, and exchange of greetings with such words as "Praise God", "Alleluia", "Amen", are common. It is equally common to hear African Christians discuss in public places, squares, markets, though not in scientific ways questions touching on christology, pneumatology, mariology, etc[170]. Indeed, in Africa today one has reason to say «this name, Jesus, grace surrounds it».[171] This feature confirms St.Augustne's own declaration in his *De vera Religione*:

> ... the way of the good and blessed life is to be found entirely in the true religion wherein one God is worshipped and acknowledged with the purest piety to be the beginning of all existing things.... In Christian times there can be no doubt at all as to which religion is to be received and held fast, and as to where is the way that leads to truth and beatitude.[172]

And Lactantius, writing of the advantage of the followers of Jesus over their predecessors and others who worship God differently said:

> here, here, is that for which all philosophers have sought throughout their life, but never once been able to track down.[173]

---

168 As if in fulfilment of the injunction: «... let these words I urge on you today be written on your heart. You shall repeat them to your children and say them over to them whether at rest in your house or walking, at your lying down or at your rising» (Deut.6,7).

169 see Francis Arinze, *Answering God's Call*, 23; also Mbiti, J.S., *Bible and Theology in African Christianity*, 3.

170 Cf. Igwegbe O.O.I., 'The Challenge of Religious Sects and the Future of Christianity', NACATHS Journal of Theology, vol.3, 1993, 72.

171 C.R.C. Allberry, *Manichean Psalmbook*, Part II, 185, no.20 (Manichean Manuscripts in the Chester Beatty Collection, vol.ii, 1938).

172 St. Augustine, *De vera Religione*, i,1, iii,3; PL 34,121.

173 Lactantius, *Divinae Institutiones*, III,30; PL 6,444-446.

The massive presence of the African religion is a factor largely responsible for the rapid spread of the Christian faith. African religion prepared the ground for many of its adherents to receive the teachings of the Bible, to reflect seriously upon them, to find a high sense of credibility in them, to discover meaningful parallels between their world and the world of the Bible, and in many cases to convert to the Christian faith without feeling a sense of spiritual loss, but on the contrary gaining a new enlargement in their religious experience.[174]

1.3.3.2 FEATURES OF CONCERN

After barely one or two generations of Christianity in Africa, serious areas of concern are already parts of its dynamism. Signs of old age and cracks can already be read on its face.

The African Church, as young as it is and faced with initial problems of growth, has her own share of problems and challenges of the contemporary world. In many aspects, the Church in Africa is a young Church with an old face. Anti-Christian or sometimes anti-religious tendencies of western society have their echoes in Africa as well. Her experience is peculiar.

In her youth, the African Church is forced to face the same problems as her elder-sister-Churches. In such a situation she is always tempted to address these problems in the same ways as her elder-sister-Churches to the detriment of special attention to her peculiarity.

Another area of preoccupation is what concerns African cultural heritage. Serious clashes exist between the two. Up till now African cultural heritage has not been positively appreciated. While the Church in some areas has rejected African culture as a manifestation of the devil, and almost as "an agreed language between men and demons",[175] some cultural Revivalists and Nationalists, have divinized the traditional culture as the gifts of the gods to men.[176]

To avoid this conflict leading to bigger tears, African thought and culture has been introduced in some universities and theological schools.

---

174 Cf. Mbiti. J.S., Op.cit., 20 and 185.
175 St. Augustine, *De doctrina christiana*, II,xxiv,37; PL 34,15; see also J.B. Zoa, 'Committed Christians Building a new Africa', AFER, 8, no.2, 1966, 99-104, esp.102.
176 Cf. Baynes, N.H., 'The Hellenistic Civilization and East Rome', *Byzantine Studies and Other Essays*, Boston, 1955, 15-16.

The aim is to discover those vital elements of African culture which are imprinted on the African soul. The result of these studies have yet to be utilized by African Catholicism. Meanwhile, Independent Churches and New religious movements are exploiting these loopholes. And the future of Christianity in African much depends on getting the right balance between the old and the new.

Another very difficult and slippery problem which African Christianity has to live and contend with is the reality of a divided Christendom, a division brought and sown by the early evangelizers, a division that still remains a serious wound in the bosom of a culture that valued common living and worship.

It is my contention that at this stage in her life, African Christianity is somehow living the experiences of some of the early Christian communities.

The stark question that tormented the first Antiochian Christian community is alive in many African Christian communities, namely, who saves?, Jesus or the Law?, the old religion or the new faith?, the traditions of the ancestors or the Eschatological Word in Jesus? (Acts.15). A dry "either or" solution adopted by some parties cause painful frictions or double allegiance.

Equally verifiable is the situation of the Corinthian Community where many baptized Christians carried some practices of their former belief and life-styles into the new sanctuary. Such believers practise the Christian Religion, but they also do not omit the beliefs and life patterns of their former system.

In his days, Augustine, who faced similar pastoral problems, said that such Christians invoked the name of God in His house amidst the antiphon "the righteous shall enter in", while wearing amulets, assiduous clients of sorcerers, astrologers; the same crowds that press into the Churches, also fill the diviners' cottage after Church service.[177]

Again I still dare to argue that the very experiences of the early Hebrew Christian community are very much reflected in many African Christian communities. Many Christians have found waned or waning their initial enthusiasm for the new faith. Some are looking back with

---

177 Cf. St.Augustine, de cat. rud. xxv,48; PL 40,309; Sermon 311; PL 38,1248; Ep.245,2; de doct. christ. II,xx,30; Enaratio in Ps.88, sermo 2,4, PL 27,1140: 'Ad idolam quidem vado, arreptitios et sortilegos consulo, sed tamen Dei ecclesiam non relinquo: Catholicus sum'.

nostalgia to the ceremonies and rituals and some practices of the old religion which they abandoned at the moment of their baptism.

Like the Isrealites on Exodus, many African Christians are already tired and are tempted to go back from where they departed; many indeed have broken their journey, and many are reluctantly marching on. Here is what one may term "the beginning of protests". Such protests have different outlets: the tone of many African theological literature[178] and the life style of many African Christians. According to Arinze some people are of the opinion that one of the reasons for this development is that,

> Christianity was not presented to them in a way that is appealing but rather in a manner that sets their culture aside, a way that leaves them culturally impoverished and thus fails to satisfy the yearnings of the African soul.[179]

Yet these are souls that came to the brook of Christianity with the yearning of the uncomplete in order to be filled, "like the deer yearns for running water".

It is this phenomenon that permits one to say that «the mixed religion of today is as real as the paganism of yesterday».[180] Many African Christians feel a serious religious vacuum that needs to be filled by a Christianity with an African face and soul.[181]

While it is true that inadequate attention to the African genius is to some extent responsible for "protests" within the African Church, it is equally true that most of the protests are due to the fact that many African Christians thought that by opting for Christ they were embarking on a journey, on a flat and smooth road leading to a land flowing with milk and honey. Many thought that they were called by a meek and gentle

---

178 The fact that most of the protest is coming from theologians and pastors is an indication of the depth of the question.

179 Francis Arinze, *Living Our Faith. Lenten Pastorals 1971-1983*, Onitsha, 1983, 48.

180 Geoffrey Parrinder, *West African Religion*, 187.

181 Cf. Moila, M.P., 'The African Version of Christianity' in Journal of Black Theology In South Africa, vol.5 no 1 May 1991, 33-39. see also MAC (Meeting for African Collaboration, a body acting within the Symposium of the Episcopal Conferences of Africa and Madagascar, SECAM), 'New Christian Movements in Africa and Madagascar' in Catholic International, vol.4 no 1, January 1993, 29-37, esp. 34.

Jesus without a cross. Some thought that option for Jesus dispenses one automatically from problems[182].

Instead they have realised that to be a Christian means to renounce oneself, not to drop but to take up one's cross daily, and a readiness to lose one's life in order to save it. Many thought that they can remain Christians while at the same time holding tight to their "old ways", thus creating for themselves what may be called "a double security". Instead some of these believers have realised that the Christian God is a "jealous God" who, abhors double standards, who, wants either all of their hearts or nothing. This heavy cost of discipleship is the core of this development.

The fact is that the presence of Christianity in the African religious culture has given birth to "another kind of culture, a new culture, ... a new consciousness",[183] a new kind of culture that requires a new attention and response.

From the encounter, a new synthesis is yearning to emerge, a synthesis which consists not in replacing the God of the Africans but rather of enthroning the God of Jesus Christ.

It is not to be expected that Africans have made, or can make, quam primum, a complete break with the past, however much they profess to do so. Deep conversion and maturity in faith is gradual. In the words of Newman, «Great acts take time».[184] Not even Augustine could shed off his old background at once:

In the five years between his conversion in 386 and his ordination as a priest in 391, Augustine spent much of his time living in monastic seclusion with groups of friends, engaged in meditation, discussion and writing. Some of the treatises of this period are so exclusively philosophical that it has been argued that it was to neo-platonism rather than to Christianity that he had been converted.[185]

Since the mantle of leadership in African Christianity fell on Africans, efforts have been made to present anew and to hear the Christian message again, and to respond directly to the question: «And you, who do you say I am?» in African idioms, symbols and imageries in a way that

---

182 see Igwegbe O.O.I., Op.cit.67.
183 Mbiti, J.S., *African Religions and Philosophy*, 127.
184 Apo 169.
185 Louis O.Mink., *Introduction, Of True Religion*, translated by Burleigh, J.H.S, Chicago, 1953, xi.

makes the orderly transition from the old to the new faith without loss of any of its ancient values possible.

The pioneer missionaries arduosly laboured to announce to us what God has said. But today Africans strive to discern what God is saying to them. Surely, the missionaries did not say things as they are; but only as they were able to describe them, because they were men speaking about God. No doubt they were assisted by the Holy Spirit for they said something: if they had not been under divine assistance, they would have said nothing. But, because those who were assisted were men, they did not say everything: they said only what men could say.[186]

The work of African theologians and pastors is an integration of Christian heritage and African genius in a single theological system in order to create a Christianity with an African soul, yet with an open heart towards the universal Church. The best elements in African religion are yearning to be sublimated into the new dispensation:

> on the credal side recognition in daily life of ubiquitous spiritual forces working in the universe; on the practical side by the transference to the new religion on a higher level of something of the symbolism, the colour, the artistry, the gaiety that marked the old.[187]

Each group of people encounters God in their historical context. It is remarkable that divine truth is one, though the revelation made to Isaiah is different from that made to Jeremiah, neither is the revelation made to Ezekiel the same as that made to Daniel.

In the same manner the final Revelation made by God to all in Jesus Christ has to be "coated" in African symbolic categories in order to be understood and lived by those to whom the revelation is made after the example of the Son of God, who became the Son of man that man might become the son of God[188]. Revelation and its expression has to pass through the symbolic path in order to bring the addressee to the sacramental level.

---

186 see St. Augustine, In *Joannem*, tract,1, no 1; PL 35,1379.
187 Geoffery Parrinder, *West African Religion*, xiv.
188 Cf. St.Irenaeus, *Advers. Haer*.3,19,1, PL. 7,939.

1.4 THE PERMANENCY OF SYMBOLIC THINKING

Africans had themselves believed with the fervor they always displayed, many of the views which they later abandoned. They had believed them because they answered their questions, and their conversion to Christianity did not mean abandonment of the questions but the discovery of a better Answer[189].

One of the cardinal points of continuity verifiable in the the reality of African Christianity and African religion is in the use of signs and symbols - the symbolic mentality.

Behind this symbolic mentality is the belief that one God alone rules all things, acting and manifesting through various modes in a world in which the activities that characterize life are a reflection of the invisible world of God and the ancestors. African symbolic mentality sees beyond external objects, to discern deeper and more mysterious realities beneath.

Imbued with a deep sense of wonder while living in close vicinity to nature, Africans discern the presence of the Infinite in the finite, the Eternal in the temporal, the Sacred in the profane, the Invisible in the visible, the Divine in the worldly, God in the world.

They possess eyes that see God's presence in the world, ears that hear the sweet melody of Divinity and echoes of the Infinite in the cosmos, and a general demeanour that proclaim these evident truths. This way of understanding or viewing the world, is called symbolic thinking.

The traditional African world is conceived to be goal-oriented. It can be said to have an "intentional stance". And in such an intentional world, events are supposed to have a meaning and a purpose and nothing happens by chance[190]. From this point of view, the field of symbolic forces throws a different light on the signs of salvation or the nearness of God. And it this that permits one to speak of the African symbolic world.

Signs and symbols are among the privileged ways God speaks. The sphere of religion is the arena of symbolism. The exchange of contact between man and his maker is realised through words, and where words fail, symbolic language takes over.

---

189 Cf. Adrian Hastings, *African Catholicism...*, 89. Jesus of Nazareth is the Answer to the fundamental interrogations to which traditional religion has hitherto offered solutions. Jesus is the Answer!

190 see Kwame Antony Appiah, In *My Father's House*, New York, 1965, 46.

No man or group of people ever had contact with God in a naked, un-adorned, unmediated, unsacramentalized, unsymbolized manner. It comes through gestures, rituals, objects, things which are in turn made sacred[191]. For African religious minds symbols are the best expression of religious mysteries.

The special capacity of a symbol to "put together", "join together", "compose together", "throw together" sacred and the secular, the material and the spiritual, in short the various aspects of a reality, and the force to produce a superior meaning strongly linked to but different from its point of departure, tallies with the Greek etymology of symbol: syn - ballein[192].

Symbol in itself then has a unifying function. And the words of Origen come to mind when he affirms that Christ as He appeared in history is a sign of contradiction since;

... in Him one thing is seen, but another is believed; He is seen in human flesh, but is believed to be God.[193]

There is therefore, a symbol when from a visible *quid* the human spirit makes a "qualitative jump" to the other profound aspect; there is the mysterious presence of symbol when one thing is seen, experienced or lived but another comes to mind. John Chrysostom affirms the presence of divine Mystery,

... not when we believe what we see but when we see one reality, and from this we believe another.[194]

In the light of the above affirmations, symbols help to lift up the heart from the visible to the invisible, from the temporal to the eternal, from

---

191 see Owen Chadwick, The Spirit of the Oxford Movement. Tractarian Essays, Cambridge, 1990, 307.
192 On the very meaning of the word "symbol", viz. bringing together of two parts that originally belonged together, numerous African myths which hold the skies and earth as originally belonging together immediately come to mind. For the Yorubas, for instance, the invisible world is intimately joined to this world, like the top and bottom halves of a single calabash.
193 Origen, In *Rom. Comm.*4,2 PG 14,396 A.
194 John Chrysostom, In *1Cor 1-2, Hom.*7,1, PG 61,65.

the finite to the infinite[195]. A major characteristic of the symbolic universe is its openness to the world of the Sacred, the Infinite.

African religion often sees signs of God's presence or rather his immanence in ordinary events and in the extraordinay powers which are at work in the natural world. This is possible because their cosmology considers everything as related to the will of God. African religion is richer in signs and symbols than it is in concepts. It is a religious world where all things speak.[196]

Consequently, Africans live and worship symbolically: some symbols can be looked as objects, acted or danced out as music, painted or carved out as art, spoken and lived as words and rituals, revered and respected as institutions, Ancestors, or Community.

In these diverse expressions of its wealth, symbol does something to Africans, it moves them, shifts their centre of awareness, changes their values. And to these concretizations of symbolic thinking we now turn.

1.4.1 LINGUISTIC SYMBOLS

African linguistic symbols constitute a non-material-real group of symbols wrapped in imageries, short stories, wise sayings, myths or legends, proverbs, riddles or epithets. In such symbolic codes, which need to be decodified for their meaning to be unveiled, the ancestors enclosed their religious life experiences and the expression of the same.[197] Thus, words have a sacred and quasi-sacramental character. And thus weaved in special linguistic codes, they are preserved from abuse.

Systematic use of symbols is a dominant feature of most societies without written language. And since African culture is overwhelmingly oral, speech and communication between people is filled with an infinite variety of symbols drawn from the concrete universe of their experience wherein language finds its expression. The spoken word itself contains a system of symbols of reality. For example, among the Ewondo and the Bulu, to "count the nights", means to live as man and wife.[198]

---

195 Cf. Lürker Manfred, *Dizionario delle Immagini e dei Simboli Biblici*, Milano, 1987, v-vi.
196 Cf. Bastide, R., 'Religions africaines et Structures de civilisation', Présence *Africaine* 66, 1968, 101.
197 see Chinua Achebe, *Morning Yet On Creation. Day Essays*, London, 1982, 35.
198 Cf. Jean Marc Ela, *My Faith as an African*, 35.

In the African universe of symbols, many animals feature in the countless myths. Thus the lizard or the toad is the messenger of death, and the chameleon or the snake, of resurrection or immortality, the spider and the tortoise, the epitome of wisdom. Since African traditional religion and Christianity encountered each other, a new vocabulary is emerging among Christians. It has become common to hear such "figurative languages" as a "Methuselah", a "Jezebel", a "Solomon", a "Job", a "Jonah", a "Judas", "to have an Abraham as one's father", etc.

1.4.2 RITUAL SYMBOLS

Ritual symbols by their characteristic involving nature, arouse "not only thought, but delight, fear, awe, ..."[199] in man and thus, transport him to the realm of the transcendence. They are vehicles for communication of divine truths and values to the participants in the second person singular, you, in order to qualify the subject for an active role in the religious universe:

This property derives from the involvement of all key ritual symbols in the dialectics of thought and communication event, and more especially - in their capacity as sacred objects to integrate for man all areas of experience in the transcendental centre of real meaning.[200]

In a society where everything is within a sacred cosmic order, birth, marriage, puberty, death, planting and harvesting, the critical moments in the life of individuals or the community are given due attention and accompanied by special ceremonies.

The different transition rites or rites-de-passage are intended to transform the subjects from outsiders to insiders, from on-lookers to participants, from neophytism to expertise, from consumers to producers, in short, from nobody to somebody, from non members to full members of a social group. And exactly because ritual symbols are corporate property, they are obligatory:

---

199 Victor White, God and the Unconscious, Cleveland, 1952, 234.
200 Ejizu, C.I., *Igbo Ritual Symbol*, Enugu, Publishers, 1986, 5.

Rituals reveal values at their deepest level...men express in ritual what moves them most, and since the form of expression is conventionalised and obligatory, it is the values of the group that are revealed.[201]

The ritual ceremony is more than a language of gestures and symbols; it is a decisive experience that changes the subject's state of being granting him or her a new form of existence in the larger world.

The transformation undergone is often manifested in the new identity, role, or name which the initiate assumes. Through the ritualised sequence of instructions and ordeals, the slowness of passage through life and the contest between life and death are represented and the triumph of life is ultimately highlighted.

One of the most important properties of symbolism is that it gives not a speculative but a participatory knowledge normally not accessible to discursive thought,[202] a knowledge of a self-involving type, conferring an experience that enables the subject to speak like one who saw, like one who was there.

Symbols in this sense are environments to be inhabited, places to live that help us discover new horizons and the possibilities that life offers. "It speaks to us only insofar as it lures us to situate ourselves mentally within the universe of meaning and value which it opens to us".[203]

Ritual symbols are capable of working on people like incantations. They stir the imagination, release hidden energies in the soul, give strength and stability to the personality, and arouse the will to consistent and committed action.[204]

Ritual symbols have these capacities because of their close relation to Mystery which they disclose not by presenting their meaning for inspection but by drawing the participants into their movement and by carrying them out of themselves[205] and thus giving rise to thought in the same participants.[206]

---

201 Wilson, M., quoted by Victor W.Turner, *The Ritual Process*, Penguin, 1974, 6.

202 Paul Tillich argues well that a symbol «opens up levels of reality which otherwise are closed to us ... and also unlocks dimensions and elements of our soul which correspond to the dimensions and elements of reality» (*Dynamics of Faith*, New York, 1957, 42).

203 Mitchell, N., 'Symbols are Actions, Not Objects', in *Living Worship* 13/2, February 1977, 1-2.

204 Cf. Avery Dulles, 'Symbolism' in *New Catholic Encyclopedia* 13, 861-63.

205 Cf. Polanyi, M., & Prosch, H., *Meaning*, Chicago, 1975, 66-67; see also Wilbur Urban, who argues very well that the peculiar character of 'insight symbols', "lies

1.4.3 SYMBOLIC OBJECTS

The African symbolic mentality also finds expression in the use of objects, colours, animals, stools, wood, stones, calabashes, pots, etc. In African religious culture, spirits are believed to be embodied in, or attached to, or conveying influence through material objects. Material objects are believed to be "alive", to "speak", and to transmit some message which does not come from man but from above. The theory of Sacramentalism rests on a similar assumption.

In African Christianity, the theory of Sacramentalism[207] is to a large extent so real in the lives of the people that one can speak of practical Sacramentalism. Many African Christians believe in the power of the Psalms; sacramentals are in daily use: crosses and scapulars are largely worn, holy water is widely used, and even pagans frequent Churches on Ash Wednesday in order to receive ash. Such religious objects instil in worshippers or in pious minds sentiments of fear, reverence, and devotion.

Through the instrumentality of certain material objects, worshippers have access or insight into mysteries beyond the ordinary limits of reason. Direct, mystical intuition or direct interior illumination and knowledge of religious truths which dispenses with mediation finds little or no reception in African religious experience.

Africans are convinced that for mortal man revelation must be mediated by signs given in history - signs which Barth in his later works describes as sacramental embodiments of revelation.[208] It is this role that African symbolic objects fulfil.

---

in the fact that they do not point to or lead to, but they *lead into*; ... they are, or at least are supposed to be, a vehicle or medium of insight" (*Language and Reality*, London, 1939, 415).

206 Cf. Paul Ricoeur, Symbolism of Evil, Boston, 1969, 348. And in the preceding pages we said that symbols help us to lift up our souls.

207 Of course the theory of sacramentalism present in African Religion is different from its equivalent in Christianity. African religious sacramentalism falls short of important requisites of christian sacramentalism: institution by Jesus Christ, efficacy in the power of the Spirit, communication of salvific grace, etc.

208 Cf. Karl Barth, *Church Dogmatics*, vol. I/2, Edingburgh, 1956, 223; also vol.II/1, Edingburgh, 1957, 53; see also Avery Dulles, *Models of Revelation*, Maryknoll, 1992, 151.

This conviction is strong since to some extent symbols have the capacity of indicating the presence of what they symbolise. For Karl Rahner, a symbol constitutes the thing symbolized, proclaims the thing symbolized, and is itself full of the thing symbolized.[209]

In the African religious world all things are symbolic. In such a religious environment, the "sacramental vocation" of symbolic objects is almost taken for granted and highly valued. God communicates with men initially through the veil of symbols and the response of men, in the form of adoration and worship is given in the first instance under the network of symbols, of which objects are part. The second phase of men's response is sacramental. And this phase is consonant with Christian revelation.

1.4.4 SYMBOLIC GESTURES, MUSIC AND ART

African culture and religious worship, ceremonies or gatherings are characterized by music and songs. This is in part due to their conviction of the ontological goodness of life. Thus they celebrate, sing and dance their religion.[210] The average African Christian's answers to such vital questions as who is the Christian God and what does he do?, who is Jesus Christ?, who is the Holy Spirit?, are documented in hymns, songs and choruses.

Through such "practical theological expressions", the average African Christians manifest their "bias" towards a God who is near and relevant to them while remaining transcendent[211]. Such a "practical profession" of the mystery of faith, is understandable in a cultural context where systematic speculation is rare. African Christian theology can therefore, be said to be condensed in hymns and songs: lex credendi, lex orandi, lex vivendi, lex celebrandi. The theologically dense hymns of St. Ephraem of Syria can buttress this point namely, that hymns are one of ways of expressing the mystery of faith.

---

209 Cf. Karl Rahner, *Theological Investigations*, vol.4, Baltimore, 1966, 251-254.
210 see Mbiti J.S., *An Introduction to African Religion*, 61.
211 It may be pertinent to point out here that the chosen people resisted the seemingly abstract definition or conception of God: "I Am who I Am" by conceiving him in different terms, representing him in an image and giving him relevant names with which they composed choruses.

It is generally believed that the gods taught man the art of music. African musical tunes are also believed to be an imitation and "type" of the sweet celestial tune resounding through the cosmos.

Africans communicate with words, but also with mimicry and body gestures, all of which are part of their expressive symbolic power. When Africans dance in lines, it is a "picture" of cosmic orderliness and equilibrium; when they dance in circles it reflects the movement of the planets around the sun.

The African style of dancing in circles is a reflection of the rotation of the mysterious chariots and celestial beings around the "Cosmic Axis",[212] the Life Principle. It symbolizes the movement of the entire creation around the "pillar" which upholds all things in unity.

And often when Africans dance, they tend to bend or to point towards the ground, a gesture that indicates the earth as the mother of all men, from which they came, and to which they will return. It is also an indication of the immanence of God in history and is intended to instil religious fear and reverence.

Hence, during celebrations Africans are "divine dancers", imitators of cosmic symphony. It has been highlighted by Crichton that,

Gestures and objects refer away from themselves to events they are recalling but *at the same time* arrest the attention of the participants in such a way that they knew they were in touch with those events. This is the first function of symbols.[213]

In Africa as elsewhere religion has inspired art: yet, African artists have invested their skill in temples and drums and masks and not upon representation of the gods in human form. Carvings and paintings on wood, ivory and stone of certain figures - animals, birds, insects etc. are often found in temples. These make a striking contrast to the houses of ordinary folk, which are usually undecorated, except for the dwellings of chiefs.[214]

---

212 The famous vision of Ezekiel (Ezek.1,4-24) has some affinity with the African spirit.
213 J.D.Crichton, Christian Celebration. *The Mass, The Sacraments, The Prayer of the Church*, London, 1971, 19.
214 Cf. Geoffery Parrinder, Op.cit., 61.

1.4.5 SYMBOL - THE APT EXPRESSION OF FAITH

Man, in the whole richness of his own being, wishes to meet God, desires that God should be real and present to him. He achieves this in the first instance by faith but faith best expressed symbolically.[215]

Symbols are concerned with reality, but in worship they transcend themselves and lead men to a world that would otherwise be beyond their grasp.[216] Thus, religious minds respond symbolically to God, who approached men in his Son Jesus of Nazareth, who also operated symbolically[217] - through deeds, works, signs and wonders,[218] and when his time was up, he returned to the Father leaving behind his "symbolic imprint" in Word and Sacraments.

To call Jesus a Symbol today is ambiguous or even repulsive to some. This is due to the deflated meaning of "symbol" to the modern mind. Yet the Fathers used this for Jesus. In the following pages, whenever "Symbol" is used for Jesus, what is meant is what the Fathers meant by this word in relation to Jesus, namely the Revealer of God the Father and what modern theologians mean when they call Jesus "Sacrament of God".

Whatever, Jesus as "Symbol" cannot be confused with symbol as it features in the traditional religion. Just as Jesus was man but not an ordinary man, so he is "Symbol", but not an ordinary symbol. When therefore Niebuhr said: "Jesus ... is a "Symbol" with the aid of which men tell each other what life and death, God and man, are ....",[219] one can intuit the depth of meaning hidden behind his words.

Jesus is a "Symbol" but not just any type of symbol. When "Symbol" is used for Jesus it is invested with a completely new and higher meaning. He is a sacramental-symbol, one who reveals God to men, and presents men before God.

The Fathers of the Church adopted Symbol to emphasize its power and concreteness. Origen and Ambrose speak of the bread as being the

---

215 see J.P.Magnine, *Pour une poétique de la foi:essai sur le mystère symbolique*, Paris, 1969,15.

216 Cf. M.D.Chenu, 'Antropologie de la Liturgie', in Yves Congar (ed.), *La Liturgie après Vatican II*, Paris, 1967, 173

217 In conformity to his nature as the Primordial Symbol: agere sequitur esse.

218 Cf. Vatican II Council, Dei Verbum, art.4; see also Yves Congar, *The Revelation of God*, New York, 1968, 70-71.

219 H.R.Niebuhr, *The Responsible Self*, New York, 1963, 15.

homoioma (likeness), the *figura*, of the body of Christ.[220] And they were right. The bread is a symbol of the body of Christ who is "the bread of life".[221]

In Sacramental Theology, it is commonly taught that Christ is really present in the sacramental elements and actions. The great Protestant theologian, Karl Barth, for instance, calls him the basic substance of the «sacramental reality of Revelation»,[222] the first sacrament, the foundation of everything that God instituted, used and still uses in His Revelation.[223]

Thus other symbols, be they words, stories, rituals or gestures, are such in that they participate in the quality which the Son of God imprinted on symbols by acting symbolically. Other symbols can be said to be such to the extent they show forth Jesus' power and meaning, namely, that:

... story of Jesus ... experienced as the transforming symbol which discloses to our understanding the depth-dimension of our finite existence. What was expressed in Jesus' words and deeds, his life and death, is evocative for our human experiences: it discloses our own existence to us; it illumines what authentic human life can be when we are aware that we are safe in the hands of the living God and can accept it as challenge.... People come to know themselves (again) in Jesus the Lord.[224]

Once religious symbols are able to play this role, they can be said to have made a jump from the natural symbolic to the Christian symbolic or sacramental level of being.

Hence the African is deeply touched when he hears Jesus called a "Symbol" or when he sees Jesus and what Jesus stands for symbolically expressed.

For the African, in this man from Nazareth who lived, worked, laboured, suffered and died; in this man, God was present; in him there was a unity of God and man, that unity which formerly existed between God and men and which unfortunately was broken. This is why the "per

---

220 To say that something or even somebody is a symbol is not to deny its or his reality. On the contrary to call something or somebody a symbol is to affirm its or his reality.

221 J.D.Crichton, Op.cit., 18.

222 Karl Barth, *Church Dogmatics*, vol II/1, 53.

223 Cf. Ibid., 54.

224 E. Schillebeeckx, *Interim Report on the Books Jesus and Christ*, New York, 1981, 60.

ipsum, cum ipso et in ipso" strikes a strong note to the ears of an average African Christian.

For Africans, Jesus is a "unifying factor", a "relational factor". That Jesus is a "Symbol" says much to African religious minds. It is such a symbolic qualification that corresponds best to African mental categories.

On account of their symbolic understanding, the question of the Christian faith, is for Africans more of ritual practice and celebration than of creed[225]. On the first "level", by calling Jesus a "Symbol", African religious spirit is captured; from there it can then be drawn to the second "level", viz. the Christian symbolic or sacramental level.

1.5 CONCLUSION

One can therefore say that the "itinerary" of faith for the African is from the natural to Christian symbol, from the natural to Christian symbolic or sacramental understanding. Such an "itinerary" for the African is a change in mentality; it is a conversion from the natural to the Christian vision; it is a *sursum corda*

This is the consequence of African symbolic thinking as it finds purification and an elevation in the Christian Mystery. The symbolic expression of what they believe makes of the Africans symbolic theologians.

Newman's experience of God and expression of the same were indispensably weaved in symbolic clothings. However, they were symbolic underpinings that transcend themselves in the understanding of Newman.

For in the arena of Christian religion, symbols are pointers to "more" than Solomon and when the symbols contain, commmunicate and effect this higher reality, they change their identity from symbols to sacraments. How Newman understood and expressed sacrament and sacramentality, his sacramental theological thought documented on his reflection on the "catena sacramentorum" is the focus of the next chapter.

---

225 This does not imply a separation between ritual and creed. In fact through rituals Christians celebrate what they believe; celebrations ritualise the content of creed. It is this ritual aspect that speaks most to many African Christians.

PART TWO:

NEWMAN'S SACRAMENTAL THEOLOGICAL THINKING POSITION AND EXPOSITION

2.1 PRELIMINARY REMARKS

In Christian "dogmatic thinking", God is the point of departure for everything. Without God there is neither faith, nor sacraments, nor theology. And God's relationship with believers is always mediated. Consequently, this part opens with an examination of the Sacramental Principle which is pivotal for the understanding of Newman's Sacramentology.

And since this study deals with "the Christian Newman", and knowing full well that the Incarnation is decisive for Christians, the relationship of the Sacramental Principle with the Incarnation will be discussed.

It will also be demonstrated how the Church's sacramental system flows from and is an application of the Sacramental Principle. It will then become evident that this sacramental system forms a chain, a catena sacramentorum, in which to touch one part is to shake others. The extent to which Newman found in the chain the finger of God, and what relevance this chain had for him will be shown.

2.2 THE COMPONENTS OF NEWMAN'S SACRAMENTAL THOUGHT

2.2.1 THE SACRAMENTAL PRINCIPLE

For Newman, "Principle" means a central idea, a determining or underlying factor of a particular system or action. This can be infered from such statements as " ... Christianity started with the principle that there was but 'one God and one Mediator'"[1]. From the reality of one God and a unique mediation realised in the incarnation derive other principles

---

1 Dev.356.

which distinguish Christianity from other religious, ethical, or political systems. Such principles include:

i) The principle of dogma, that is, supernatural truths irrevocably committed to human language, imperfect because it is human, but definitive and necessary because given from above.

ii) The principle of faith, which is the correlative of dogma, being the absolute acceptance of a divine word with an internal assent, in oppositon to the informations, if such of sight and reason.

iii) The doctrine of the Incarnation is the annoucement of a divine gift conveyed in a material and visible medium, it being thus that heaven and earth are in the Incarnation united. That is, it establishes in the very idea of Christianity the sacramental principle as its characteristic.

iv) Another principle involved in the doctrine of the Incarnation, is the necessary use of language, e.g., of the text of Scripture, in a second or mystical sense. Words must be made to express new ideas, and are invested with a sacramental office.[2]

v) It is our Lord's intention in his Incarnation to make us what he is himself; this is the principle of grace, which is not only holy but sanctifying.

vi) It cannot elevate and change us without mortifying our lower nature: here is the principle of asceticism[3].

It may be pertinent to point out here that Newman's doctrine of the Sacramental Principle has four sources: i) Newman's own very nature,[4] ii) Bishop Butler, iii) J.Keble, and iv) the Eastern Fathers of the Church.

Already as a boy, Newman was inclined to think of the "unreal" quality of material phenomena. And in Joseph Butler's Analogy, he found a formulation of this principle which had already germed in his own mind.

Succintly put, from bishop Butler Newman learnt the Sacramental System, that is, the doctrine that material phenomena are both the types

---

2   Some partial parallels can be noted between the mystical principle and what is said above on linguistic symbols.

3   Dev.310-312. Newman noted a close link between principles and doctrines. "Doctrines", he said, "are developed by the operation of principles, and develop variously according to principles. For him, " ... the difference between the two sometimes merely exists in our mode of viewing them; and what is a doctrine in one philosophy is a principle in another" (Ibid., 179 and 180).

4   More will be said on this in the third part.

and the instruments of real things unseen.[5] This doctrine sees that God performs his works through the instrumentality of men and of material things which he makes the channels of grace in the economy of salvation.[6]

For Newman, the Sacramental System is not a figment of the imagination, but an objective quality inherent in creation, impressed in it to give us an index or token of the invisible.[7]

The basis of the Sacramental Principle is therefore the truth that the created world comes from God and leads back to him. This in turn indicates that the blessings of grace which the Spirit of God poured on the world at creation have continued to point to the Lord of creation[8] and to serve his purpose:

God does not make for us new and miraculous instruments wherewith to convey His benefits, but He takes, He adopts means already existing. He takes water, which already is the means of natural health and purity, and consecrates it to convey spiritual life. He changes the use of it. Again He selects bread and wine, the chief means and symbol of bodily nourishment. He takes them, He blesses them; He does not dispense with them, but He uses them. He leaves them to appearance what they were; but He gifts them with a Divine Presence, which before they had not.[9]

In this optic, the created order in its totality is understood to be a "sacrament" of God. Consequently, nature as a whole and natural objects in particular, and even natural cycles are channels of grace, instruments of the divine, symbols of truth.

It can be said that the "message" of the Sacramental Principle is directed to the human heart and conscience. It is therefore, human conscience as the voice of God which receives what may be called the "transmission" of the Sacramental Principle. Human conscience is able to receive this "transmission" or to apprehend the dictates of God for it is " ... a messenger from him, who, both in nature and in grace, speaks to us behind a veil... Conscience is the aboriginal Vicar of Christ, a prophet in

---

5 see Apo 18.
6 Cf. PPS III, 194-97 (29.8.1829); see also J.Keble, Tract 89, 152.
7 Ibid.; see also J.D.Dalgarins, *Dante, and the Catholic Philosophy of the Thirteenth Century*, 121.
8 Sacramentality is the vocation of material things, of the created world. They proclaim the Glory of God: 'res clamat ad dominum', as their maker and sustainer.
9 PPS IV, 173ff (27.11.1825); also Apo 10; R.I.Wilberforce, The Doctrine of the Holy Eucharist, London, 1853, 21.

its informations, a monarch in its preremptoriness, a priest in its blessings and anathemas..."[10]

In the Apologia, Newman recounted how, in 1827, the reading of Keble's *Christian Year*, dense in poetic dictions and spirit, had reinforced in his own mind the principle he had learned from Butler, «though recast in the creative mind of his new master».[11] Newman does not however tell us in what way Keble had recast this idea of Butler's.

For him the material world was not just a sign, pointing to the world of the supernatural: it was the instrument of the supernatural world, its symbol and index. In an Essay titled 'Milman's View of Christianity', Newman wrote:

> ... all God's dealing with His creatures, have two apsects, one external, one internal. They are two fold, 'having one part heavenly, and one part earthly'. This is the law of Providence here below; it works beneath a veil, and what is visible in its course does but shadow out at most, and sometimes obscures and disguises what is invisible. Ordinarily speaking, nothing happens, nothing goes on in the world, but may be satisfactorily traced to some other event or fact in it, or has a sufficient result in other events or facts in it, without the necessity of our following it into a higher system of things in order to explain its existence, or give it a meaning.[12]

Butler, who exercised a strong influence on Newman, argued that in the natural realm, God uses various means to accomplish his ends: «In the daily course of natural providence and in the dispensation of Christianity, God operates analogously, in both making use of a series of means».[13] Newman had no difficulty in using this to read the entire Church system.

All that exists or happens visibly, within or outside the religious circle, conceals and yet suggests, and above all subserves a system of institutions, facts, and events beyond.

He understood this to be the driving principle of religion and the Church system.[14] Thus «all that is seen, - the world, the Bible, the Church, the Civil polity, and even man himself, - are types, and, in their

---

10 Diff.II.,248.
11 Cf. Apo 18f.
12 Ess.II. 190-191 (Milman's View of Christianity).
13 J.Butler, *The Analogy ...*, 206.
14 Cf. Ess.II. 192-193.

degree and place, representatives and organs of an unseen world, truer and higher than themselves».[15]

In this line of thought close to Butler and Keble, it is no wonder that Newman could comment upon reading the philosophical works of Neoplatonists like Clement and Origen:

> Some portions of their teaching ... came like music to my inward ear, as if in response to ideas, which, with little external to encourage, I had cherished long ago. These were based on the mystical or sacramental principle, and spoke of the various Economies or Dispensations of the Eternal. I understood this passages to mean that the exterior world, physical and historical, was but the manifestation to our senses of realities greater than itself. The visible world still remains without its divine interpretation; Holy Church in her sacraments and her hierarchical appointments. Her mysteries are but the expressions in human language of truths to which the human mind is unequal.[16]

Newman even went to the extent of formulating what he called "... the theory of double sense ..."[17], to describe this doctrine that every single phenomena has two sides: the side that is immediately self-evident and the truth to which it points, represents, and contains.

In the light of this "theory of double sense", one can easily understand the role of Newman's catena sacramentorum.[18]

The catena sacramentorum is an extension or application of the Sacramental Principle. On this he would say: «... some things are historically creations of the supernatural system, or are perceptibly instrumental, or obviously symbolical»,[19] index or veil, of the invisible world.

From these influences, and the *modus cogitandi* which most of the members of the Oxford Movement shared, Newman found himself engulfed in a continuous research into the full role and meaning of the sacraments in salvation history; an enterprise which left a special mark on his theology viz. "sacramental thinking".

It is necessary to point out that Newman was not a kind of poet with disregard for evidence and prove. His insistence on the Sacramental Principle was a reaction against a Protestant mentality which has no such principle.

---

15 Ibid.
16 Apo 23; also 36-7.
17 Ess.II.193.
18 Subsequently we shall be evidencing the significance of this catena.
19 Ess.II.193.

2.2.2 THE CENTRALITY OF THE INCARNATION

The doctrine of Incarnation is the good news that divine love, divine life and gift have been summed up in a historical figure, Jesus of Nazareth, and dispensed through his visible body.

The mystery of Christ-Incarnate is the content of Christian preaching. Newman considered Incarnation to be the most particular of all the Christian mysteries, which was verified in "those days" when a decree went out from Caeser Augustus that the world should be enrolled (Lk.2:1); it was God's assumption whole and entire of the lot of creation in his Son.

For Newman, like in Catholic doctrine, the decisive truth of Incarnation, is that the Almighty Son of God, who was in the Father's bosom, became man as truly as he was God, having all the perfections of the Father. The Son of God became man without ceasing to being in any respect what he was before.[20]

Hence the most solemn and transporting doctrine of the Incarnation is the cornerstone of the whole Church system; «the Word was made flesh», being the divinely appointed way, whereby we are regenerated and saved.[21]

Consequently, the central object of the Christian faith, in the mind of the theologian of Oxford, is not a certain number of articles, but the whole of Christ in whom are hidden all treasures of wisdom and knowledge with which the eye of faith is blessed[22]: the object of faith is Christ's history and his doings among men.

For Newman as for the Fathers of the Church, especially Athanasius and Basil, and in line with the teaching of St.Paul and St.John, we are saved not only *by* Christ but *in* Him. In other words, we are redeemed from sin, adopted by God, made partakers of His divine glory through the Holy Spirit, not only *because* of Incarnation of the Son of God, but literally, *in it*[23].

The humanity of Christ was instrumental in bringing about salvation. Through Incarnation, the Invisible God manifests and communicates

---

20 Cf. PPS VI, 71-2 (1.4.1836).
21 Cf. Ibid., 74.
22 Cf. MS Sermon 354,23 (28.8.1834).
23 Cf. Louis Bouyer, *Newman's Vision of Faith. A Theology for Times of General Apostasy*, San Francisco, 1986, 167.

Himself, together with his invisible gifts, in bodily forms.[24] Jesus is the Sacrament of God, and those acts and ordinances which reveal Jesus and what he stands for are in themselves sacramental.

Since the Christ-event is the foundation, content and measure of Christian faith[25], Newman held the Christ-event to be the key doctrine around which others are to be grouped, and to which the source and force of other truths are to be traced.[26] In other words, the underlying factor is the image of that «whole circle of doctrines, of which our Lord is the subject.[27]

As early as 1830, Newman had insisted that one of the differences between Natural and Revealed Religion lay in the fact thanks to the Incarnation, only the latter offered to man an object on which the affections could be placed, and the energies concentrated.[28] From Incarnation, the central aspect of Christianity, the three main aspects of its teaching derive, the sacramental, the hierarchical, and the ascetic.[29] Newman's tendency to give priority to Incarnation was his own reaction to what he understood to be a lack of equilibrium in the Western Christianity of that time.[30] In fact, "popular theology of the day" in Protestant England emphasized the Atonement as "the chief doctrine of the Gospel".[31]

Such emphasis on the Atonement relegated the Christ-event to a religious subjective utility: "my sinfulness and my salvation". Jesus Christ was not considered except in relation to the salvation of the sinner.

---

24 Cf. J.H Walgrave, Newman the Theologian, London, 1960, 129.
25 In fact a more precise theological formulation would read: 'The Trinity is the foundation, content and measure of Christian faith and therefore, is the central content of the Gospel'. The statement presupposes a systematic nexus in which, to speak of one of the three divine persons is to speak of the other two. Newman was aware of this systematic link.
26 Cf. Dev. 324, also 35-36: «For the convenience of arrangement, I will consider the Incarnation the central truth of the Gospel, and the source whence we are to draw out its principles».
27 Ibid., 10.
28 Cf. OUS, 23 (13.4.1830).
29 Cf. Dev. 35-36; see also Ian Ker, Newman On Being a Christian, 39.
30 Cf. Mix., 321-22 (14.10.1849); also 358.
31 Cf. Ibid. Emphasis on Atonement as against "external forms of religion" was one of the features of Evangelicalism to which Newman was converted as a young man.

In Newman's thinking, the mystery of Incarnation was a part of a mediatorial plan which providence always followed in dealing with the created world. The difference is that among the many and diverse mediatorial ways, Incarnation was special and thus constituted a reference point in a way that no other can equal:

There were mediators many,[32] .... But now all is superseded by One, in whom all offices merge, who has absorbed into Himself all principality, power, might and dominion ... He is the sole self-existing principle in the Christian Church, and everything else is but a portion or declaration of Him ... There is under the Gospel but One proper Priest, Prophet and King, Altar, Sacrifice, and House of God. Unity is its characteristic sacrament; all grace flows from One Head ....[33]

In this sense Incarnation is the central moment of the divine economy and the fundamental principle of the Christian religion and the Church; and from this "central truth" all other Christian doctrines justly derive.[34] The Incarnation explains other Christian doctrines and sheds light on them.

In as much as the Incarnation constitutes the identity of Christianity, in as much as it is the principle of Christian confession, it stamps a fundamental christological "seal" on the Christian faith.

Thus, Newman sees in the mystery of the Incarnation the *Articulus stantis vel cadentis Ecclesiae*. The only Christian "proposal" or "offer" is Jesus Christ, the God-Man. To preach the Gospel is to preach Jesus Christ, who is salvation Himself. The Tractarians led by Newman never thought of the Church and the sacraments except in relation to Christ.

Not only were the sacraments instituted by him, but as channels of grace they were considered instrumental causes of that grace which Christ had merited. The mediation of the Church, as the sacrament of Christ, is linked to the salvific mediation of the Incarnate and glorified Word, present through and in his Spirit.

---

32 In the light of the Sacramental Principle, creation in its entirety has hitherto mediated the goodness and message of God. The Patriarchs, kings, prophets, institutions, have in different ways lived this mission. But now Christ has assumed these roles and henceforth he is the only mediator in whose service other mediators are.
33 Jfc., 196-8.
34 Cf. OUS, 27 and 35 (13.4.1830); see also Dev. 42.

2.2.3 THE INCARNATION AS THE ARCHETYPE OF THE SACRA-
MENTAL PRINCIPLE

Jesus of Nazareth was God among men. Newman was full of admiration for this condescension. «Jesus was man indeed, but He was more than man; He did what man does, but then those deeds of His were deeds of God ...»[35]

That the man of Nazareth was the Christ, that the young rabbi was the Law-giver, the "one who was before Abraham", is to the mind of New-man a unique way which God used to reveal himself to believers or to impart noble truths to them. Thus for Newman, Incarnation is the arche-type of the Sacramental Principle.[36]

God's dealings with the world does not come as though between a pure Spirit and a "naked spirit". He communicates with us through the instru-mentality of things, events and persons, and through a series of means.[37] Newman therefore, saw in Incarnation God's consistent faithfulness to the way He had always dealt with the world:

> The mediatorial plan of salvation ... is quite parallel to the methods which provi-dence has adopted in imparting His blessings both in the ordinary course of this world's affairs, and in His extraordinary dealings with the patriarchs and the Jewish people. God's mode of acting by means of His Son, is thus not in itself new or unu-sual, and displayed for the first time in the Christian system, but one which He has made use of everywhere and in every age for the preservation and benefit of the human race.[38]

However, Incarnation remained in the thoughts of Newman, an un-duplicatable master-piece in the divine mediatorial plan of salvation. For in the Son of God, mediation assumes a truly special dimension. Jesus Christ is the channel not only of all God's actions directed to man, but also of all mankind's actions directed to God.

Christianity is erected on the truth that there is one God and a sole Mediator. Such a single Mediation belongs to Christ and to him alone:

---

35 PPS V, 20 (4.11.1838). Even here one can catch glimpses of the Sacramental Principle. Jesus of Nazareth was more than a simple carpenter, rebel, teacher, or prophet. In him, the invisible God was present; his words and actions were the words of God.

36 Cf. Dev. 104.

37 see J.Butler, *The Analogy of Religion* (ed. Gladstone), 206-7.

38 MS Sermon 176,2 (14.2.1828).

... there is this plain and clear distinction between the mediatorship of Christ and that of all other beings, that Christ has a *power* and a *claim* with God which others have not ... Thus His mediation, and His only, is meritorious ....[39]

The leader of the Oxford Movement believed that Jesus' unique role was due to his identity. He was man but not in exactly the same sense in which any one of us is a man. We may not, Newman sustained, speak of him as we speak of any individual man. He was not an ordinary man, but God-man.[40] And his taking on our nature is a necessary condition for him to impart to us those great benefits which we accrued from his death.[41]

Divine Providence deemed it fit that divine blessings were communicated through Incarnation. And such forms as the Church, Tradition, Scripture, Authority, Fathers, Rituals, are closely associated with the Incarnation.

The whole of the Christian sacramental system is Christ's continuous assumption of what is human and created through which he dispenses to us the fruits of his redemption. Thus the Incarnation, Church, Tradition, Sacraments, Fathers, Authority form one single organic system.

2.2.4 THE PLACE OF THE CHURCH IN THE SACRAMENTAL SYSTEM

Newman's reflexion on the New Testament led him to a deeper understanding of the Church. For him, God has asked us to seek him and told us where to find him. Christ came and went back to God. But He who is gone has left the Church to teach us in his stead and to remind us of him:

He has left His Church, in which His Spirit dwells. This gifted company, ranged into a society by Himself and His Apostles, has lasted from the time of His ascension to this day. This Church is the spiritual mother of us all and the liturgy is her voice.[42]

For the author of "Lead Kindly Light", it is in the Church that we are to find traces of Jesus' having walked our earth and the concrete signs of

---

39 PPS VI, 79 (1.4.1836).
40 Ibid., VI, 62 (24.4.1836).
41 Cf. PPS V, 117 (17.1.1839).
42 MS Sermon 225,22f (7.2.1830).

His name as God with us. Jesus of Nazareth has interposed something between his first coming and his second coming, namely the Church, whose office is to apply the blessings which Christ has purchased to the individual.[43]

In his understanding, the actions of Jesus as Mediator have their continuation, not only in His heavenly intercession but also in His presence in the Church. Consequently the Church is an instrument, a visible representation of Christ, Christ's very self below, an organ of the Paraclete.[44] So she is not just a reminder of, or pointer to Christ, she is a locus where he makes himself present and active.

From this Newman argued for the importance and even the necessity of the Church while refuting any kind of individualistic and "spiritual" concept of religion, as being not only a form of undutifulness but also theologically mistaken. Since the external Church is the divinely instituted means of grace, a Christian life is impossible without reference to this Church.[45]

Newman maintained that Christ has set up the Church as "a city on a hill", to be a "visible power" in the world. It is therefore, a privilege to enjoy communion with the Church.

In the sermon *On the Christian Scheme of Mediation*, Newman worked out the Sacramental Principle and explicitly applied it to the Church system. In this sermon, the Church is regarded as a part of the "mediatorial plan of salvation" and thus analogous in character to God's manner of acting in His general providence. The Church then is a "Mediator", that is to say, a "means in the hands of God" for the conveyance of the gift of the Holy Spirit; a mediator "under the one accepted and meritorious mediator, the Son of God",[46] since she only conveys "to

---

43 Cf. PPS II,311 (29.6.1830). It is interesting to note that even though the texts quoted belong to different periods, the substance of his ecclesiology was the same. Evolution took place in his thoughts but it was a deepening of that truth of the Church which Whately and Froude had taught him.

44 Cf. Dev.xxxix.

45 In a sermon of 14.4.1833 on 2 Cor.6,17, he bemoaned those who followed only spiritual religion which knew nothing of outward forms and rules, rites, this or that particular communion. The "sad truth" is that there are "persons who think that Christianity will flourish more, when the Church is removed" (MS Sermon 347, 12,15).

46 MS, Sermon 176,2,5f (28.11.1824).

us spiritual blessings, whereas Christ not only *conveys* them from God, but *gains* them from Him".[47]

Newman insisted that since the Church is the sacramental medium through which the blessings of redemption realised by Christ are dispensed, reception of the blessings is connected to participation in its assemblies.[48]

Newman spoke of the Church as "the representative of our Lord, divinely interposed between the soul and God".[49] And as such she is not just the Lord's juridical representative but the "instrument of Him who is unseen".[50] God who once manifested Himself in the flesh, is continually manifested in that Church where He still dwells as Emmanuel. In the visible structures and activities of the Church, the Risen Lord is in operation:

> We reverence and love the Church as that which, if we may speak, detains Him on earth though He is gone away; which gives Him to us in a closer approach ... The Church is the sacramental body where Christ continually *exercises* His ministerial functions as the Mediator.[51]

This close link with the Lord and the Church's status as his instrument, means that among other things, the Church resembles her Lord and acts like him; it also means that she is a sacrament and acts sacramentally.

The external forms of the Church therefore, are means which God uses as the extension of that manhood of Christ. So the Church sacramental system is, in effect, the sacramental presence of the God-Man.[52]

For him, the Church, as the representative of the absent-present-Lord, continues sacramentally the mission of the Redeemer. She has been sent to do the work of God as her Lord did it and would have done it were He to be in the flesh today. The life of her Lord is her only yardstick for measuring her performance.

Newman's Ecclesiology is faithful to the meaning of the Sacramental Principle, that from the moment that our Blessed Lord assumed flesh, He sanctioned, for all ages to come, the great truth upon which the whole

---

47 Ibid., 6f; also MS Sermon 178,3 (12.10.1828).
48 'On the duty to public Worship', MS Sermon 213,6f (25.10.29).
49 PPS IV, 171 (27.11.1825).
50 Ibid.; see also Jfc., 270.
51 LD XXIV, 346-7 (7.10.1869).
52 Cf. VM II, 147 (Note III. The Anomalous Statements of St. Basil, St. John Chrysostom, and St. Cyril about the Blessed Virgin).

ecclesiastical dispensation is built, that God comes to us, in the form of earthly veils.

As a divinely instituted means of grace, in which the event of the Nativity is continuously made present, Newman affirmed the necessity of participation in the life of the Church:

> It is quite plain then, that if we would gain God's favor in Christ, we must come together into one place for it - we can only gain it as a body - we cannot gain it as individuals, unless any solitary sacraments can be discovered appointed by the author of our salvation.[53]

Newman calls the Church, "the voice of our Lord".[54] As for the scandalous lives of her leaders, this did not stop them, any more than Balaam or Caiaphas, from speaking religious truths:[55] He prayed:

> Let me never forget that Thou hast established on earth a kingdom of Thy own, that the Church is Thy work, Thy establishment, Thy Instrument, that we are under Thy rule, Thy laws and Thy eye - that when the Church speaks Thou dost speak. Let not familiarity with this wonderful truth lead me to forget that it is Thou who dost speak and act through them.[56]

Newman became the champion of the Church once he realised that through her God gives Himself to us and leads us to holiness. The Church imposes a creed, remits sins or rebukes and punishes because she stands for Christ and conveys the power of the Spirit.[57]

For Newman, the Church as a visible reality transcends herself: «The holy Church has been set up from the beginning as a solemn religious fact ... as a picture, a revelation of the next world, as itself the Christian Revelation».[58] She is, therefore, not a mere gathering of individuals as she may appear to the uninformed eyes of an ordinary observer.

Rather she is a mystical body, representing realities both visible and celestial: «they are on our right hand and our left, martyrs, confessors,

---

53 MS Sermon 213,12 (25.10.29).
54 LD XXIV, 346-7.
55 Ibid., 330.
56 Meditations and Devotions, V, 378-79.
57 Cf. Essays, II, 172-73 (The Protestant Idea of Antichrist).
58 PPS II, 66 (3.4.1831).

and the like, high and low, who used the same creeds, and celebrated the same mysteries, and preached the same Gospel as we do».[59]

Against subjective and individualistic tendencies in religion, Newman insists that Christ has so willed it, that we should seek Truth, not by investigations of our own, but by being taught[60] through the Church.

For Newman, the Church is the divinely blessed symbol and pledge of the true faith and the obvious means of securing it.[61] It is hard to imagine a higher view of the Church than one in which the Church and Christianity are synonymous;[62] The Church for Newman «is a visible body, and, to appearance, an institution of this world».[63]

The Church for Newman is "full of God". Indeed his Ecclesiology is very profound. «The Church», is the Body of Christ, erected in His image, «her priests His delegates, her people His members ... His instruments are not even so much as instruments, but only the outward lineaments of Him».[64]

For our author, encounter with Christ after the Ascension happens in the Church. It is in the Church that He is to be seen and heard. He who wants to see Him operate should look at the operations of the Church.[65]

In the divine dispensation, the Church is not only possible but necessary since, she alone delivers the human mind from the feeling of insecurity in its quest for an objective religion.[66] Already as an Anglican Newman called the Church the "pillar and ground of Truth".[67]

Newman was convinced that the Church was the guarantor of the veracity of the supernatural doctrine which surpasses every contingency.[68] As he said in 1849, the Church bears on her the signs of divinity, which

---

59 PPS, III,386 (1.11.1835).
60 PS II, 66 (3.4.1831).
61 VM II, 143 (Letter Addressed to a Magazine on behalf of Dr. Pusey's Tracts on Holy Baptism and of other Tracts for the Times).
62 Cf. Ian Ker, Newman on Being a Christian, 73.
63 PS II, 391 (11.11.1834).
64 Jfc., 196.
65 Cf. PPS II, 121 (24.1.1832); see also Giovanni Veloci, Newman al Concilio, Alba, 1966, 45.
66 Cf. Diff. II, 86 (Belief of Catholics about the Blessed Virgin coloured by their devotion to her).
67 Cf. Tract 11 (1833); see also GA 149-150.
68 see Diff. I, 217 (The Providential Course of the Movement of 1833 Not in the Direction of a Branch Church); see also Tract 11, 20.

make striking impression on the mind of whoever is not possessed by prejudices, or educated in suspicion.[69]

He noted that between the visible and invisible Church there is an interchange of living relations, relations of sign and grace. The invisible Church develops itself in the visible, the rites and external forms are nourished and animated by the force it has in it.[70]

Preaching in 1849, Newman pointed out that it is God who takes the initiative to call men and to lead them into the divine society.[71] In his own definition, the word "Church" means a gathering, a convocation whose author is God Himself:

> The word "Church", is used to indicate the community of Christians in this world, in the Bible a visible body endowed with invisible gifts of grace.[72]

In a sermon on *Waiting on God*, he told his audience that it is through the sacrament of Baptism that one is admitted into the visible Church,[73] the storehouse and direct channel of grace.[74]

2.2.5 THE IMPORTANCE OF TRADITION IN THE SACRAMENTAL SYSTEM

For Newman, Tradition is a fact in the history of all peoples. It is substantially derived from that Word of God or seed of Truth announced or sown by God in the heart and community of religious men, how religious men have received, developed, cultivated this word or seed, how they have elaborated its fruits and their experiences as they care for this seed throughout the history of their search for God and relationship with him.

The ultimate source of Tradition is therefore God. Newman wrote that:

> There never was a time when God had not spoken to man, and told him to a certain extent his duty. ... all men have had more or less the guidance of Tradition, in

---

69 Cf. Mix., 262.
70 Cf. PPS V, 41 (2.6.1839).
71 Cf. Mix. 262.
72 PPS III, 221 (4.12.1825).
73 Cf. MS Sermon 2, 6,8 (23.6.1824); see also Vincent Ferrer Blehl, 'The Spiritual Roots of Newman's Theology', 21.
74 Cf. TT II, v (1833).

addition to those internal notions of right and wrong which the Spirit has put into the heart of each individual.[75]

It is the inquiry into what God revealed and its locus that brought Newman to examine the question of Tradition. In other words, Newman was confronted with the question of the relationship between written and unwritten Gospel,[76] viz. Scripture and Tradition. On account of his family background and some influences he had, Newman grew up a proponent of biblical unilateralism, that, the Bible and the Bible alone is the norm of Christian faith.

Through Hawkins Newman understood another side of the truth.[77] It dawned on him that Tradition comes from God and that faith is more than the Bible. The ultimate source of Christianity lay in the Person, words and works of Jesus Christ, in the context of the Revelation of which He was the climax.

Hawkins taught Newman that the words, works of Jesus are accessible in the light of living Tradition which thrives within the bosom of the Church,[78] and outside Tradition, Scripture was mute, blind and dead.[79]

In this understanding and growing consciousness, Newman indicted Evangelicals, Protestants and heretics who create conflict between the Church and Scripture and limit Chrisitian faith and doctrine to sciptural evidence alone.

In Tract 85, *Lectures on the Scripture Proof of the Doctrines of the Church*, he explicitly criticised the notion that the essentials of belief can be clearly found in Scripture. For if we ask what these essentials are which, Scripture contains, the different schools which maintain biblical unilateralism will be found to disagree on the answer.[80]

Newman learnt that the Bible is the book of the Church, and as such the Church is its custodian and the place of its elaboration. He realised that Scripture is the Word of God. But the same Word of God also became incarnate, died, rose from the dead and now indwells his followers

---

75 Ari. 80.
76 The good tidings addressed to man by God is a complex whole, with a part written and another part unwritten. The written part is Scripture; the unwritten part, (but documented all the same) is known as Tradition.
77 Cf. Apo 112. see the first part.
78 Cf. Apo 112; see also Dev.97.
79 see OUS 33 (13.4.1830).
80 see Tract 85, 15, also 28 (1838).

through the power of the Spirit thus making them members of his body, the Church.

He saw an intimate relationship between the written Word and the embodied Word which is the Church so that the Bible is to be accepted on the authority of the Church.[81]

Newman sustained that «the sacred text was never intended to teach doctrine, but only to prove it», and that «if we would learn doctrine, we must have recourse to the formularies of the Church; for instance to the Catechism, and to the Creeds.

The Church is the teacher, while the proofs of its teaching are to be collected from Scripture».[82] Heretics, on the other hand, like the Arians, relied on a private study of Holy Scripture to elicit a systematic doctrine from the scattered messages of truth Scripture contains.[83]

For Newman therefore, Tradition meant the form of instruction given by the Church in its creed, catechism, liturgy, rituals, prayers, hymns, etc. Tradition gathers the fundamental teachings of sacred Scripture in a systematic but simple form. It is the key which unlocks the treasures of Scripture.[84]

Thus one can intuit that for Newman, Tradition is richer and wider than Scripture, for Tradition includes also the Sacred text. We are taught from the Bible not by the Bible. Already as an Anglican Newman believed that Christians derive their faith not from Scripture but from Tradition.[85]

In the light of the relationship between the written Word and the embodied Word, Newman maintained in a sermon from 1830, that

The same Spirit which inspired Scripture is necessary for its interpretation. And that Spirit is still with the Church and lives within Christ's true servants, and such composed the Church services; in the prayers of the liturgy we have Scripture digested and commented on by those whose hearts the Holy Ghost had cleansed and made His temple. The same Spirit is speaking in Tradition as in Scripture.[86]

---

81 Cf. LD XIX, 448 (2.1.1861).
82 Apo 9; see also Ari.50; Tract 71,8.
83 Cf. Ari. 50-51.
84 Cf. Ibid., 51.
85 Cf. VM I, 26-27 (Nature and Ground of Roman and Protestant Errors); also 244, 245 (On the Essentials of the Gospel).
86 MS Sermon 225, 19,22 (7.2.1830).

For him, both Tradition and Scripture necessarily exist and complementarily too because the mystery of Revelation transcends material documentation. It was not possible to commit to writing all that the Apostles experienced, lived, saw, heard, touched, and contemplated:

> No one you fall in with on the highway, can tell you all his mind at once; much less could the Apostles ... digest in one Epistle or Treatise a systematic view of the Revelation made to them. It (tradition) is latent, but it lives, like the rapids of a river, before the rocks intercept it. It is the Church's unconscious habit opinion and sentiment; which she reflects upon, masters, and expresses, according to emergency. Tradition in its fulness is necessarily unwritten.[87]

Newman's discovery of Tradition represented a great enhancement of his ecclesiology and spirituality. It constituted a conversion from the "religion of a book"[88] to the religion of history and of the Fathers. It was a change from a Protestant mentality to a Catholic one. It was a shift of mind from the Evangelical to history[89].

Our author, however, was aware of the fact that "appeal" to Tradition is not so simple. He therefore, made a distinction between Episcopal and Prophetical Traditions. Episcopal Tradition is the creed, a collection of definite articles descending directly from the apostles, received and committed from bishop to bishop.[90] To the Church therefore, Newman ascribed the duty and authority to decide what has been revealed, and to teach it.[91]

The Prophetical Tradition on the other hand, is not a definite article. It is, Newman says,

> ... rather what St. Paul calls 'the mind of the Spirit', the thought and principle breathed in the Church.... It is partly written, partly unwritten, partly the interpretation, partly the supplement of Scripture, partly preserved in intellectual expressions, partly latent in the spirit and temper of Christians; poured to and fro in closets and upon the housetops, in liturgies, in controversial works, in obscure fragments, in sermons, ... in local customs. This I call Prophetical tradition, existing primarily in

---

87 VM I, 31-34; also 281f (On Scripture as the Record of Faith).
88 This is not to be understood to mean that Newman believed in the letters of the Bible and not in the doctrines that the letters teach or that he believed in the material teachings of the Bible no matter what the bible teaches.
89 Newman underwent an evolution. More will be said on this in the pages on the sacraments.
90 Cf. VM I, 134 (On the use of Private Judgment).
91 Ibid., 249.

the bossom of the Church itself, and recorded in such measure as Providence has determined in the writings of eminent men.[92]

To the Church, represented by the Episcopal Tradition, Newman reserved the authority and right to discern, discriminate, define, promulgate, and enforce any portion of the Prophetical Tradition.[93] It is on the authority of the Episcopal Tradition that doctrines are to be accepted or refuted.

For Newman, the Church's living Tradition is a safe bay in the midst of doubt and uncertainties, a faithful and reliable guide, that never fails all those who appeal to it. It is that which is held because it is true.

Tradition is of great and legitimate use as an initial means of gaining notions about religious and historical facts and others; it is an important and reliable informant we make daily use of. Life is not long enough for proving everything by oneself; we are obliged to take a great many things as given as true by others.[94]

In the light of the above, one can infer that for our author, Tradition includes that "deposit of religious values" in the bosom of the Church which developed and took shape and accumulated as the children of the Church responded and reacted to the Eschatological Word addressed to them in Christ. And as such it includes Scripture, Sacraments, Institutions, and all that which enhanced the life of the Gospel and life in the Gospel. Tradition and these others are applications of the Sacramental Principle.

2.2.6   THE PLACE OF AUTHORITY IN THE SACRAMENTAL SYSTEM

Previously we have seen how for Newman, God's dealings with the world are realised through the *instrumentality* of persons or things. According to the Oxford theologian, God does not reveal himself to men without providing someone to decide, conserve, and transmit what He has revealed.

---

92   Ibid., 250-1.
93   Cf. Cons.63.
94   Cf. Dev.46.

A revelation is not given, if there be no authority to decide what it is that is given. And so in order to distinguish true from false developments, a supreme authority is necessary ...[95]

Thus is the place and importance of Authority in the religious sphere. In the Apologia, Newman acknowledged that Rev. William James had taught him that Christianity possessed hierarchical principles,[96] a truth he later deepened with the help of the Fathers.

And thus viewed through the "lens" of the Sacramental Principle, authority and wielders of authority are "types", "pictures" of a higher reality. Wielders of authority therefore stand and act in Christ's stead. Consequently Newman said:

> Christ is in His ministers, who are to be received as Him, even as Jesus Christ, as His representatives and ambassadors. The minister is therefore in his most honoured place when in the public liturgy he gathers up the prayer of the congregation, and much more when he celebrates the sacraments. He is then like Christ esalted, presenting redeemed sinners to the Father and granting the gifts of grace.[97]

Newman understood that wielders of authority in the Church were divinely guided to teach, to preserve the purity of doctrine and to hand on age after age the sacred torch of truth.[98]

He went on to argue that the ministers of the Church are representatives of Christ, and his instruments. And since they stand in Christ's stead, to their custody are committed «those blessings which flow from Christ as a Saviour, as a Prophet, Priest, and King».[99]

In an ordination sermon of 1831 *On the Ministerial Order, as an Existing Divine Institution*, the ministry is proclaimed as «the first principle of the visible Church, the centre around which it is to grow». The ministerial order is the appointed «guardian and channel»[100] of spiritual privileges conferred on the Church by Jesus the Lord.

Thus, Newman affirmed the truth that the hierarchical structure is an essential part of the Church system.[101] Growth in holiness then is the

---

95 Dev.79-80; also 88-90 and 92.
96 see Apo 150; also 152-157 and 10; see also Ari.38-39.
97 MS Sermon 121,17 (12.9.1824); also 224,6 (31.1.1830).
98 Cf.MS Sermon 157,17 (19.11.1826); see also VM I, 190f; Pusey, Letter to the bishop of Oxford, 29.
99 PPS II, 302 (14.12.1834).
100 Cf. MS Sermon 323,8f (18.12.1831).
101 Cf. MS Sermon 2, 6-8 (23.6.1824).

result not merely of God operating through the Holy Spirit in the individual soul but also in and through a visible community of believers, interrelated, and hierarchically ordered.

Conscious of the role and mission of the hierarchical set-up in the Christian sacramental system, Newman offered unalloyed respect, regard and obedience. As if professing an act of faith, he said: «The essence of all religion is authority and obedience».[102]

He once prayed for the grace to discern daily the voice of God in the Church hierarchy: «Let not the weakness of Thy human representatives lead me to forget that it is Thou who dost speak and act through them».[103]

In the mind of the leader of the Oxford Movement, men who exercise functions in the Church, especially the bishops, are the instruments of the Spirit.[104] Consequently the Anglican convert obeyed his bishop as he would the pope, not simply because he cared for order and discipline or hated anarchy, but because the voice of his bishop communicated the will of God.[105]

Always in the light of the Sacramental Principle, Newman gave a special consideration to the bishops whom he revered as "Angels of the Churches", representative of the Apostles, and dispensers of the grace of Christ's redemptive work. And considering the sacred treasures in their custody, which were those peculiar spiritual blessings which flow from Christ, Newman added:

> The gift or office cannot be named which belongs to our Lord as the Christ which He did not in its degree transfer to His Apostles by the communication of the Spirit through which He Himself wrought; one of course excepted, the one great work which none else in the whole world could sustain, of being the atoning sacrifice for all mankind. So far no one can can take His place, and "His glory He does not give to another".[106]

In these words, Newman exposes the dignity and limits of the hierarchy. They represent a perfect mediator but cannot arrogate to themselves

---

102 Dev. 86.
103 Meditations and Devotions, 378-379.
104 Elsewhere it has been seen that, for Newman, defects and shortcomings of wielders of authority does not hinder them from speaking religious truths.
105 Cf. Apo 97; see also AW 263 (22.2.1865).
106 PPS II, 304-305 (14.12.1834).

His Place and Claims. They can identify themselves with Christ but only to some extent.

They represent Christ but they are not Christ. While they are instruments of Christ's mediatorial work, Christ alone is the mediator. For our author, the relevance of authority remains as long as there is guilt to be washed away, sinners to be reconciled, believers to be strengthened, matured and comforted.[107]

2.3 EXPOSITION

2.3.1 NEWMAN'S DOCTRINE ON THE SACRAMENTS IN GENERAL

One of the perennial traditions of the Church is the praxis of the sacrament. Newman considered this such a crucial area to the Christian religion that from his "first conversion", the meaning of sacraments and their relation to faith occupied a great part of his intelligence of faith.[108]

Added to this is the fact that men react and think in relationship with their environment. This is particularly true of the members of the Oxford Movement. How they understood the Word of God, the Church, the means of grace, and their theology was coloured by their world.

They experienced the state of the Church as one of captivity: the Church broken into fragments, revealed truth a matter of controversy, the ordinances of grace profaned, and penitential discipline slighted or even unknown.[109]

However, the members of the Oxford Movement did not content themselves with mere protests. They felt themselves to be apostles of what was known as the "Catholic Church System", a system of doctrine and sacred ordinances.[110]

Their fervor and zeal, courage and determination was such that for me it is most accurate to say that the "means of grace", Word and Sacraments were at the core of the Tractarian spirit and enterprise.

---

107 Ibid., 306-7.
108 see AW 152 (18.9.1817).
109 Cf. SSD, 432 (17.7.1831). Already we have indicated that Evangelicalism to which Newman was converted was not an elaborate sacramental religion.
110 Alf Härdelin, Op.cit.,p.9

Thus the central doctrine of the Tractarians championed by Newman is undoubtedly the doctrine that the Church is to be understood as a visible society, having divinely empowered ministers, and having *Sacraments and rites* which are the channels of life-giving grace.[111]

Consequent to the Sacramental Principle, Newman believed that in some cases, the objects of nature become not only "types", but also channels of grace. This is why the Church gladly makes use of them in her worshipping life:

She interposes between God, the Sole Object of her adoration, and the mind of man, certain symbols, which the Christian may use as a medium to lift up his soul to his Creator, inasmuch as they are faint images of Himself.[112]

Therefore when the Church in her worship uses material things, she acknowledges their original vocation in the light of the Sacramental Principle.

2.3.2 UNDERSTANDING OF THE SACRAMENTS

Newman has a flair for "appeal" to Authority and to Tradition.[113] This is reflected in the formulation of his understanding of the sacraments: he defines "Sacrament" in the words of the Anglican Prayer Book, as «an outward and visible sign of an inward and spiritual grace»,[114] through which we enter into communion with Christ and with each other.[115]

---

111 Cf. Apo 49, see also S.C. Carpenter, *Church and People, 1789-1889. A History of the Church of England from William Wilberforce to Lux Mundi*, London & New York, 1933, 112.

112 Cf. Ibid.

113 It has already been seen above how Newman always delighted in perusing through the Fathers and the Tradition of the Church, how he saw in them the real image, spirit and expression of the riches of the faith and how he cites them extensively. In the following pages this shall be more evidenced.

114 *The Book of Common Prayer and Administration of the Sacraments...*, Article XXV; see also MS Sermon 24, 156 (11.3.1827).

115 It is interesting to note the conspicuous presence and meaning of the sign-symbol keyword in this definition.
It is pertinent to point out that even when the texts cited in this section belong to different periods, the central idea of Newman after his discovery of the sacraments is according to our understanding the same.

In another expression which clearly portrays the sacraments as an instance of the Sacramental Principle, Newman explained the sacraments of the Church as visible signs of invisible reality, through which the grace of Christ is communicated to the believer.[116]

It is interesting to note that the words of this definition are all in function of *grace*, that which happens whenever man meets God. Together with other Christian ordinances, sacraments are appointed bonds of communion with the Saviour, blessed channels of intercourse, ladders let down from heaven, and gifts from the Him. The author of "Lead Kindly Light" knew quite well that in every encounter with the Divine, the human counterpart is "implicated". God comes to fulfil his redeeming promises and man, the beneficiary of God's promises undertakes to serve God.

In the sacraments, Newman saw a pact between God and man, in which believers undertake to serve God. Newman expresses the truth of this in the following beautiful words:

> The word Sacrament properly means an oath - and in the sacraments there is a kind of compact and covenant entered into between us and our Merciful God - He promises to bless us with spiritual blessings - we promise through His grace to serve and obey Him.[117] Sacraments have three aspects in which they differ from other means of grace - first in that they are pictures[118] (as it were) and *signs* of the grace given, second in that they are *pledges* of grace, i.e. tokens appointed by God to witness to us the faithfulness of His spiritual promises, third and lastly that in them *we* on our own part make a promise and take an oath to God *that we will obey Him.*[119]

---

116 Cf. Ess. I, 247-248 (Theology of St. Ignatius); see also PS III, 277-278 (6.10.1834), V, 139 (19.1.1840); VI, 242 (15.11.1835).
117 Newman was quick to point out later that «the reason why many people keep away from sacraments is that they believe that the sacrament binds them to live very much more strictly and thoroughly in the pursuit of holiness than they do at present. They want a Saviour who delivers from sin, one who gives His gifts freely, without imposing at the same time "a heavy yoke". (PPS VII, 152 - 27.2.1831). Such people can be likened to the rich young man who wants all for nothing, desirous of receiving but without committing himself.(Cf.PPS I, 299 - 8.5.1831). It does not mean that we should be too familiar with the sacraments. We should approach them in fear and trembling, in the real attitude of mind of those who confront the triple holy God, the Lord of hosts.
118 In this word "pictures of...", one hears echoes of the Sacramental Principle.
119 MS, Sermon 24, 150, 156 (23.4.1826).

In expressing the spiritual experience of those who draw and nourish themselves from the "deposit of divine bounty" enclosed in the sacraments, Newman called the sacraments, «means and pledges of grace - keys which open the treasure-house of mercy».[120] God's effectual promises are locked in them and when they are rightly approached they do not fail for «sacraments are symbols of truth».[121]

Newman also understood Christian sacraments to be «witnesses and types of precious gospel truths»,[122] and Christians are to «religiously adhere to the form of words and the ordinances under which they come to us, through which they are revealed to us, apart from which revelation does not exist, there being nothing else given us by which to ascertain or enter into it»;[123] sacraments are the continual pledge of God's unseen mercies, and «... channel of invisible gifts to our souls».[124]

Revelation, Gospel, and doctrine for our author, are tangibly accessible in the sacraments, so that we have no better way of understanding the main truths of the Gospel than through Word and sacraments.

2.3.3 REASON FOR SACRAMENTAL ECONOMY

Judging from the Sacramental Principle and from Newman's understanding of the sacraments above, one can say that for the theologian of Oxford, the reason for sacramental economy is *ex voluntate Dei*. The "symbols of Truth", "pictures of grace", "efficacious signs", etc. derive their existence and meaning from Jesus' meritorious life, words, and actions. They are, therefore, associated with Jesus and what Jesus stands for.

In the salvific economy God always comes to man,[125] and He knows and chooses the best way to do this. His options are unlimited and include, among others, him assuming human nature. In the range of his

---

120 PPS III, 290-291 (29.6.1828).
121 LD V, 191-2 (17.1.1836; repeated on 18.3.1838).
122 PPS II, 77 (1.1.1831); see also Tract 34, 1; Froude, Remains, I:I, 10.
123 Tract 73, 13 (1836); see also Jfc., 252.
124 PPS II, 256 (11.12.1834).
125 In the encounter between God and man, the initiative always comes from God. He always takes the first step and every reaction of man, positive or negative, is a response to the God who acts or speaks first.

infinite options, God, in his expert paedagogy, digests for the simple and little ones in word, sacraments and ordinances his very self.

One can infer from Newman's thesis that the sacramental system is a part of God's design in his dealing with a composite creature of his, namely, man[126]. The compound nature of the sacraments, being outward signs of inward grace, make them «a singularly appropriate medium of intercourse between things, which are themselves compound, i.e. man, who is to be renewed, and the mediator whose presence renews him».[127]

In the mind of Newman therefore, God's mode of acting by means of the sacraments is thus not in itself new or unusual, but one which continues to mediate in concrete terms those salvific goods which He communicated definitively to the world in His Son.

The sacraments are the "extension of the Incarnation", for through them Christ's human nature is communicated to men, that sanctified human nature which is men's link with the Deity. It is through the sacramental system that He continuously carries out His work of mediation.

Newman argued convincingly that as long as men are in this world, they have need for mediatory means to God. What we call sacramental communion is necessary in some mysterious way, for preparing human nature to bear the sight of Him.[128]

According to him, when Moses came down from the Mount, and the people were dazzled at his countenance, he put a veil over it.[129] In the same way are Christian sacraments veils, through which we receive the glorified Christ lest we be dazzled by his transfigured face.

A denial of the sacramental system, in the mind of the leader of the Oxford Movement, implies that there is a means of intercourse between God and man apart from Christ's humanity.[130] The sacred rites and ordi-

---

126 see MS Sermon 176, 2 (14.9.1828).
127 Apo 49; see also Carpenter, S.C., *Church and People, 1789-1889. A History of the Church of England from William Wilberforce to Lux Mundi*, London & New York, 1933, 112.
128 Cf. PPS V, 8-9 (2.12.1838).
129 Cf. Ibid.
130 The sacramental and Anti-sacramental systems are two different religions, and to rest our hope of salvation on the one, is to say anathema to the other. To affirm the doctrine of Mediation and to deny it - to assert the reality of those things, which the Son of God effected by coming in the flesh, and to call their reality in question - are as much opposed as light and darkness, as truth and error. (see R.I.Wilberforce., *The Sacramental System. A sermon preached at St. Mary's Church before the University of Oxford...*, London, 1850, 14f.).

nances are expressly adapted to bring Christ before us, and to show him forth.[131]

In simple terms, Newman sustained that since the Son of God first entered the stage of human history, he has never left it. He chose to be present, to be approached and to be available in the sacraments.[132]

Newman expressed the necessity of the sacraments in terms of "Accomodation". According to him, the gifts of the Spirit which the Church receives from God, she conveys to the world by word, sacraments or ordinances.

Newman called the Church our "spiritual mother". And like a good mother, the Church, after the example of her Lord and Master, translates and interpretes in infantile language the teachings of the Lord to her children; she breaks down into concrete signs and adapts the Lord's Word to them.

In this way, her ordinances are "outward signs" and "tokens" for knowing, and means for entering that living shrine in which He dwells; means to draw up weak and infirm men to the source of their joy and aspiration.

In the sacramental economy, Newman saw as vividly "displayed" and "represented" in the Church, the things that are described in words in Scripture. As such they are "objects pleading through the visual sense", and, "capable of issuing appeals stronger than discourses to the ear". They are adapted to reach and move the soul and can "force the unseen truth upon our senses and stimulate our fainting faith".[133]

For him, the religious mind needs certain symbols, which it can use as a medium to lift his soul to his Creator[134]. Newman is convinced that

---

131 Sacraments follow a similar divine plan as the humanity of the Jesus of Nazareth which bore and showed forth the person of the Christ of God, and the face of the invisible God.

132 Cf. PPS III, 277 (15.11.1835).

133 MS Sermon, 388, 16 (31.5.1835); also PPS III, 250f (14.9.1834); Isaac Williams, *The Baptistery, or the way of Eternal Life*, Oxford & London, 1838, ix.

134 In Newman's early sermons we see how the question of the relation between inward and external religion recurs again and again. In a sermon *On the sacraments* of 1826, he dealt with the relation between religion as "an inward principle seated in the heart" and "the use of outward rites and observances".
It is a common "error", he says, to think that since religion is an inward principle, outward ordinances are therefore "mere forms". (MS, Sermon, 156, 1 (10.9.1826).
On a different ocassion Newman said: «... it is through these outward forms that God gives grace, they are the means of grace ... so that a man who despises it un-

111

«religion must be realized in particular acts, in order to be kept continu-ously alive»[135]. And the sacramental economy enters into such acts.

2.3.4 THE NECESSITY OF THE SACRAMENTS

Since sacramental economy is a part of God's design, since God comes to us in sacramental form, so it follows that they are necessary. In fact, Newman is categorical in affirming that «it is only in the form of sacra-ments that we are attracted to the Lord, that we go to him, that we recei-ve him». For him, a rejection of the sacraments, is a rejection of the divi-ne offer of grace:

> To slight or disregard the outward forms of religion, as if their use were without any connection with being religious, reveals a complete misunderstanding of the nature of prayer. Now since God has promised to give us blessings at common pray-er and through the sacraments, it is absurd to hope for His grace if we wilfully reject the means which he has ordained for obtaining it.[136]

In the Preface to the second volume of the *Tracts for the Times*, Ne-wman said that it may be set down as the essence of sectarian doctri-ne,[137] «...to consider faith, and not the sacraments, as the proper instru-ment of justification....»[138] He insisted that the sacraments, therefore, cannot be excluded from the economy of salvation, and "pure" faith allowed to remain alone.[139]

---

der the idea that God looks only to the heart, would (if he were consistent) neither come to public worship of any kind» (MS Sermon 157, 20 - 19.11.1826).
135 PPS II, 74 (1.1.1831).
136 MS, Sermon, 156, 2 (10.9.1826).
137 "Sectarian" is an adjective from the noun "Sect". The Sects in this context most probably refers to the Evangelicals whom we have seen as having little or no room for external ordinances of grace. Most of what Newman said in his Ecclesi-ology, Sacramentology, etc. is an invective on these Evangelical Sects.
138 TT II, vi.
139 The Tractarians dwelt much on this point. Pusey argued that «Our Lord places two conditions of salvation before us; one required on our part, the other prom-ised on His; one a requisite *in us*, through His gift *in us*, the other His gift *to us*; Faith, whereby we desire to be healed, and his gift, whereby he heals us...It is then a grievous fault in our habit of mind, if any...should dissect and sever what He has thus conjoined, and hold that we were *in such sense* 'saved by faith only', as [if] Baptism was of secondary account, an outward exhibition of what had already

Commenting on the words of the eleventh article of the Church of England, where it is said that "we are justified by Faith only", Newman sustained that both faith and the Dominical sacraments each have their proper office and are not mutually exclusive. Faith, is unique in being "the sole internal instrument", while sacraments are the "outward instruments".

Newman compared sacrament and faith with the hands of the giver and receiver, respectively. The mysterious virtue of faith is thus not made void. On the contrary through the sacraments it is established, as it coalesces with the sacraments, brings them into effect, dissolves what is outward and material in them, and through them unites the soul to God.

In the scheme of salvation both have their proper place. Justification, for Newman, comes *through* the sacraments; is received by faith; consists in God's inward presence; and lives in obedience.[140]

Newman thought, the Sacramental economy became necessary in the physical absence of the Saviour. Since «... historically speaking, time has gone on, and the Holy One is away, certain outward forms are necessary, by way of bringing us again under His shadow; and we enjoy those blessings through a mystery, or sacramentally in order to enjoy them really».[141]

In the light of the above, one can interpret Newman as saying that sacraments are necesary because they refer us back to Christ; they recall, represent and effect his acts and promises. While Jesus of Nazareth walked the earth and operated among men in the flesh, there was no need for sacraments, for in Him was something greater than Solomon and Jonah. Sacraments became necessary after his Ascension.

Appealing to a higher Authority, Newman firmly argued that sacraments were not optional religious practices or observances:

...the Church Catechism tells *us* that they are "generally" necessary for salvation. The Catechism tells us that the sacraments are means of grace[142]. The means of grace then are the ways God has appointed for

---

taken place inwardly. Sacraments are not only means to kindle men's faith but actual means of grace. No degree of faith, repentance and love can therefore render God's "birth from above" through baptism superfluous» (Tract 67, 47, 81f, 135).

140 Cf. Jfc. 225f; see also 237,278,282,303; Ward, W.G., Heurtley's four Sermons. In British Critic 31 (No.62) 1842, 428-451 esp.434f.
141 PPS VI, 242 (29.11. 1840), The title of this sermon is "Waiting for Christ".
142 see *The Book of Common Prayer and Administration of the Sacraments...*, Article XXV.

gaining grace, gaining His heavenly help, without which we cannot be spiritually minded...[143]

He strongly maintained that no serious religious person can do without the sacraments: to refuse them, to deny their necessity, is to call unclean and unnecessary what God had recommended and commanded, a God who can neither deceive nor be deceived.

He reminded some Evangelical extremists that «St.Paul even after the heavenly vision was baptised to wash away his sins»,[144] a simple demonstration that no amount of faith can dispense with the sacraments, an argument that no degree of illumination can annul a divine ordinance, an illustration that 'faith is a whole', a *totus*, in which there is no "either or", a system in which everything is closely linked.

2.3.5 SACRAMENTS - EFFICACIOUS SIGNS AND SYMBOLS

Newman believed that inasmuch as sacramental ordinances and signs were willed, ordained and commanded by God, they bear the imprint of divine infallibilty,[145] which qualify them as efficacious instruments and signs of that redemption realised *pro nobis*.

Between 1824 and 1825, Newman's ideas on sacraments were not completely clear: "Yet I do not even actually maintain that the Spirit always or generally accompanies the very act of baptism..."[146]

By 1828[147], Newman's understanding had deepened and his ideas had become clearer: "Sacraments are not only promises of grace, means of grace, pledges of grace, they *convey* grace".[148]

---

143 MS Sermon, 24, 150 (23.4.1826).
144 MS, Sermon 26,360 (10.10.24). I am inclined to think that Newman is not limited here to saying that Baptism causes Regeneration for in 1824, his ideas about Baptism were not yet clear. His words can be taken as a counter attack on those who reject ipso facto the baptismal ordinance as unnecessary.
145 «It is characteristic of God's word in Scripture that it «effects what it announces» (Jfc.81). Christian sacraments are efficacious by the force of the infallible promise and word of the Lord. He who has given the commission was one whose words were creative. They were and they remain creative whether proclaimed by Him in the flesh or by those who have received the power to do likewise (Cf. Froude, *Remains*, II:I,141f).
146 AW 206 (29.5.1825).

114

He rejected the idea that sacraments are «mere forms and shadows»,[149] and called them «effectual signs of grace», «instruments which the Holy Ghost uses»[150], through which are communicated invisible privileges promised by Christ the Lord to believers. Not only were the sacraments instituted by the Lord, but as channels of grace they were considered instrumental causes of that grace which Christ had merited.

According to Newman, it is therefore only in relation to Christ and to His Spirit that the sacraments and their meaning are to be understood. The sacraments are efficacious in the name of and for the sake of Christ because they are the "extensions of the Incarnation".

It follows therefore that outside Christ and outside the sphere of influence of His Spirit, no outward means are in any objective sense the instrumental cause of grace. The power of Christ shines forth in and through the sacraments. Newman saw the efficacy of the sacraments in the fact that they contain and are charged with the blessings which Christ purchased.[151]

Thus for Newman, the whole meaning of sacramental efficacy lies in the fact that weak, finite matter is adapted and empowered to mediate divine gift,[152] thanks to a force and animation that comes from above.[153] In this way Newman explains the marvel that even though sacraments are composed of humble elements, simple gestures,[154] and short words they create and effect what they represent.

---

147 We have indicated above how Newman came to the discovery of the sacraments namely, through Froude, from the Anglican divines and from the Fathers of the Church.

148 MS Sermon 20, 172 (13.7.1828).

149 PPS II, 93 (23.11.1834); see also III, 221f, 226 (14.12.1825 and 15.10.1835) respectively.

150 Ibid, see also The Book of Common Prayer and Administration of Sacraments..., Article XXV.

151 Cf. PPS II, 311 (29.6.1830). Newman made a similar statement on 14.12.1834; see also Pusey: «In the sacraments, there is the pleading of Christ for us. This pleading gets its force from the fact that God is not approached solely with what is men's own, but with the "pledges of His love", Christ Himself sacramentally present» (Letter to Bishop of London, 25,35).

152 Cf. SSD VIII, 116f (3.7.1831); see also Dev.325.

153 Cf. PPS V, 41 (2.6.1839).

154 Such humble elements like water of Baptism, bread and wine of holy communion, oil etc. (Cf. PPS VI,3 - 4.3.1838).

In these "extensions of the Incarnation" in the power of the Spirit, the theologian of Oxford saw a unique application of the Sacramental Principle. He saw this in the very fact that the Almighty, the All-powerful, acts through weak elements to lift up our souls. On this note, Newman maintained that sacraments urge believers to "go higher", "to transcend", and thus transport them to that wonderful truth that lies beneath all phenomena.

With this conviction, Newman argued that those who, sincerely receive the sacraments experience a sort of heavenly fragrance and a flavor of immortality, which is aroused in their souls as a pledge that God is with them and has filled with the rays of glory what formerly appeared earthly.[155]

From the moment that Newman discovered the "hidden power" of the sacraments, he formed the conviction that frequent and worthy reception of these privileges into the soul draws the receiver closer to the Redeemer, imprints in him the seal of the elect of God, and brightens the image of God in him. Through the reception of the sacraments, our souls are drawn closer to the transfigured Jesus and are themselves transfigured:

The perfect reaches the fullness of Christ; he is that which Christ is; he is privileged to participate in the passion of the Redeemer, to die with Him and to rise again.[156]

---

155 Cf. PPS VI, 134 (6.5.1838); see also SSD, 322: «In the very act of partaking of the sacraments, man, reinforced by the life of God, transcends himself and binds himself with heroic promises» (28.11.1841).

156 PPS III, 363 (22.1.1835). Constant reception of the sacraments deeply infuses the sentiments of Christ in the believer so that «Christ is really present in the believer and should be discernible in and through his words and actions. Thus the believer becomes a kind of sacrament of Christ in the world» (Ath.ii.88).

According to R. Strange, the sacraments are one of the means by which the real presence of Christ is set up in the believer. This teaching on the sacraments is an integral part of the doctrine of the divine indwelling (Cf. Roderick Strange, *Newman and the Gospel of Christ*, New York, 1981, 144-145).

Newman maintained that we are "redeemed by the precious blood of the Son of God, born again and sustained by the Spirit through the invisible virtue and strength of sacraments, and called, through self-denial and sanctification of the inward man, to the Eternal Presence of the Father, Son, and Holy Ghost" (Cf. PPS II,317-318 - 29.6.30).

For Newman, the grace of the sacraments confer divine tasks and inclinations. The power of the sacraments according to him are such that they can quicken Christian perfection:

One receives a rectitude of thought and taste, a clarity or stability of principles: this is the power of the secret grace of God, which is at work in these rites which He had established.[157]

As if reminding his audience that in the sacraments are concentrated the force of Jesus' touch to the man born blind, the power of his words to the paralytic, and to his dead friend, Lazarus, Newman once said in a sermon, that they live in divine friendship and joy those who are nourished with the hidden food of angels, who tasted the sweet Word, who made contact with the powers of the invisible world, the amability of the Lord, and the peace which transcends all comprehension.[158]

Christian rites in Newman's thought are "full of Christ" and Him alone. He understood them to be a continuation of what the Lord started in the flesh:

Henceforth whatever is done is His doing.... As He is the unseen source, so must He be acknowledged as the Agent, the present Object of worship and the thanksgiving in all that is done...[159]

Such an understanding confirms that sacraments are integral parts of the Gospel and Faith Tradition and cannot be either excluded from the economy of salvation or understood outside this context.

Inasmuch as the sacraments are charged by and with the power of Jesus' mantle and His Spirit, Newman refuted any attempt to relegate them to simply means which kindle men's faith. For him, it is Christ Himself who comes to us in the sacraments by the agency of the Holy Spirit while remaining on high, so that they are efficacious ex opere operato Christi:

Thus Christ shines through the sacraments as through trasparent bodies, without impediment. He is the light and life of the Church, acting through it, dispensing of His fullness, knitting and compacting together every part of it; and these its mysteries are not mere outward signs but effluences of His grace developing themselves in

---

157 PPS IV, 230 (10.12.1837).
158 see SSD, 313 (28.11.1841).
159 Jfc. 196-198.

external forms.... He has touched them and breathed upon them when He ordained them; and thenceforth they have a virtue in them which issues forth and encircles them round till the eye of faith sees in them no element of matter at all.[160]

Since the life-giving Spirit operates through material elements infusing them with spiritual qualities, Newman called the baptismal font the washing of «*regeneration*», not of mere washing with water, «and renewing of the Holy Ghost which He has poured out on us richly through Jesus Christ our Saviour».[161]

However, and above all, Newman was careful enough to affirm that Christ's presence in the sacraments is imperceptible to the bodily sense faculties, but apprehended by the eyes of faith. To be received for what they are, he sustained, sacraments need grateful approach, devotion, respect and faith from religious minds.[162]

The problem of the office of faith in relation to the sacraments was a central problem in the Tractarian critique of Evangelicalism. The Tractarians criticised the Evangelicals for having no place for an objective sacramental grace. For the Evangelicals, the sacraments were merely outward signs and emblems of God's saving grace, while faith was the objective means for gaining God's favours.

Newman rejected Evangelical theses on the ground that the sacraments are efficacious means of grace. By the force of God's creative word and promise, sacraments cause and convey grace. He admitted that faith is necessary for the fruitful acceptance of divine offer of grace, but maintained that faith is not the objective cause of grace:

Faith is the necessary condition from the human side for a beneficial reception of the sacramental grace which is there objectively offered by God as something entirely from above. It "makes the sacraments open their hidden virtue, and flow forth in pardon and grace".[163]

---

160 PPS III, 277-278 (15.11.1835).
161 Ibid, 280-281. According to Newman, Christ lodged virtue in his Church, and she dispenses this virtue in all her words and works. To view Christ as visibly revealed, to look upon His ordinances, not in the themselves, but as signs of His presence and power, as the accents of His love, the very form and countenance of Him who ever beholds us, to see Him thus revealed in glory day by day, is to believers an unspeakable privilege. (Cf. Ibid. 285).
162 Cf. Ibid., 277-78.
163 PPS II, 126 (24.1.1832).

Newman was adamant that it is not any act of the recipient which makes the ordinances of the Church become means of grace. The virtue contained in the ordinances of grace derives solely from above, faith being but the *sine qua non*, the necessary condition on our parts for duly receiving it.[164]

Newman believed that the efficacy of the sacraments is completely realised in faith and through faith. God "speaks through the sacraments", but only in faith can religious ears hear this language. Without faith, the sacraments are mute. Sacraments, and ordinances of grace, are mysterious instruments of the presence of divine grace for him who has faith. For faith is the means of His imparting his grace.[165]

Hence our author categorically stated that: «A proper disposition, preparation, and faith, are certainly necessary for a blessed reception».[166] Newman seems to be saying that "May it be done for you according to your faith", is completely true and valid in the sacramental ordinances of the Church.

In his sermons and other works from the years 1831 to 1837, Newman constantly reminded his audience of the truth that God's gifts are conveyed to individuals, not by a faith which can dispense with sacraments, but through sacraments which must be used in faith:[167]

Only by faith is He known to be present, he is not recognised by sight. When He opened his disciples' eyes, He at once vanished. He removed His visible presence and left but a memorial of Himself. He vanished from sight that He might be present in a sacrament; and in order to connect His visible presence with His presence invi-

---

164 Cf. TT II, v-vi (1833).
165 see Jfc., 209; also PPS VI, 122,132, and 137; VM II, 236f.; Letter to Rev. Godfrey Faussett On certain points of faith and practice, Oxford & London, 1838, 58. «Faith alone makes the Lord's Supper a means of grace to a man - without faith there is only an outward sign - i.e. a form or what is worse, a means of condemnation...»(MS, Sermon 17, 381 - 12.9.1824).
166 PPS III, 315 (2.11.1834); see also Keble, Tract 4,2, 52,8.
167 To come to Christ and receive life from him is not an internal process only, for «He has shown us, that to come to Him for life is a literal bodily action; not a mere figure, not a mere movement of the heart towards Him, but an action of the visible limbs; not a mere secret faith, but a coming to Church, a passing on along the aisle to His holy table, a kneeling down there before Him, and a receiving of the gift of eternal life in the form of bread and wine» (PPS VII, 149). These outward signs are simply the means of a hidden grace (see PPS I, 274 - 22.4.1832; OUS ,153f - 4.11.1832). They are not mere symbols, but actual vehicles of the divine gift (cf. Tract 82,xxi).

sible, he for one instant manifested Himself to their open eyes, manifested Himself, if I may so speak, while He passed from his hiding place of sight without knowledge to that of knowledge without sight. Our faces are as it were, turned from Him; we see Him not and know not of His presence, except by faith, because He is over us and within us.[168]

For Newman, the grace which is necessary for a holy life is given through the sacraments and other ordinances of a sacramental character. Nothing, he reasoned, can move us to holiness but God's grace and our will "co-operating",[169] that is to say, working in unison.

All that Newman is saying is that the sacraments are rich in the gifts of the Lord, which He wishes to lavish on souls, but these have to be disposed to receive them - they are received fruitfully in proportion to the disposition of souls. In other words, men have to "realise" the sacraments.

2.3.6   THE NUMBER OF THE SACRAMENTS

2.3.6.1   MULTIPLE SACRAMENTS AS "EXTENSIONS OF THE INCARNATION"

For Newman, the core of Christianity was the history of God's own saving and self-revealing offer which culminated in the hypostatic union of humanity and deity in the person of Jesus the mediator.

Following the logic of the Sacramental Principle, the Incarnation is sacramental[170] and the sacraments incarnational. Jesus of Nazareth is therefore the new and only hermeneutical principle for the comprehension of the sacramental economy.

In the sacraments just as in the man Jesus, we see one thing but what we see is in function with another;[171] we have a tangible matter and form but these are in function with an invisible power and reality.

---

168 PPS VI, 131-133 (6.5.1838); also 121-122.
169 Our "will" in this context refers to our faith in who God is, what God can do, and what God has promised. "Co-operating" with God means not to doubt God, not to forget or resist him. see MS Sermon 290, 7 (25.7.1824).
170 The man Jesus of Nazareth was the sacrament of God. This man whom the Jews saw, knew and lived with, in him was the Father present.
171 Just as Jesus was a sacrament of God so are the sacraments, sacraments of Jesus. Sacramental signs are more than what they appear to the naked eye. The Sacra-

In the logic of the Sacramental Principle and the mediatorial plan of Providence, the saving work and message of the mediator were effectually "represented" in the Church by means of certain sacramental "extensions of the Incarnation".

In the new era inaugurated by the Jesus-event, God dispenses his grace through a series of means rightly called "extensions of the Incarnation".

For the leader of the Oxford Movement, Christianity is both a Mystery and a Revelation: as Mystery it has rites and ordinances, as Revelation these rites and ordinances transcend themselves. The ordinances and sacraments of the Church are but expressions in human language and rites of those magnificient truths which fill eternity and to which the human mind is unequal[172]. It behoves one therefore, to inquire into the means by which his blessings are mediated,[173] how they are and how many they are.[174]

2.3.6.2 THE NUMBER OF THE SACRAMENTS IN CHRISTIAN ANTIQUITY

A special characteristic of early Tractarian theology was its appeal to and high esteem for early Christianity in which it found the best interpretation of the Lord's Gospel.[175] Tractarian theology saw also an inseparable connection between apostolic faith and apostolic worship.[176]

---

ments transcend themselves. They belong to two spheres of existence. However, it is necessary to comment that the sacraments of the Church are not sacraments in the same way that Jesus is Sacrament. Jesus is a person. The sacraments are things. When Jesus is called "Sacrament", the word is invested with a new office and higher meaning (see Dev.325).

172 Cf. Apo 37.

173 In the new scheme of mediation after Jesus Christ, the Church itself is the next most important mediator. What she receives from God, she conveys to the world through sacramental ordinances (see Ari.71f).

174 Evidently we have been speaking of the sacraments in the plural, a supposition that they are many. But the question that arises and which we are poised to answer gradually and systematically is how many there are.

175 Cf. Tract 6,4 (1833); also 71,29; VM I, 199.

176 Christian liturgy is nothing but a celebration of faith, practical living of dogma and creed. It is interesting to note that the oldest christological formulations were born within liturgical precincts, they were liturgical hymns.

In the mind of our author, the present Church system is the heir and successor to this Christian golden age which was the model in all matters of doctrine.[177]

When Newman understood the Roman Church to be the true Church, he understood and accepted the Church's sacramental praxis as an integral part of that Faith-Tradition by which the Fathers lived.

He believed that to be without sacraments was to be very much unlike the early Christians. And to be unlike them is to be short of a fundamental privilege and patrimonial tradition.[178]

2.3.6.3 MULTIPLE SACRAMENTS AS "DEVELOPMENT"

Initially Newman had the impression that the number of the ordinances of grace and sacraments had been inflated by the Roman Church. But gradually he resolved the discrepancy he suspected existed between biblical evidence and Rome's sacramental praxis.

Earlier on we saw how Newman realised that Christians are taught from the Bible, but not by the Bible. Here the role of the Episcopal Tradition is evident. For Newman, some practical matters, such as formularies and rites of the Church belong to the competence of Episcopal Tradition, on which the New Testament offers only fragmentary indications.

The Church has the office to complete the general indications by Scripture, for while the Bible gives the Spirit of religion, it behoves the Church to provide the body in which that Spirit is to be lodged.[179]

Through her attentive listening to the promptings and manifestations of the Spirit in her bosom (Prophetical Tradition), the Church completed what is contained in Sacred Scripture, and one of the outcomes of this process, is the Church's multiple sacramental life.

---

177 Cf. Tract 71, 29f (1836); see also VM I, 199 (The Indefectibility of the Church Catholic).
178 Cf. PPS III, 310 (2.11.1834).
179 PPS II, 73 (1.1.1831); see also J.Keble, SAO:VIII, 203; W.J.A.M.Beek, John Keble's Literary and Religious Contribution to the Oxford Movement. Dissertation, Nijmegen 1958, 114-125; Greenfield, The Tractarian Attitude, 135. However, it is necessary to make the following remarks: The ultimate norm of faith is the Word of God. Consequently, the Church is not to introduce what was not in the mind of the Lord. What her Lord abhorred should not appeal to her. Otherwise she would be an adulterous Church.

In this optic, to the query: «How are we to explain that the New Testament is silent about a multitude of rites and ceremonies which the writings of the Fathers show to have been generally received in the primitive Church?»,[180] Newman could answer that the principle of the rites and ceremonies are sanctioned in Scripture, but the form in which they are delivered to the Church is determined by Tradition.[181]

Thus, says Newman, the incidental character of the information which the Bible offers on liturgical customs is «sufficient to reconcile us to the complete ritual system which breaks upon us in the writings of the Fathers. Until it can be proved that this system - in part or in whole is *contrary* to Scripture, we are bound to venerate what is certainly primitive, and probably is apostolic».[182]

The best key for the understanding of this,[183] is Newman's theory of Development of Doctrine.[184]

Under this theory, Newman understood multiple sacramental practices to be the inevitable result of the intelligence of faith by the children of the Church under the guidance of the Spirit. They are the fruits of the Church's continuous meditation on her faith in Jesus the Lord. Particular historical factors prompted the Church at particular historical moments to formulate dogmas as the expressions of the fruits of her meditation.[185]

---

180 Tract, 34, 1f (1834).
181 Ibid.
182 Ibid., 4; see also Biemer, *Überlieferung*, 59.
183 What is being said here is not limited to the question of the number of the means of grace alone. The message of Newman's theory of doctrinal development is valid for sacramentology in all its ramifications.
184 This does not apply hundred per cent to the Anglican Newman.
185 It is necessary to point out that Tradition and the life of the Church are the best commentary on Scripture. Revelation sets before the mind of the believers certain supernatural and thrilling truths. Fired and aroused by such a lovely impression, the mind tries to to give accurate utterance to the blessed vision that holds it spellbound.
    Clear and explicit formulation of the inward vision is not easy, and the process of formulating it, naturally gradual. Even centuries might pass without an adequate formal expression of an aspect of the original idea.
    Thus Newman accounts for how certain dogmas, formulations, rites, ceremonies, which are found in the Catholic Church are in accord with the ancient creed. They have been there from the beginning but are proclaimed explicitly at the fullness of time, just as Jesus, the Messiah was there unnoticed to many until John the Baptist pointed him out: 'Behold the Lamb of God...' Jesus was not made Messiah by the

Thus, Newman responds to accusations of "corruption" and "additions"[186] he and his colleagues had previously levelled at the Catholic Church with regard to the growth of ritual and definitions of dogma.

In any living system, there are changes which, far from being corruptions, are merely response of a living social body to changing conditions. As Christianity grows into a philosophy or sytem of belief, under varying and expanding circumstances, "old principles reappear under new forms",[187] as developments of the original deposit. Newman understood the Roman Catholic multiple sacramental system and religious ceremonial as but a bringing out of the rich deposit of the Christian faith.

The idea of doctrinal development helped Newman and some of his colleagues to accept Rome as the true representative of that Catholic Church which before they had seen in its fulness and purity only in Antiquity, and to accept as integral parts of *de fide*, as revealed truths, the changes which occurred and the decisions of the later Roman Catholic Church. Thus, the Tractarians were attracted to the elaborate sacramental life of Rome.[188]

For the Tractarians, the Roman sacramental and ceremonial system has, at least in some respects, better embodied and carried out that Catholic faith to which the Anglican Church lays claim.[189] Newman's Essay on Development, as far as the sacraments are concerned, can be

---

force of John's words. What was new was the striking manner in which John stated the truth, a truth that had always been there.

Development and doctrinal formulation are part of the inner life and dynamism of faith. For Newman, the Biblical revelation is characterised by development, and moves from beginning to end in a climate of increasing and growing revelation. Its earlier stages are anticipations of the latter; the Pentateuch anticipates the Prophets, and the Prophets anticipate, though dimly, the fulness of time in the New Testament. And as revelation proceeds, it is ever new, yet ever old.

From this he was convinced that: «we may fairly conclude that Christian doctrine admits of formal legitimate, and true developments, that is, of developments contemplated by its Divine Author» (Dev.65, also 74).

186 Cf. VM I, 40 (The Nature and Ground of Roman and Protestant Erors).

187 Dev.30.

188 It has already been noted that a major characteristic of the Tractarian Movement was its emphasis on the sacraments. Now, its leaders clearly saw in the Roman Communion what they were interested in promoting.

189 While Newman accused Rome of having exaggerated the number of the means of grace, at the same time he bemoaned the scarce sacramental practice of the Anglican Church. see Tract 34,2 and 4 (1834).

called a "portrait of the development of his mind" in his effort to understand the meaning of the sacraments and their relation to faith. In this Essay, Christianity, is a *living idea*, which changes with the human community which it serves. It changes with them in order to remain the same. The Essay cleared Newman's doubts and removed the obstacles on his way.

The awareness of the number of the sacraments increased as the Church gradually understood and took deeper consciousness of her faith. The Church has, therefore, not invented new means of grace, but has like a good mother and teacher expressed in new ways to her children the meaning and relevance of the deposits of grace which her Lord bequeathed to her.[190]

In the light of the theory of development of doctrine, it dawned on Newman that the Church does not possess too many sacraments. Rather she has a number that corresponds to and responds to her understanding of her faith in the Lord's life, words and actions.

In short, the body of the faithful, the Church, has developed in the understanding of the means of grace. And what the Church understood, she lived and celebrated in her multiple sacramental system, and what she lived and celebrated, she formulated into doctrines and dogmas.

And if the Church's explanation and formulation of her faith in the fourth century was right, she was also right in the sixteenth century; if she was right in the use of some philosophical terms such as substance, nature, person, relation, generation, etc., to explain her faith, she is also right in her dogmatic affirmations on the sacraments, since it is the same faith that she explains under the guidance of the same Spirit.[191]

As Wilfrid Ward ably sums up, Newman,

---

190 The Church has the gift of explaining the Creed. The function of Tradition is to guide and enlighten us in our understanding of the inspired word. Its base was continuity and development. Change cannot but happen to society; an authentic change, however, grows out of and conserves the best of the past. Newman takes it for granted that the contemporary Catholic Church, with its multitude of rites and ordinances, is the «historical continuation of the religious system, which bore the name Catholic ... in every preceeding century...» (Dev.203).

191 Cf. Dev.30. Thus Newman laid down, in a sermon from 1830, that «the same Spirit which inspired Scripture is necessary for its interpretation. And that Spirit is still with the Church ... (MS, Sermon, 225,19,22 (7.2.1830); see also Oakeley, Rites and Ceremonies, 435).

accounts for and justifies the proud claim of the Catholic Church to be semper eadem, in spite of the changes in its outward form and polity - *the growth of ritual*, the assimilation of extraneous philosophies by its theological schools, ... its fresh definitions of dogma. The Catholic Church has the identity of uninterrupted life and growth.[192]

What Newman had regarded as Roman corruptions he later admitted were genuine parts of the system of Antiquity. Rome, in other words, preserved and set forth some cardinal points of that Catholicism which they had inherited from Christian Antiquity. Thus, Newman and some of his friends underwent a "change" of mind, a "conversion".

This "sacramental conversion" meant for Newman, "an exodus from his people" to his "former enemies"; it meant "violence" to himself and to the education he had received; it meant a "new vision of faith"; it meant "questioning and even jettisoning" some convictions he had lived with and taken seriously for granted till now.

For the Oxford theologian, it was a conversion from a scarce-sacramental religion to an elaborate-Sacramental religion. And a conversion from the one school to the other necessarily involved a reconsideration of the question of faith in relation to the sacraments.[193]

2.3.6.4 THE SEVEN-FOLD NUMBER OF THE SACRAMENTS

While Newman remained a staunch member of the Anglican Church, he seemed to hold private opinions different from his Church's official position[194]. In some of his preachings, he manifested his belief in more than two sacraments recognised by the authority of his Church. Already in 1824, in a sermon on *Christian sacraments contrasted to Jewish Rites,*

---

192 Wilfrid Ward, *Life of Newman* I, 88.
193 Newman later formulated the results of his reconsideration of this question. According to him, we grow in our understanding of the object of our faith. What we understand we formulate in words; and these formulations change as we grow in our faith. And «growth is the only evidence of life» (Apo.109). Newman's crossing from one type of sacramental religion to another was part of the dynamism of faith: «To live is to change», and ,«to be perfect is to have changed again and again» (Dev.40).
194 In Article XXV of the Church of England, it is categorically stated that: "There are only two sacraments ordained of Christ our Lord in the Gospel, that is to say, Baptism, and the Supper of the Lord" (The Book of Common Prayer and Administration of the Sacraments...)

126

he explicitly enumerated and defended multiple elemenents in the sacramental system:

The Church's multiple sacramental system - baptism, the Lord's supper, Ordination, absolution, holy matrimony, public prayers, Saints' days and holidays is not slumping the soul into bondage or leading it away from Christ...[195]

Shortly after, Newman vigorously argued that our Lord himself instituted the sacramental ordinances - such "ordinances as baptism, confirmation, ordination, absolution, ... and therefore one would think they *could* not possibly interfere with supreme devotion to Him, as the Jewish rites did".[196]

He was unbudging in his defence of multiple sacraments as means of grace against the current polemical understanding of the same. He once launched an appeal to his audience, inviting them to see in the sacraments what God offers to man, and what the Church teaches, namely, efficacious means of grace:

O brothers, do not come to Church, or to Holy Communion, nor be present at wedlocks, funerals or any other rite, without the feeling and belief that there is a reality greater than what we see.[197]

One can say that Newman underwent an evolution in his understanding of the sacraments. He grew in faith as he understood that sacraments are more than two and why they are so. It is no longer enough to rely on the evidence of the material pages of Scripture.

It is safer to travel with and under the infallible and secure guidance of Tradition. In the light of the truth that the Church's living Tradition is the pledge of the true faith and the means of securing it, Newman said,

It is from the visible Church, and not only in her - from her sacraments and rites, which are *so many tokens* of Christ's active presence in her through the Spirit - that the invisible Church does not cease to be born.[198]

---

195 MS Sermon 281, 9 (8.8.1824).
196 MS Sermon 17, 381 (12.9.1824).
197 SSD, 179 (30.10.1831).
198 PPS III, 250-253 (14.9.1834). The emphasis is mine. The phrase "so many", can be interpreted as referring to different forms of the celebration of the Eucharist. But I am more inclined to interprete it as referring to sacraments in the strict sense of the word. However, Newman can be understood in both ways.

He regreted the meagre sacramental praxis of the Anglican Communion. In his last sermon preached as a priest of the Anglican Church, *The Parting of Friends*, of 25 September 1843, Newman almost wept: "O my mother", he addressed the Church of England, "... who hath put this note upon thee, to have a 'miscarrying womb and a dry breast, ...?"[199]

For the Oxford theologian, the Church dispenses and recommends the sacraments because they were instituted by Christ. And to argue that Christ did not institute the sacraments, is to misapply Scripture, since whatever is not contrary to the Spirit of the Gospel is in support of it.

In the light of the above, one may observe that Newman recognised a wide range of ordinances of grace: Baptism, Holy Communion, Confirmation, Absolution, Ordination, Holy Matrimony, Extreme Unction,[200] Funerals, Public prayers, Saints' days, holidays, etc.

But a Catholic is supposed to accept and profess the teachings of the Church. Was not Newman under the anathema of the Tridentine Council?[201] Quo vadis?

It can be said that Newman resolved this incongruency when he entered the Roman Catholic Church. By accepting this Church, he accepted its dogmas, doctrines and ordinances. And as such it was no longer necessary for a "Catholic Newman" to explicitly profess all the articles and propositions defined by the Church as a manifestation of being in complete syntony with its beliefs and teachings.

Newman himself expressed this truth in a very beautiful line. For him, by professing the Church and the faith of the Church, a Catholic implicitly professes the teachings or dogmas of the Church even when he cannot resolve all theological queries surrounding the same:

As for the many dogmatic propositions to which a Catholic is required to give ... assent, his assent is implicitly given when he gives ... assent to the Church».[202]

---

199 SSD, 407.
200 According to Newman the character or grace received through this sacrament is bodily health (LD XIII,454; also Dev.92; Apo 312).
201 One of the canons of the Council of Trent reads: "If anyone says that the sacraments of the New Law were not all instituted by Jesus Christ our Lord; or that there are more or fewer than seven, that is, Baptism, Confirmation, the Eucharist, Penance, Extreme unction, Order and Matrimony; or that any one of these is not truly and properly a sacrament, *anathema sit" (DS 1601).*
202 GA 72; see also 251.

Thus Newman, on becoming a Catholic, accepted all Catholic dogmas, doctrines and disciplines: «... I had no difficulty in believing (it), as soon as I believed that the Roman Catholic Church was the oracle of God».[203]

One can therefore say that for Newman, the sacraments are seven because the Church, which stands for Christ, teaches it. The Church has a divine mandate to apply to the individual the blessings of Jesus the Lord. And this application the Church does through the seven-fold sacramental ordinances.

According to Newman, there is a hierarchy within the sacramental system. Before establishing this hierarchy, a brief comment shall be made on the individual sacraments as they are delineated in his writings.

2.3.6.4.1 THE SACRAMENT OF BAPTISM

In the Tractarian sacramentology, Baptism is the first and fundamental sacrament by which one is incorporated into Christ, and subsequently admitted into the visible Church.[204] This sacrament was of a special importance to the Anglican Newman because it emphasizes the necessity of belonging to the Church as opposed to the Evangelical stress on individual salvation through faith, which can dispense with the Church.

At the moment of baptism, «a wonderful change» is wrought in the soul, for through the entrance of the Spirit it is regenerated and becomes the temple of the Spirit.[205] The gift of the Spirit is imparted to every member on his baptism:

... by this new birth the Divine Shechinah is set up within him, pervading the soul and body ..., raising him in the scale of being, drawing and fostering into life whatever remains in him of a higher nature, and imparting to him, in due season and measure, its own surpassing and heavenly virtue.[206]

Great indeed is the transformation which the 'baptised' undergoes. The great work which the Spirit realised in Christ is realised in us as well. Just as Christ was generated through the Spirit, likewise we are regener-

---

203 Apo 215.
204 As early as 1825, Newman would say in a sermon on 'Our Admittance into the Church our Title to the Holy Spirit': «How do we become entitled to the gift of Christ's Spirit? We answer by belonging to the body of His Church - and we belong to His Church by being baptized into it».
205 PPS II, 222f (11.11.1834).
206 PS III, 266 (8.1.1835).

ated with the intervention of the Spirit through His action; in the sacrament of baptism, men become parts and members of the mystical body of Christ;[207] they become like Him, they become Christians.

In Newman's mind, baptism, according to the most explicit teaching of the New Testament, involves the actual gift of regeneration:

As there is one Holy Ghost, so there is one only visible body of Christians which Almighty God "knows by name", and one baptism which admits men into it. But more than this is taught us ...; not only that the Holy Ghost is in the Church and that baptism admits into it, but that the Holy Ghost admits by means of baptism, that the Holy Ghost baptizes; ... that each individual member receives the gift of the Holy Ghost as a preliminary step, a condition or means of his being incorporated into the Church; or in our Saviour's words, that no one can enter except he be regenerated in order to enter it.[208]

The baptised is privileged to share in the spiritual heritages of the Church: «The sanctity which belongs to the Church as the Spirit-bearing body is through baptism extended to the individual».[209] The depth, significance and beauty of the work of the Spirit in Baptism is such that Newman called the baptismal font, «the washing *of regeneration*».[210]

From the time Newman understood the efficacy of the sacraments, his prefered word for the description of what happens in baptism became *regeneration*, a term which is charged with mystical meaning, change of being, new birth, birth from above, nearness to the Godhead, etc. Baptism is God's first indelible claim and demand on the baptised.

Every baptised person is under a process of divine influence and sanctification, a process often interrupted, often given up, then resumed, irregularly carried on, heartily entered into, finally completed, as the case may be.[211] Newman took pains to explain to his congregation that baptism does not operate magically: «we but slowly enter into the privileges of our baptism; we but gradually gain it».[212]

Newman reminded his congregation that what God performs in the sacraments transcends human empirical calculations. Certainly, «nothing

---

207 Cf. PS VIII, 232 (30.4.1843).
208 PPS III, 271 (15.11.1835).
209 PPS IV, 176 (27.11.1825).
210 PPS III, 285 (15.11.1835).
211 see AW 78 (13.1.1825); see also 77 and 80.
212 PS VI, 98 (31.2.1839).

shows, for some time, that the Spirit of God is come into, and dwells in the child baptized».[213]
But that, according to him, is no pretext to defer infant baptism. «To defer Baptism till persons actually have repentance and faith», Newman likened to «... refusing to give medicine till a patient begins to get well». Above all he argued that

It is certain that children ought to be instructed in religious truth, as they can bear it, from the very first dawn of reason; clearly, they are not to be left without a Christian training till they arrive at years of maturity. Now ... Christ seems distinctly to connect teaching with Baptism, as if He intended to convey through it a blessing upon teaching, - "Go and teach all the nations, baptizing them." If children, then, are to be considered as under the teaching, as learners in the school of Christ, surely they should be admitted into that school by Baptism.[214]

2.3.6.4.2 THE SACRAMENT OF PENITENCE

Newman knew that officially the Anglican Church did not acknowledge Penitence as an ordinance of sacramental character instituted by Christ.[215] Consequently it had little or no relevance to the faithful of this Communion.

One could therefore imagine the amount of trouble and the degree of resentment the "Radicals of the Oxford Movement" were provoking with their Sacramental Revolution, in which, among other things, they were encouraging and even introducing the penitential discipline in their pastoral work.[216]

---

213 PPS VIII, 57 (25.4.1837).
214 PS VII, 224, also 226-227 (15.6.1828).
215 Cf. Jfc. 152ff; also Tract 90,43ff; Pusey, *Letter to Bishop of Oxford*, 97-100.
216 Elsewhere we have referred to how Newman pictures the ecclesiastical situation of the Church of England as the leaders of the Oxford Movement saw it before and during their rise: « ... revealed truth as a matter of controversy; the ordinances of grace profaned; and *penitential discipline slighted or even unknown»* (SSD,432). I purposely emphasized this preoccupation with the penitential aspect of the "Sacramental Movement" in the hope of expressing within my limits, how the Tractarians felt this problem. Pusey has himself admitted that the tracts on baptism ought to have been followed up with a work on "Christian Repentance, on Confession and Absolution". What prevented him at that time from carrying out his plan was his uncertainty about a series of theological questions connected

In this regard, the Tractarians, in spite of their deep respect for authority, differed from their Church authority especially in her interpretation of Scriptural evidence[217] on questions concerning the penitential ordinance.[218]

In fact, Newman heard his first confession back in March 1838, early one Sunday morning in St.Mary's, while he had sat at the altar-rails with his penitent kneeling before him.

He found the absence of sacramental confession, particularly at a time like Christmas, painful.[219] This lack of confessional practice in the Anglican Church seemed to him a serious lacuna in the Anglican "pastoral care": «I cannot understand how a clergyman can be answerable for souls, if souls are not submitted to him».[220] And in answer to Keble's inquiry about his pastoral practice in matters concerning this sacrament,

---

with the matter (Cf. H.P.Liddon, *Life of Edward Bouverie Pusey*, ed. by J.O. Johnson & R.J. Wilson, vol.I, 352-353).

217 Newman, in a private note of 1838, related the theological confusion he felt when, for the first time, he was asked to hear a private confession. Such theological confusions, in a man like Newman, who nurtured deep respect for Authority (and in this case, the Authority of the Anglican Church) were complex: is this really an ordinance of grace or a simple means of comfort to troubled consciences?, is it efficacious on divine commission of the minister, or on his personal character and his ability to help?, what did the other divines think of this question? (Cf. AW 214 - 18.3.1838).

218 While the theological uncertainties regarding this sacrament lingered, popular piety saw its practical revival during the later thirties. And it began, as Pusey asserted, not as a consequence of much preaching recommending it, but as a relief sought for by earnest penitents, looking "for a remedy for post-baptismal sin" (Letter to bishop of London,177; see also H.P.,Liddon, *Life of Edward Bouverie Pusey*, III,269). Keble spoke in 1844 of private confession and absolution as "the appointed way" for the penitent who has been defiled with grievous sin after Baptism" (SOP;XXXIX,465f).

219 Cf. Letter to W.H.Anderson, August 1 1842, quoted in A.Withey, *John Henry Newman. The Liturgy and the Breviary. Their Influence on his life as an Anglican*, London, 77. This letter is not found in the edited volumes of Anne Mozley; and the volumes of Letters and Diaries of Newman in which they are to be contained are not yet available.

220 To Mrs J.Mozley, September 15 1843, in P.Murray (ed.), *John Henry Newman. Sermons 1824-83, vol.I: Sermons on the Liturgy and the Sacraments and on Christ the Mediator*, Oxford, 1991, 102. What we said above is true of this letter.

Newman replied with a surprising vehemence: «Confession is the life of the parochial charge - without it all is hollow ...».[221]

This type of reasoning and the consequent praxis which it provoked is enough to label the Oxford Movement, "a penitential movement".[222] Newman himself sustained: «... it is certain from Scripture, that the gift of reconciliation is not conveyed to individuals except through appointed ordinances».[223]

The Church rightly imposes a creed, remits sins or rebukes and punishes because she stands for Christ and conveys the power of the Spirit. It is through a particular ordinance that the Church exercises this office of remission of sins.

2.3.6.4.3 THE EUCHARIST

Very early in life, Newman developed a deep devotion for this sacrament. We have already seen above how he voraciously read books that dealt with preparation for the Eucharist. He strongly believed this sacrament to be the most privileged and chief channel of grace to the redeemed humanity.

His Eucharistic piety was so deep that he saw in this sacrament Christ's personal inhabitation in the hearts of the faithful. According to him, in the Eucharist the Lord is received by the soul as a guest who comes in order to assimilate the host to Himself and in order to be one with him.[224]

For this reason, he called the Lord's Supper,«*a feast of inward and spiritual strength*, not only pledging us God's favour through Christ, but actually conveying to us the gracious influences of His Spirit»,[225] and assimilating the soul to the Lord. This assimilation is possible because Christ is really present in the Eucharist:[226]

---

221 To J.Keble, December 20 1842, in Anne Mozley (ed.), *Letters and Correspondences of J.H.Newman*, II, 405. This letter is not found in the volumes of the published editions of Newman's Letters and Diaries.
222 Cf. Alf Härdelin, *The Tractarian Understanding of the Eucharist*, 333.
223 Jfc. 280; see also Froude, *Remains* II:I,71.
224 Cf. Jfc. 201; see also MS Sermon 24, 16 (3.10.1824).
225 MS Sermon 24, 16 (3.10.1824).
226 Cf. Ess.I. 247-248 (The Theology of St. Ignatius); see also PS III, 277-278.

He who is at the right hand of God, manifests Himself in that Holy Sacrament as really and fully as if he were visibly there .... Such is the glorious presence which faith sees in the Holy Communion, though every thing looks as usual to the natural man. Not gold or precious stones, pearls of great price or gold of Ophir, are to the eyes of faith so radiant as those lowly elements which He, the Highest, is pleased to make the means of conveying to our hearts and bodies His own gracious self. Not the light of the sun sevenfold is so awfully bright and overpowering, if we could see as the angels do, as that seed of eternal life, which by eating and drinking we lay up in our hearts against the day of his coming.[227]

As an Anglican, Newman had believed in the real presence of the Lord in this sacrament. Writing as a Catholic, he appealed to his memory on this question: «... And when I was at the early Eucharistic service at St.Mary's (I thus specify it, because I am appealing to my memory distinctly), I had an absolute and overpowering sense of the Real Presence».[228]

For Newman, the reservation and adoration of the Eucharist is concrete proof of the presence of Christ in this sacrament and the guarantee of the unity of believers. Writing in 1846 to Mrs Bowden, Newman said: «... There is nothing which has brought home to me so the Unity of the Church as the presence of its Divine Founder and Life wherever I go - All places are as it were, one ...»[229]

His Eucharistic spirituality and joy was almost ineffable. The presence of the Lord in the tabernacle produced in him «the deep impression of religion as an objective fact»[230]. And, almost overwhelmed with joy and gratitude, Newman confessed: «... I never knew what worship was, as an objective fact, till I entered the Catholic Church».[231]

It is not surprising then that when the hero of his novel *Loss and Gain* attends the Catholic Church for the first time, it is not the singing, the rituals, or the beauty of the liturgy that impresses him as much as «the Great Presence, which makes a Catholic Church different from every other place in the world».[232]

Newman shows a reluctance to explain the manner of the Eucharistic presence; how and when the Spirit of God acts upon sacramental ele-

---

227 PS IV, 147-148 (6.11.1836).
228 LD XI, 101 (27.1.1846).
229 Ibid., 254 (4.10.1846).
230 LD XI, 129 (26.2.1846); also 131 and 65.
231 LD XI, 249-250 (24.8.1846); also 232-233.
232 LG 427.

ments is not necessary for us to know, he reasoned. We indeed say *spiritually, sacramentally, in a heavenly way*, but this is in order to impress on our minds religious, and not carnal notions of it.

This spiritual, sacramental, or heavenly[233] presence implied a presence which is unapproachable and imperceptible to the bodily sense faculties, but perceived through faith.[234]

He is rather more emphatic with regard to the effect or blessing that is contained in this sacrament. The effect of the holy Communion is *life*, and life to the whole man who, by partaking of this sacrament, is vested with the sentiments of Christ, the Lord:

> Bread sustains us in this temporal life; the consecrated bread is the means of eternal strength for soul and body. Who could live this visible life without earthly food? And in the same general way the Supper of the Lord is the "means" of our living for ever .... We eat the sacred bread, and our bodies become sacred; they are not ours; they are Christ's; they are instinct with that flesh which saw not corruption; they are inhabited by His Spirit; they become immortal; they die but to appearance, and for a time; they spring up when their sleep is ended, and reign with Him for ever.[235]

2.3.6.4.4 THE SACRAMENT OF MARRIAGE

Newman did not dedicate any special attention to this particular ordinance of grace. His treatment of this argument was closely linked to his consideration of the Christian life in the world as "sacrament":

> To be a Christian is one of the most wondrous and awful gifts in the world. It is in one sense, to be higher than angel or archangel. If we have any portion of an enligh-

---

233 A sacramental, a spiritual or a heavenly presence does not here mean a presence of a *mere sacramental sign*, but a presence *under* a sign (Cf. Pusey, Letter to Bishop of London in Explanation of some statements contained in a letter by W.Dodsworth, 1851,157.

234 Cf. PPS VI, 242 (29.11.1840); also 122; Jfc. 209. According to Newman: «There are some truths addressed solely to our faith, not to our reason; not to our reason, because we know so little about the 'power of God' (in our Saviour's words), that we have nothing to reason *upon*. One of those, for instance, is the presence of Christ in the sacrament. We *know* we eat His Body and Blood; but it is our wisdom not curiously to ask how or whence, not to give our thoughts range, but to take and eat and profit. This is the secret of gaining the blessing promised» (PPS I, 276 - 22.4.1832).

235 PPS I, 274 (22.4.1832).

tened faith, we shall understand that our state, as members of Christ's Church, is full of mystery.[236]

From this he passed over to a consideration of the sacramental aspect of Christian marriage. Newman thought of Matrimony as one of the mysterious ways divine providence uses for educating and training each other[237] in the knowledge of good and evil, and invited and encouraged his congregation to understand this and to live accordingly:

> When a man at all enters into such thoughts, how is his view changed about the birth of children! In what a different light do his duties, as a parent, break upon him! The notion entertained by most men seems to be that it is a pleasant thing to have a home - this is what would be called an innocent and praiseworthy reason for marrying .... Doubtless wife and children *are* blessings from God: and it *is* praiseworthy and right to be domestic and to live in orderly and honourable habits. But a man who limits his view to these thoughts, who does not look at marriage and at the birth of children as something of a much higher and more heavenly nature than anything we see, who does not discern in Holy Matrimony of divine ordinance, shadowing out the union between Christ and the Church, and does not associate the birth of children with the ordinance of their new birth, such a one, I can only say, has very carnal views.[238]

Thus, already as an Anglican, Newman recognised Matrimony as an ordinance of grace and urged his audience that behind what one may see materially in Matrimony, there is something of a higher order, something divine, an ordinance of grace.

2.3.6.4.5 THE SACRAMENT OF ORDERS

For Newman, Jesus is the only Priest of the Church and the only dispenser of messianic blessings. «... There is under the Gospel but one proper Priest, Prophet and King, Altar, sacrifice, and House of God; all grace flows from One Head».[239]

Others are priests, in the understanding of Newman, because they participate in the priestly office of Jesus, the only meritorious Mediator and Priest before God, from whom all life circulates in the members of the

---

236 PPS III, 298 and 300 (4.3.1826).
237 Each other in the mind of Newman, in this context can be the couple themselves, their children, neighbours and friends.
238 PPS III, 298-300.
239 Jfc.196 and 198.

one body, the Church. Those who share in this ministry are one with Christ and are extensions of the role that belongs by right and nature to the Son of God:

Christ's priests have no priesthood but His. They are merely His shadows and organs; they are His outward signs; and what they do he does; when they baptize, he is baptizing; when they bless, he is blessing. He is in all acts of His Church.[240]

Priests are the instruments of His grace, through the mysterious but all-powerful action of His Spirit. Just as the Christians are «His members», so are «Priests His delegates».[241] With this understanding, he drew a good definition of a priest of the New Testament:

By a priest, in a Christian sense, is meant an appointed channel by which the peculiar Gospel blessings are conveyed to mankind, one who has power to apply to individuals those gifts which Christ has promised us generally as the fruit of His Mediation.[242]

It is clear from this definition that a priest is a dispenser of the "Gospel blessings", the sacraments. This simple definition exposes the nobility and greatness of the ministry and the weakness and unworthiness of him who is called to this ministry. It is an awesome sacrament.

For Newman, ministers should always live in the consciousness of their nothingness and lowliness and consequently should tread around the threshold of the triple holy God in fear and in trembling just like Jeremiah and Jonah did.

He realised that such an attitude towards this sacrament was not always there. «Alas for us!», Newman groans, «we feel none of those terrors about it, which made the early Christians flee from it!» For them «it was so solemn a function, that the holier a man was, the less inclined he felt to undertake it».[243] He invited those who embrace this calling to beware of what is at stake:

So again they who enter Holy Orders promise they know not what, engage themselves they know not how deeply, debar themselves of the world's ways they know not how intimately, find perchance they must cut off from them the right hand,

---

240 PS VI, 242 (29.11.1840).
241 Jfc.16.
242 PS II,305 (29.6.1830 and repeated again on 14.12.1834).
243 PS IV, 61 (22.1.1835).

137

sacrifice the desire of their eyes and the stirring of their hearts at the foot of the Cross, while they thought, in their simplicity, they were but choosing the easy life of quiet "plain men dwelling in tents".[244]

While an Anglican, Newman believed in the validity of the Anglican Orders.[245] But on the day he was received into the Catholic Church, he wrote: "The Church of Rome has never acknowledged English Orders, though she has never formally denied them. Practically, I am a layman in her eyes".[246]

For him, the Eucharist and Holy Orders are linked. Therefore, "... If the Anglican Church has not Orders it has no Eucharist ...."[247] and vice versa:

... If the English Church has the sacrament of the Eucharist, I cannot imagine anything more frightful than priests consecrating and people receiving who *do not believe*, the careless disposal of Christ's own flesh, the crumbs under which it lies left on the plate, the pieces suffered to fall about and kicked aside, the blood drunken as a refreshment or a treat after a service, or poured back into the bottle ... and certainly it is an argument, which has for sometime weighed with me, in corroboration of other more direct ones, in proof that the Anglican Church has not the Apostolic succession.[248]

2.3.6.4.6 CONFIRMATION

Very often Newman reveals his admiration for and devotion to Christian Antiquity. This is true in his thought on the sacrament of Confirmation. His thought runs in the same direction as the patristic writers who group together as the sacraments of Christian initiation, baptism, confirmation, and eucharist.

His sermon portrays a connection between baptism and confirmation. This is because in his mind, Confirmation is a completion of the operation which the Spirit begins in the soul:

---

244 PS IV, 304 (28.2.1836).
245 In 1841 he styled himself "a priest of the English Church and vicar of St.Mary the Virgin's" (Apo.146).
246 LD XI, 15 (9.10.1845).
247 LD XII, 249 (21.7.1848).
248 LD XII, 293 (11.10.1848).

Confirmation seals in their fulness, winds up and consigns, completes the entire round of those sanctifying gifts which are begun, which are given inchoately in Baptism .... It is properly an integral part of the Baptismal rite; I do not say of the essence, or an essential part, of Baptism, but an integral part, just as a hand is an integral part of our body, yet may be amputated without loss of life. And in ancient times it was administered at the time of Baptism, as its ratification.[249]

Commenting on the fact of a close connection within the sacramental system, Newman described the sacraments as " ... members of one family, and suggestive, or correlative, or confirmatory, or illustrative of each other..."[250]

Newman felt the Anglican Church's praxis of not administering this sacrament at an early age very inapt. He urged its reception as early as possible, for he was convinced that it is the confirming of the good works started[251] by the Spirit in the believer at Baptism:

When persons are young, before their minds are formed, ere they have sullied their baptismal robe, and contracted bad habits, this is the time for Confirmation, which conveys to them grace whereby they may perform that 'good work' which Baptism has begun in them.[252]

As to the effect of Confirmation on the receiver, Newman believed it transforms the receiver into an active militant of the Victorious Lord. It «is directed to arm the Christian against his ... enemies, which, when entering into his field of trial, he at once meets».[253] For Newman, the bishop is dispenser of confirmation. Through a highly indicative gesture of the imposition of hands, the bishop administers the rite.[254]

2.3.7 THE HIERARCHY OF THE SACRAMENTS

Having established the sacramental role of material phenomena in the divine economy, and having seen that the sacraments of the Church

---

249 LD VI,80 (4.3. 1837).
250 Dev.110.
251 He called the sacrament of Confirmation, «... the completion of Baptism since it grants its recipient entire fellowship with the body of believers, and allows them to join in the Communion of the Lord's supper» (MS Sermon - 31.1.1830).
252 PS IV, 63 (22.1.1835).
253 Ibid.
254 Cf. LD VI, 79 (4.6.1837).

though not exhausting in themselves the sacramentality of creation are *sacraments within the sacramental system*, it is interesting to observe what Newman said about these ordinances of grace at different periods and how he classified them (if one may say so).

The sacraments are all necessary and the same Spirit of Christ operates in all but in different degrees according to what God wants to realise:

And what is true of the ordinary services of religion, public and private, holds in a still higher or rather in a special way as regards the sacramental ordinances of the Church. In these is manifested in greater or less degree, according to the measure of each, that incarnate Saviour who is one day to be judge and who is enabling us to bear His presence then by imparting it to us in measure now.[255]

What is therefore at stake is not a hierarchy of necessity or importance, but hierarchy of degree of divine presence and operation quo ad recipientes.

Already in 1824 Newman reserved a special consideration for the Eucharist as the most majestic. According to him, the eucharist is the commemoration of Jesus' passion and the sacrament of his resurrection.[256] As he matured in faith, he continued to give vent to such a high regard for the eucharist. In 1831, he called it a special moment of encounter with the God of Love and the love of God:

Christ is uniquely present to each Christian when the Church is gathered to form the Eucharistic community, since this is that special mode of approaching Him which He has bequeathed.[257]

He emphasized that Christ's splendour and most awful presence in the Eucharist than in any other service is even testified in the architectural style of church buildings. He remarked that Christians express this belief by making the chancel, if they could, more beautiful and majestic and awful, than the rest of the church.[258]

Nor did Newman hesistate to consider the Eucharist the core of the Church's liturgical life, the absolute and essential centre of all worship,

---

255 PPS V, 10-11 (2.12.1838).
256 Cf. MS Sermon 18,459 (5.9.1824).
257 PPS II, 144 (3.4.1831); see also C.S.Dessain, 'The basis of Newman's Ecumenical Theology', 109.
258 Cf. SSD, 439 (17.7.1831).

its sole indispensable element, the signal for the gathering together of all the faithful, and the primary instrument for the building up of Christ's body, the Church. For him, the Eucharist is «a Feast, the chief Gospel Ordinance, ... our destiny of joy and thanksgiving ...»[259]

For Newman, among other ordinances of grace, the Eucharist, is a moment of revelation, when believers are drawn to Christ and together with Him are elevated to that unique sphere of heavenly vision:

> The Eucharist, the most precious of his gifts offers us that heavenly food by which our eyes shall be opened, not as Adam's were to know good and evil, or as Balaam's to see God's angel of wrath but as the two disciples, to know *Him* who is life, and moreover to become of one family, of one blood and nature (so to speak) with Saints and Angels.[260]

In a sermon on "The Eucharistic Presence", in 1838, Newman told his congregation:

> The text speaks of *the greatest and highest of all the sacramental mysteries* which faith has been vouchsafed, that of Holy Communion. Christ who died and rose again for us, is in it spiritually present, in the fulness of his death and of His Resurrection.[261]

For Newman, the reservation of the consecrated eucharistic bread is another credit to the singularity of this Sacrament among the ranks of other sacraments and sacramentals, for in it is verified the prolongation of the Atonement:

> The Atonement of Christ is not a thing at a distance, or like the sun standing over against us and separated off from us, but that we are surrounded by an atmosphere and are in a medium, through which his warmth and light flow in upon us on every side.[262]

Newman and his group regarded the Eucharist as the crown and summit of the sacramental system.

---

259 Ibid.; see also Keble,J., The Presence of God in holy Places,89-96, Lectures on Poetry 1832-1841, vol.I, trans.by E.K.Francis,1912,92f; Froude, Remains II:I, 134f.

260 MS Sermon 18, 459 (23.4.1837). Newman expressed the same idea again in another sermon on 6.5.1838.

261 PPS VI,136-137 (13.5.1838). The emphasis is mine.

262 LD XII, 224 (16.6.1848).

It seems to me that the reason why Newman gave this pre-eminence to the Eucharist is because the most apt description of the life and ministry of the Son of God is the Eucharist. Jesus' entire life and ministry were eucharistic.

As one of the last solemn acts of our Lord before he suffered was to institute the Eucharist, so one of the first solemn acts of his after he had risen was the celebration of the Eucharist.

And just as he continuously gave thanks to God throughout his life and before drinking the chalice of salvation, so he gave thanks for rising from the dead. The Eucharist is, therefore, a memorial of his manner of life, a memorial of his death, but above all, it is the pledge of his final triumph.[263]

Of course all the sacraments are means of grace, pledges of God's loving mercy, and signs of His unfailing presence and comfort. And whatever one says of God, of Jesus Christ, of the Church, and of the sacraments, *depends on one's personal experience* with God, with Jesus Christ, with the Church, and with the Sacraments.

The more positive, the more joyful and the more soothing is this experience, the more eloquent, wide, and explosive is the testimony and expression of this personal experience, even to the point of what may seem exaggeration to another.[264]

It is interesting to note that while recognising privileged place of the Eucharistic altar in the Church's sacramental life, Newman said of Penitence,

How many are the souls, in distress, anxiety or loneliness, whose one need is to find a being to whom they can pour out their feelings unheard by the world? .... *If there is a heavenly idea in the Catholic Church, looking at it simply as an idea, surely, next after the Blessed sacrament, Confession is such ....* Oh what a soothing charm is there, which the world can neither give nor take away! Oh what piercing, heart-subduing tranquility, provoking tears of joy, is poured, almost substantially and physically upon the soul ... when the penitent at length rises, his God reconciled to him, his sins rolled away forever![265]

---

263 see MS Sermon 21, 449 (19.3.1837).
264 Of course it happens that what is enough to one may be exaggeration to another, and what says much to one, may be to another either little or nothing or indifferent.
265 Prepos, 351-352. The Emphasis is mine.

And it is here that one finds the kernel of the whole point. God's presence, operation and grace are special in each of the sacraments. Theologically speaking God is not more present in the one than in the other.

But room is left for personal experience and individual spiritual sensation which may feel and live this experience differently and diversely. With such statements as: the Lord is *really* present in the Eucharist, the Church makes a qualification of the "experience of God" in the Eucharist by the collective soul of Christians.

However, this strong expression does not exclude the fact that the same Lord is also *really* present in other sacraments. Christian sacraments are what they are because the Lord is present and operates in them through the power of His Spirit.

Furthermore, the doctrine that some sacraments: Baptism, Confirmation and Orders, imprint a character, that is, a kind of indelible spiritual sign[266] on the soul does not mean that other sacraments have "short-term" effects or imprint erasable character. Surely, other sacraments have indelible effects on those who partake of them. In all the sacraments, it is the same grace of the Holy Spirit that comes into contact with human nature. And the effect of divine grace on nature is a lasting one. From this consideration one can intuit the "open-ended-nature" of the Church's doctrinal formulations.

This is why a discussion of the sacraments or sacramental theology is more a question of the believer's experience of God's wonderful operation in the divine ordinances than a question of concepts or abstract theological "vagabonding".

What happens in the sacraments is deeply personal, almost ineffable, a deep experience of God which the Christian can struggle to formulate in words. And the formulations, no matter how many they be and how perfect they may be believed to be remain always inadequate.

According to Newman, " ... Catholic dogmas are, after all, but symbols of a Divine Fact, which, far from being compassed by those very propositions, would not be exhausted, nor fathomed, by a thousand".[267]

---

266 see DS 1609.
267 OUS, 331-332 (2.2.1843). Previous to this Newman had already in 2.2.1831 made similar assertions.

2.3.8 SACRAMENTS AS "SIGNS AND SYMBOLS" OF THE SACRED

Taking into consideration the profound "sacramental spirituality" of the author of "Lead Kindly Light", one can say that "signs and symbols of the Sacred" is the most apt expression of the divine treasures present in the Christian rites and ordinances. For Newman, in sacramental signs we have the Word of Salvation condensed.

According to Newman's Sacramental Principle, sacraments, ceremonies, rituals, observances are signs, seals, means, and pledges of supernatural grace.[268] This can be called a theory of the double sense. On this basis, sacramental ordinances are signs of the Sacred.

For a sacramental thinker like Newman, Christians do not only hear the word of God; in the sacraments they also taste and eat what the Lord is. Like the physical world, Christian sacraments are but the manifestation to our senses of realities unseen, vivid expressions of sacred truths intended to stamp indelible truths of the Divinity on our souls.

This is why for him, the Sacred Mysteries of the Church are but concrete expressions of those sacred truths which surpass the human mind and which otherwise would have remained beyond our reach. In this sense, Newman reasoned, these channels of divine gifts constitute the life-line of the Church.[269]

The treasures of God's written and unwritten words are documented, preserved and dispensed in the Church's universal sacramental practice. All those things, signs and gestures, which point to Christ are part of the Gospel.

His own experience taught him that human nature is not only moved by words, but particularly also by highy symbolic gestures, and that a religious mind is much more touched, more moved by the sacramental embodiment of religious truth, for such an approach is much more able to draw the whole man to the point of commitment[270] than critical and dialectical procedures.

According to Newman, the ordinances which we behold force the unseen truth upon our senses.[271] The Lord has, therefore, deemed it fit to

---

268 Cf. Ess.II.193 (Milman's View of Christianity).
269 see PPS II, 256 (11.12.1834).
270 Cf.GA.323.
271 Newman even reasoned that the very disposition of the Church «building, the subdued light, the aisles, the altar, with its pious adornments, are figures of things unseen and stimulate our fainting faith. We seem to see the heavenly courts with

approach us and make Himself approachable in rites and ceremonies.[272]
We should therefore, says Newman,

> Religiously adhere to the form of words and ordinances under which God comes
> to us, through which He is revealed to us, and apart from which the revelation does
> not exist, there being nothing else given us by which to ascertain or enter into it.[273]

He understood the life and essence of the Church's sacramental system
to depend on, and to consist of its connection with the continual mediation of Christ. The sacraments link us with that unique historical event
which did not just happen and is now gone, they transport us to the *illo
tempore*, which was and is still efficacious pro nobis.

Newman was convinced that men live in a net-work of the sacramental
system. All is sign and symbol of Him who fills all things with His life.
«All goods are but types and shadows of God, the Giver, and they are
similar among themselves, because they are similar to God»:[274]

> We cannot look on Him, hear Him, converse with Him, follow Him from place to
> place; but we enjoy the spiritual, immaterial, inward, mental, real sight and possessi-
> on of Him; a possession more real and more present than that which the Apostles
> had in the days of His flesh, *because* it is spiritual, *because* it is invisible.[275]

In the life and activities of the Church, Christ is made present, and
through our surrender by faith, the fruits of the Paschal mystery are extended to us:

> Christ lodged virtue in his Church, and she dispenses it forth from her in all her
> words and work. To view Christ as all but visibly revealed - to look upon His or-
> dinances, not in themselves, but as signs of His presence and power, as the accents
> of His love, the very form and countenance of Him who ever beholds us, ever che-
> rishes us - to see Him thus revealed in glory day by day - is not this to those who

---

the angels chanting and Apostles and Prophets listening as we read their writings
in due course....» (PPS III, 250-253 - 14.9.1834). The Church's life is a sacramental organic system where every thing *speaks*.

272 Cf. Ari.241.
273 Tract 73,13 (1836); also Jfc., 252f.
274 PPS V, 192 (18.3.1838); also 100.
275 PPS VI, 121-122 (6.5.1838).

145

believe it an unspeakable privilege? Is it not so great that a man might well wish it true from the excellence of it and count them happy who are able to receive it?[276]

According to Newman, the power and merits of Christ's cross "spill" into the sacraments and are accumulated in them; and the benefits of Redemption are

... scattered about amid the leaves of that mystical vine which is seen and receive their nurture from its trunk and branches. They live on its sacraments and on its ministry; they gain light and salvation from its rites and ordinances; they communicate with each other through it.[277]

Thus is the immensity of wealth which Newman found in the sacramental economy. Throughout the period of his "desert experience", the wealth of the signs of the Sacred with which Catholicism is adorned remained Newman's only comfort:

... there is a depth and power in the Catholic religion, a fullness of satisfaction in its creed, its theology, its rites, its sacraments .... This is the true secret of of the Church's strength, the principle of its indefectibility, and the bond of its indissoluble unity. It is the earnest and beginning of the repose of heaven. To know that we are surrounded by an atmosphere and are in a medium, through which Christ's warmth and light flow in upon us on every side, what can one desire, more than this?[278]

We could almost say that Newman and his fellow Tractarians saw sacraments everywhere as pillars in the universe. They sang the praises of the bounty of the sacraments so much that they were once accused of sacramentalizing every where and everything.

In fact, in 1836, Thomas Arnold, the headmaster of Rugby, wrote a letter to A.P.Stanley. In it he observed: «It is clear to me that Newman and his party are idolaters; they put Christ's Church and Christ's sacraments, and Christ's ministers, in the place of Christ Himself».[279]

Some serious scholars of Tractarian literature agree with this observation to some extent. Roderick Strange for one writes:

---

276 PPS, III,285 (15.11.1835).
277 PPS,III,240-241 (14.9.1834).
278 LD XXIV, 25 (2.2.1868); see also AW 254-257.
279 quoted in A.P.Stanley, *The Life and Correspondence of Thomas Arnold*, II, London,1845,p.45;see also Thomas Arnold, 'On the Oxford School of Theology' in Christian life, its Course, its hindrances, and its helps, sermon iv, London, 1878,pp.xxii-xxiv.

There is an obvious truth in Arnold's accusation. The Tractarians turned constantly in their writings to emphasize the Church, the sacramental system, and the apostolic succession, partly because they believed them to be in danger; and it is also true that their writings on Christ often end in discussion of one or more of those issues.[280]

Above all, we have already noted that in Tractarian writings, the Incarnation is sacramental and sacraments incarnational. In the same vein one can sustain that the Christology of the Tractarians was a Sacramental Christology. Furthermore it is true that whenever Newman and his group discuss a theme of interest, they are deeply immersed in it, they deeply explore it, and in their bid to express it in the best possible way, they may be found to be riding at a speed that may appear eccessive to a biased observer.

2.3.9 CONCLUSION: NEWMAN'S WIDE UNDERSTANDING OF "SACRAMENT"

In the light of the Sacramental Principle, Newman developed the belief that created things are not "just there" casually; rather they are like the pages of a book from which to read the mind of the Writer, they are mirrors which reflect His power and goodness. In short, they are signs and instruments of the Sacred. This profoundly sacramental vision meant that Newman did not see the formal sacraments of the Church in any way isolated from a larger sacramental reality.

What may be called, in a large sense of the word, the sacramental system, that is, the doctrine that material phenomena are both the types and the instruments of real things unseen, - a doctrine, which embraces in its fulness, not only ... Sacraments properly called.[281]

In a special way the New Dispensation bears a clear sacramental seal: The man Jesus, a carpenter from Nazareth, is the Christ, the Son of God, the Church is His representative and a symbol of those heavenly facts which fill eternity, sacraments are His instruments, liturgy is the voice of the Church, bishops her rulers, their collective decisions her voice, and

---

280 Roderick Strange, *Newman and the Gospel of Christ*, 1.
281 Apo 23; also 29,36-37.

Scripture her standard of truth.[282] Widely understood, for Newman the "seven-fold" sacraments do not exhaust the "extensions of the Incarnation". At least tacitly he recognised other ordinances of grace.

And if widely understood, Sacramentality is not limited within the sevenfold sacraments of the Church by which she principally constitutes and realises her own sacramental character. Newman had this wide understanding of the sacramental economy. One can say that such a wide vision of "sacrament" made him a forerunner of modern theologians for whom sacramentality is not limited to the seven classical sacraments.

Through baptismal regeneration, Newman believed that the Christian is permeated by the Spirit and sentiments of Christ to the extent that even he himself becomes a kind of sacrament of Christ in the world,[283] in whom the face of the Father is revealed and through whom the Son acts. Such a Christian "will see Christ revealed to his soul amid the ordinary actions of the day, as by a sort of sacrament. Thus he will take his worldly business as a gift from Him, and will love it a such».[284]

In the mind of the theologian of Oxford, the Christ that is really present in the believer becomes discernible in and through his words and actions.[285]

Such a Christian is a real sign and instrument of divine love and consolation, a sacrament, and lives sacramentally. About such a Christian, Newman, writes: «These and the life of good men were the great persuasives of the Gospel, as being visible witnesses and substitutes for Him who is persuasion itself».[286]

In the Christian dispensation, all parts hang together, since they derive from and form a part of the One vast Sacrament. Thus, Incarnation, Church, Tradition, Authority, Sacraments, form a universe and one single network of sacramental system.

In this one vast sacramental network, there are 'no externals without meaning', all are essential in their place as manifestation of the Sacramental Principle. Christ's presence since His Ascension has therefore become sacramental.

---

282 Cf. Ess.II,8 (Catholicity of the Anglican Church).
283 Cf. PPS VIII, 165 (30.9.1836); see also Jfc. 201.
284 Ibid.
285 Cf. Ath.II. 193.
286 LD V, 21, (4.2.1835); also 32,39-40,44-47.

E.R. Fairweather has expressed well the systematic link between Tractarian Christology and Sacramentology and how they often over-lapped:

The Tractarians saw the Incarnation, the Church, and the sacraments as conti-guous and inseparable elements in God's redemptive economy. To their minds it was no less clearly a part of the Christian message that the saving person and work of the Mediator were effectually 're-presented' in the Church by means of certain sacramen-tal 'extensions of the Incarnation'. It was, they insisted, supremely fitting that the life-giving flesh and blood of God's Eternal Son who was made man should be commu-nicated through fleshy signs wrought by human hands.[287]

The sacraments in the strict sense of the term are therefore nothing completely new or extraordinary. They are concrete realizations per voluntatem Christi of those "eternal truths which fill eternity", and of the sacramentality of creation.

Having been affected by the redemptive gesture of Christ they have been specially charged by the Spirit and are able to draw us nearer to our First, Last, and Only Desire.

---

287 E.R.Fairweather (ed.), *The Oxford Movement*, 11; also A.M.Allchin, 'The Theo-logical Vision of the Oxford Movement', in Coulson and Allchin (eds), *The Re-discovery of Newman*, 50-57.

PART THREE:

EVALUATION OF NEWMAN'S SACRAMENTAL THEOLOGICAL THOUGHT AND ITS RELEVANCE TO THE AFRICAN CONTEXT

3.1 PRELIMINARY REMARKS

Having articulated Newman's Sacramental theology in its general ramifications in the previous pages, it is the concern of this part to examine him and his performance through the critical lens of evaluation. In this regard the mould and content of his sacramental thought are to be examined. The intention is to underscore his originality, weakness, and general relevance to the African religious mind.

3.2 CRITICAL EVALUATION OF NEWMAN'S PERFORMANCE

3.2.1 FROM THE POINT OF VIEW OF FORM: WHETHER NEWMAN REASONS SACRAMENTALLY

3.2.1.1 SACRAMENTAL MENTALITY: EARLY BEGINNINGS

Newman's modus cogitandi is deeply shaped by those factors which constitute the formative elements of his mind. His original poetic and musical mind found a boost in biblical literature whose sign and symbolic language printed an indelible character in his mind to the extent that his subsequent writings and preachings are completely weaved in scriptural idioms and metaphors.

3.2.1.2 IMMERSION INTO CHRISTIAN PLATONISM

While Newman was growing in familiarity with scriptural language he came into contact with Christian Platonism through the writings of the Alexandrian Fathers. In them he rejoiced in the confirmation of the "sacramental mentality" which had been taking root in his mind:

... Some portions of their teaching ... came like music to my inward ear, *as if in response to ideas, which, with little external to encourage them, I had cherished so long.*[1]

From Platonism he learnt such doctrine as the symbolism of the material world,[2] the identity of the ephemeral as the picture of the Real, the subsistence of the visible in function of the Invisible, the temporal as the image of the Eternal[3] etc. From his study of Origen and Clement he formed the conviction that the external world is a manifestation, to our senses of another reality that transcends this world:[4] «that which is visible is not real; if the presence of God were not invisible, it would not have been real».[5]

When Newman says, «What a veil and curtain this world of sense is; beautiful but still a veil»,[6] our attention is drawn to Newman's mystic or idealistic vision of the world.[7]

However, Newman did not fall into a radical idealism. For him the visible world is true, but only as an instrument of the invisible world; it is real, but only in the sense that it is the symbol of the invisible.[8]

It is with this principle that reality is to be interpreted; it is a question of relationship between the exterior and interior, shadow and reality, anticipation and fullfilment of truth. With this optical lense is salvific economy to be viewed, and human history, Scripture, the Church and her ordinances, Tradition, and authority to be understood.

---

1 Apo 26. Emphasis is mine. We have already referred above to this passage. The ideas which Newman had cherished so long are among other things, the Sacramental Principle, the fact that material phenomena is a picture of the invisible world.

2 «... and all things about him are but shades....» (see PPS IV, 82-3 - 27.1.1836). This affirmation does not mean that Newman's mental categories were modelled only on platonism. Newman was also a Thomist in thought.

3 With the help of this principle Newman read the whole Church system: Jesus is God, the Church is his image, priests are his instruments, and the sacraments are the outward lineaments of him.

4 Cf. Apo 35.

5 PPS IV, 192 (22.7.1837).

6 LD II, 69 (10.5.1828).

7 Cf. Philomena Rodriguez, *Newman and the Oxford Movement*, Trivandrum, 1983, 217.

8 see Ess.II, 190-193 (Milman's View of Christianity).

152

3.2.1.3 THE APPEAL OF THE SACRAMENTAL PRINCIPLE

It was while his young mind was growing within the walls of "a sacramental environment" that Newman discovered Butler's Sacramental Principle. This discovery found echoes and a fertile ground in his mind. Henceforth, the Sacramental Principle became for him one of the keys and hermeneutical principle for the interpretation of the created order and history.

In events and historical course he discovered the appeal of the Almighty, and the trumpeting summons of the Divine. Daily life, with its joys and sorrows, hopes and fears; history, with its contradictions, offers and challenges, became for Newman the flame of the "Kindly Light".

Thus he saw all that happened to him as signs and instruments of the Eternal, "the hand of God". In this light, the circumstances of his conversion were for him more than ordinary incidents. Thus, human reality in all its manifestations is appreciated, integrated, and raised through the Sacramental Principle.[9]

Newman lived and died with the conviction that the heart is reached by the testimony of facts and events. Bremond has intelligently noted that for Newman, «There are no such things as insignificant events»,[10] and proceeds to show how Newman was a master at interpreting the insignificant as meaningful.

When Sir Geoffrey Faber glossed the passage in the "Autobiographical Memoir" about the motto in the window of Oriel Hall «Pie repone te»,[11] he noted that Newman interpreted it as «clearly intended for a direct message to him».[12] His whole life and works are replete with such a Sacramental Reading of events and history.

The Sacramental Principle therefore, is, a main formula for decodifying and analysing Newman's Sacramental theology and some of his works outside the strict boundaries of Sacramentology.

---

9   Cf. GA 249-253.
10   Henri Bremond, *The Mystery of Newman*, London, 1907, 295.
11   AW 61 (18.3.1822).
12   G.Faber, Oxford Apostles. *A Character Study of the Oxford Movement*, London, 1933, 67.

3.2.1.4 SACRAMENTAL CONVERSION

The discovery of this Sacramental Principle helped Newman in the understanding and interpretation of the Christian dispensation. This means a change from an ordinary way of looking at reality to the sacramental interpretation of the same. For him it was a "discovery" of that "primitive"[13] mentality which is typical of religious minds.

Newman rejoiced at having made this progress; he delighted at having assumed this stance, a horizon that is not open or immediately accessible to all.

The intellectual itinerary of Newman concerning the understanding of the means of grace portrays an evolutive progress. He started from Neo-platonism for which material things are "shadows" and "images" to Christianity in which certain material elements are efficacious signs and instruments of the Lord for the conferment of salvific grace.

To arrive at the knowledge that the Church and its sacramental ordinances are not just there as mere shadows, but are efficacious signs and instruments of God in the power of the Spirit, is a qualitative jump.

This stance assumed by Newman can be called substantial shift from symbolism to sacraments, from symbolic to sacramental vision. It may be called a "conversion". A son of the Church, who like the Church, understands that the Church herself is a sign and instrument of God, her whole being and activities are efficacious means for the sanctification men and the glorification of God, and who lives in this consciousnesss, can be said to live or think sacramentally:

The material world is viewed by Newman as emblematic of the spiritual. Such a philosophic trend of thought, that all human knowledge, activity and experience should be brought into relation with God's revelation of Himself in the universe and in Christ's Incarnation provides a key to the sacramental life of the universe and the Church.[14]

Thus Newman understood in a new light that the Church's sacramental system is a new dimension and continuation of original sacramental

---

13 'Primitive mentality' does not mean pre-scientific level of existence. It means that pure and uncontaminated cosmovision, deeply sensitive to the mysteries and wonders of and in creation, able to remain in syntony with the poetry of nature, and capable of expressing itself in the same simple terms. This is a major characteristic of religion. African religion enjoys this trait.

14 P. Rodriguez, Op.cit., 217.

economy. Thus the Church's sacramental system is a sign and instrument of eternal verities.

We can say that Newman became a real new man the day he discovered that the Church's sacramental system is an application of the Sacramental Principle and its clear manifestation, and that it constitutes an instrument through which God brings about interior change in believers.

One can say that Newman is a true child of the Church, which being a sacrament, lives and acts sacramentally; he is a strong believer in a God who manifests himself sacramentally; he is an arch-sacramental-confessor who lived and defended the conviction that sacramental symbols are one of the the most apt languages of the mystery of faith.

The facts of religion, because of their living and developing nature, require for their expression this essentially sacramental language. Otherwise the intellect runs wild; but with the aid of sacramental signs and symbols, it advances with precision and effect.[15]

From what we have seen so far, sacramental thinking appears to be the most apt qualification of Tractarian theological vocabulary. That Newman was deeply imbued with this spirit is beyond doubt. We might dare remark that Newman's theologising can only be appreciated by those minds which while sojourning in this world, dwell in a different spiritual vision. This is why Newman has some relevance for African religious spirit.

3.2.2   FROM THE POINT OF VIEW OF CONTENT: HIS INSIGHTS AND THEIR GROUNDINGS

3.2.2.1   ON SACRAMENTS AS THE MANIFESTATIONS OF "ARCHESACRAMENTALITY"

Newman's understanding of the sacramental system of the Church as an empirical manifestation of the Eternal Truth is a credit to his sacramental theology. In the light of the manifestation of Archesacramentality which found a culmination in the Incarnation, those rings which constitute the catena sacramentorum acquire offices, vests and dimensions.

By the will of God the Father, through Jesus Christ and in the power of the Spirit, they are made effectual signs and instruments. That the

---

15   see GA 200.

sacraments of the Church are a new but faithful continuation of the Sacramental Principle, that in them God becomes palpable for frail and sinful human family is a good theological insight.

In affirming this, Newman laid foundations for what modern theology was to call primordial sacrament and concrete realizations of it.

In this light the doctrine of the seven sacraments cannot be taken as a war shibboleth and that "the seven sacraments do not exhaust the sacramentality of the Christian faith" no longer becomes a "provocative statement".

3.2.2.2 ON SACRAMENTS AS ANTICIPATIONS OF HEAVENLY JOY

The way Newman has expressed what the believer experiences in the sacraments is a big contribution to Christian piety. Sometimes sacraments have been miscontrued to be legal religious practices. But using his own experience as the point of departure Newman described Christian sacraments as «the foretaste of heaven», and as anticipation of Him whose face Christians continuously seek and «whom they shall see after face to face».[16]

In these words, Newman enuciated the vocation of the Church's sacramental system as "instruments", "means", but not the *end*, and as such implied that they will cease when Christians definitively encounter Him whose "instruments" and "means" the sacraments are. It is true that the Church's sacramental system indicates, represents, and communicates Christ to believers, but they are not Christ. In short, Newman meant that when all things are recapitulated in Christ the sacraments will become superfluous: Ubi maior minor cessat.

Through the sacraments believers prepare for the next world. Hence the «most momentous reason for religious worship ... [is] ... to prepare us for this future glorious and wonderful destiny, the sight of God - a destiny which, if not most glorious, will be most terrible».[17]

In the Christian sacramental system we have the «anticipations and first-fruits of that sight of Him, which one day must be».[18] It is with this view in mind that believers appreciate the sacramental system. In so doing, they are granted a glimpse of a Form which they shall see face to

---

16 Cf. PS VII, 158-159 (27.2.1831).
17 PPS V, 1 (2.12.1838).
18 Ibid.

face and are allowed to enter heaven though they do not yet see it.[19] Newman once reminded his Congregation of the deep sense behind active participation in public worship:

I come to Church, because I am a heir of heaven. It is my desire and hope one day to take possession of my inheritance: and I come to make myself ready for it, and I would not see heaven yet, for I could not bear to see it. I am allowed to be in it without seing it, that I may learn to see it. And by Psalm, sacred song, by confession and praise, I learn my part.[20]

Furthermore he confirms the following experience:

We shall remember ... how all things, light or darkness, sun or air, cold or freshness, breathed of Him, - of Him, the Lord of glory, who stood over us, and came down upon us, and gave Himself to us, and poured forth milk and honey for our sustenance, though we saw Him not. Surely we have all, and abound: we are full.[21]

3.2.2.3 ON SACRAMENTS AS "ENCOUNTER-MOMENTS" OF TWO SUBJECTS

Without minimising the communitarian aspect of the sacraments, Newman underscored their special role as encounter-points between two subjects, namely God and the individual. For the Fellow of Oxford, the sacraments are one of those best occasions when the believer encounters his God personally.

Human nature "requires something special», something of a personal character".[22] And so it is that Christ comes to each of us individually and personally through the sacraments:

Our Lord, by becoming man, has found a way whereby to sanctify that nature, of which His own manhood is the pattern specimen. He inhabits us personally, and this inhabitation is effected by the channel of the Sacraments.[23]

---

19 Cf. Ibid.; see also Colm Mckeating, *Eschatology In the Anglican Sermons of J.H. Newman*, Dissertatio ad Doctoratum, Pont. Univ. Gregorianum, 1992, 269.
20 PPS V,10 (2.12.1838).
21 Ibid., 283 (10.3.1839).
22 Cf. Jfc. 323.
23 Ath.II, 193.

In sacraments, according to Newman, God communicates what is uniquely meant for each soul.[24] "What is so mysterious as to receive the virtue of that death one by one through the sacraments?",[25] Newman once asked his congregation.

He insisted that in the sacraments, God condescends to speak to us one by one, to manifest Himself to each of us, to carry us with Himself. In the sacraments, God gives us something to rely on, which others do not experience, something that we cannot communicate to others, which He meant for us alone.[26]

In a sermon on Baptism, Newman, once invited his audience to look to the sacraments of Christ not as themselves, but rather as signs of his presence and power, as the true physionomy of him who sees us always, caresses us always, nourishes and protects us.[27]

This is what happens in souls that worthily receive the sacraments. Sacraments are not received in proxy. It is in this context that one understands the depth of Newman's words: «the thought of two and only two supreme and luminously self-evident beings, myself and my Creator».[28]

Thus through the sacraments Christ establishes a dwelling in the soul of the believer[29], and in this way becomes the source of «spiritual life to each of His elect individually through the mysteries». And «while we are in the flesh, soul and body become, by the indwelling of the Word, so elevated above their natural state, so sacred, that to profane them is a sacrilege».[30]

It is the confession of a soul schooled in experience of "real encounter" with God in the ordinances of grace. This is an encounter that is possible in the different manifestations of sacramentality. So that the questions: who is God?, has he revealed himself?, what did he reveal?, where and how?, can be answered in the affirmative by pointing to the sacraments.

Newman, reminds everyone that for belief to be living, it must always be linked with personal experience. A theologian therefore, should, be

---

24 Cf.Ibid.
25 PPS III, 298 (24.4.1835).
26 see SSD 325 (24.4.1831).
27 Cf. PPS III, 265 (8.11.1835).
28 Apo 4; also 127; PPS I, 10.
29 Cf. PPS IV, 265 (7.5.1837).
30 Ath.II, 193 and 195.

someone with an encounter with God, who speaks as "someone in-volved" in an experience of God; one who speaks from or of a direct experience of God. Such a personal encounter and experience with God Newman saw in the sacraments.

This can be said to be one of the messages Newman is delivering when he denies being a theologian[31] . He denied being that kind of theo-logian who knows the history of different theological schools of thought, who can quote them at ease, and who can fluently discuss or formulate the experiences and intuitions of others but who may perhaps remain an "outsider" because he lacks a "personal encounter" with God.

But if theologian is taken in this perspective of one who speaks from experience and of experience of God, then Newman is one in the same way as the prophets and hagiographers are theologians.

3.2.2.4   ON THE QUESTION OF THE RELATIONSHIP BETWEEN THE SACRAMENTS AND JUSTIFICATION BY FAITH

In the *Lectures on Justification* Newman deals with this question. He convincingly argued that in the religious realm, sacramental signs are inevitable in as much as what is at stake is the relationship between the eternal and temporal, visible and invisible.

Religion implies «belief in such sensible tokens of God's favour, as the sacraments are accounted by the Church ...».[32] Newman cited St.Paul's encounter with the Risen Christ as an example. This encounter was realised in the arena of sacramental signs. His point is that sacra-ments are among the necessary conditions for justification:

---

31   " ... and really and truly I am not a theologian. A theologian is one who has mas-tered theology - who can say how many opinions there are on every point, what authors have taken which, and which is the best - who can discriminate exactly between proposition, argument and argument, who can pronounce which are safe, which allowable, which dangerous - who can trace the history of doctrines in suc-cessive centuries, and apply the principles of former times to the conditions of the present. This is to be a theologian - this and a hundred things besides. And this I am not, and never shall be", Newman wrote on February 10 1869 (LD XXIV, 212-213).

32   Jfc. 323.

Though faith comes before baptism, yet before baptism it is not the instrument of justification, but only one out of a number of qualifications necessary for being justified.[33]

Newman reduces to absurdity the antagonism between sustainers of justification by faith and those who thought that just by receiving the sacraments they are assured of justification. Faith «... unites the soul to Christ through the Sacraments ... Justification comes *through* the sacraments; it is received *by* faith; *consists* in God's inward presence; and *lives* in obedience». And again he writes:

... whether we say we are justified by faith, or by works or by sacraments, all these but mean this one doctrine, that we are justified by grace, which is given through Sacraments, impetrated by faith, manifested in works.[34]

In a sermon on *Moral Effects of Communion with God*, Newman described the spiritualising and elevating effects of faith and sacraments on souls that worthily receive them:

A man is no longer what he was before: gradually, imperceptibly to himself, he has imbibed a new set of ideas, and become imbued with fresh principles. He is as one coming from kings' courts, with a grace, a delicacy, a dignity, a propriety, a justness of thought and taste, a clearness and firmness of principles, all his own. Such is the power of God's secret grace acting through those ordinances which He has enjoined us; such the evident fitness of those ordinances to produce the results which they set before us.[35]

3.2.2.5 ON THE THEORY OF DEVELOPMENT AS REGARDS SACRAMENTAL THEOLOGY

With the aid of Newman's theory of development most of the "hard nuts" on matters concerning sacramental theology can be loosened. When one ponders on the question of scarce biblical evidence for the dogmatic teachings on the sacraments Newman's theory is a good point of contact.

Faith is never complete. It is never received "ready-made". Faith is a continuous inquiry for new insight. Evidence abounds that nobody ever understood quam primum the word of God. Sometimes one needs study,

---

33   Ibid., 189-90; also 231,240-41.
34   Ibid., 251, also 278,303.
35   PPS IV, 230 (10.12.1837).

research, meditation, reflection which may last as long as possible in order to comprehend what God has communicated.

This has been the lot of the Church. Revelation is therefore in a continuous process of unfolding. As it unfolds, it grows with those to whom it is addressed. This is particularly true about questions concerning the sacraments. One can say that questions concerning what they are, how they are, their number, how they operate, etc. have been gradually answered and are in a continuous process of being answered as the Church meditates on the Revelation God has made.

Dogmas on the sacraments are nothing but formulations of the product of the Church's meditation on what her Lord said, and did.

If understood in this perspective, the question is no longer so much of one knowing whether this or that doctrine is contained in Scripture, but rather of knowing whether it is the outcome of a series of developments begun by Scripture. The Word or idea was at first only a seed, which developed gradually under the influence of a great number of causes and minds.[36]

Just as the Word is dynamic so is the believing community dynamic; what the apostles could not immediately understand they understood later through the illumination of the Spirit; just as there is progress in life so there is progress in the spiritual life.

Thus the complex of theologising which has been done around the sacraments and which cannot be directly found in the literal pages of the Scripture or in the volumes of the Fathers are fruits of this on-going meditation on the Word by those to whom it has been addressed.[37]

Dogmas and Church doctrines are the Church's formulation of what she understood to be the mind of her Lord and master. On this very point Newman's theory of development is very helpful.

In fact, from the time it was widely known many theologians appealed to it for the understanding of Church teachings:

---

36 Cf. Emile Saisset, "De l'origine et de la formation du Christianisme, à l'occasion du livre de M.Newman" in *La liberté de Penser*, 15 March 1848, 337-58.

37 God is king and it is worthy of a king that when he speaks his subjects take him serious. This means paying attention, listening well, dedication to the sense of the words, study of the words, asking questions, research into what is said or understood and carrying it out.

The Essay ... brought new light to the understanding of Catholic dogma. New light is what it was for many; and several theologians were only brought around to accepting certain definitions of the Church by calling on Newman's help.[38]

About Newman's theory of development Richmond has argued:

> The truths of revelation ... lie like leaves in the bud, destined to be unfolded, not at once, but gradually, in the long process of time. As the world grows in knowledge and experience, so there come to be displayed to the world, not contradictions, of the old truths for that could not be, since they were divinely revealed - but new facts, new aspects of them.[39]

In other words, just as Jesus commissioned the Spirit to teach the Apostles other truths as they matured in faith, Jesus could,

> ... have confided to the same Holy Spirit the mission of unveiling all the riches of the sacramental system, when the needs of the growing Christian society would demand it. It can thus be understood how, according to the testimony of history, the Church did not have from the beginning, a full and entire consciousness of some sacraments.[40]

It can be continued that the Holy Spirit who, continues the mission of Jesus gradually brought to the consciousness of the Church[41], certain truths about the sacramental system. After all it is only God who knows when to reveal himself to men, how to reveal himself, and when men are disposed to receive Revelation

All said and done, one can interpret Newman to be saying that the mystical experience which pious minds enjoy in the sacraments is ineffable; it is an experience better lived than described, and better understood from within.

3.2.2.6 ON THE CHURCH AS THE LOCUS OF DIVINE PRESENCE

Once Newman discovered the meaning of the Church in the economy of salvation, he held tenaciously to it. The Church was a "privileged object" of Newman's aspiration and devotion. Speaking on the occasion of the

---

38 Emile Saisset, Op.cit., 150.
39 Geo Richmond, *Scenes from the Life of J.H.Cardinal Newman*, London, 1945, 6.
40 P. Pourrat, *Theology of the Sacraments*, Freiburg, 1910, 301.
41 God does this in his own 'fullness of time'.

Symposium on the first centenary of the death of Newman, Pope John Paul II said:

the mystery of the Church always remained the great love of J.H. Newman's life. His writings project an eminently clear picture of his unwavering love for man in every phase of history. His was a truly spiritual vision capable of perceiving all the weaknesses present in the human fabric of the Church, but equally sure in its perception of the mystery hidden beyond our material gaze.[42]

Throughout his trials, his "desert experience", and throughout his long life, Newman lived with the conviction that the Church is God's instrument, and the locus of divine life and love.

For our author, man's encounter with Christ as a "personal visitation" and "personal presence", occurs always through the Church as a public body.[43] «If a number of things disappointed him in the Catholic Church», observed Stern, «he never experienced any deception with regard to the fundamental question of the presence of God»[44] in it. People with such a vision and fidelity are rare.

3.2.3 CRITICAL OBSERVATIONS

In spite of the above merits, some critical observations can be made on the corpus of Newman's sacramental theologising. The Oxford Movement led by Newman has rightly been called «a revival on Church principles»,[45] that is to say a promotion

... of a more ecclesiastical piety in which the liturgy and the sacraments functioned not only as a source of inspiration and strenghth for the individual worshipper but as a focus for the common life in the body of Christ.[46]

---

42 John Paul II, *Address to Participants of the Symposium on the First Centenary of the death of J.H. Newman*, L'Osservatore Romano, ed. It. April 28th, 1990, p.4; Engl. ed., April 30th, 1990, 1,11.

43 Cf. J.Coulson, *Newman and the Common Tradition*, Oxford, 1970, 64.

44 J.Stern, 'The Institutional Church in Newman's Spirituality', 84.

45 Georgina Battiscombe, *John Keble:A Study in Limitations in Lawrence N.Crumb*, The Oxford Movement And its Leaders. A bibliography of secondary and lesser primary sources, New York, 1988, xvi.

46 L.S.Thornton, *The Common Life in the Body of Christ*, Westminster, 1942, 120.

Despite the fact that Oxford Movement was a sacramental movement, concerned with the ordinances of grace and their revival, the leader of this group in the person of Newman produced no systematic work on this all important question of the day. It is a pity that Newman did not address adequately this theme.

One can rightly suspect Newman here of not having invested to the full his genius and talent to produce what he was unquestionably capable of doing.

Traces of "hard tones" can be found in some of Newman's utterances. These utterances cannot be explained away as sentiments of a prophetic uncompromissing spirit and avowal.

One of the most notorious of these occasions occured in 1862 when he wrote to the editor of the Globe in reaction to rumors that he was about to return to the Anglican Church. He declared devastatingly:

... with an absolute internal assent and consent, that Protestantism is the dreariest of possible religions; that the thought of the Anglican service makes me shiver, and the thought of the Thirty-nine Articles makes me shudder. Return to the Church of England! no; 'the net is broken, and we are delivered'. I should be a consumate fool (to use a mild term) if in my old age I left 'the land flowing with milk and honey' for the city of confusion and house of bondage.[47]

Such affirmations carry a special personal force[48] in defence of particular positions. Is Newman acting on the spur of the moment? If we are to take serious his doubt and rebutal of his first conviction about Anglicanism as hewn from the Fathers and Christian Antiquity, are we not right to nuture the same attitude toward the second and contrary position?

Notwithstanding the above "loopholes", Newman has remained «... a man whose work has a compelling charm even for those who cannot accept his beliefs ... it is still a fact that Newman remains for many people a fascinating or repellant enigma».[49]

---

47 LD XX, 216 (28.6.1862); see also Diff.II, 339 (The Vatican Definition).
48 Cf. G. and K. Tillotson, *Mid-Victorian Studies*, London, 1965, 250-56.
49 Charles Frederick Harrold, *A Newman Treasury*, 1975, 1-2.

3.3 A DISCERNED RELEVANCE OF NEWMAN'S SACRA-MENTAL THEOLOGICAL REASONING FOR THE AFRICAN

Of course it is not every detail of Newman's sacramental theology that has consequences for the African religious mind. It is those key concepts within Newman's theologising, the catena sacramentorum that merit discussion as having some relevance for the African.

What Newman said after reading the Fathers of the Church, some Africans can say of him: Some portions of his teaching, magnificient in themselves came like music to our inward ear, as if in response to ideas, which, with little external to encourage them, we had cherished so long.

These were based on the mystical or Sacramental Principle, and spoke of the various economies or Dispensations of the Eternal. We understood him to mean that the exterior world physical and historical, was but the outward manifestation of realities greater than itself.

Nature was a parable: Scripture was an allegory: African religious structure: Community, Ancestors, Rituals, were historical creations of the supernatural system, and consequently instruments or veil of the invisible world. Properly understood they were anticipation of Church sacramental system and a preparation for the Gospel.[50]

3.3.1 AFRICAN RELIGIOUS EXPERIENCE

The following relevant conclusions can be drawn from Newman's biography for an African context: Many Africans have been faithful to their "Kindly Light" which has led them through the storms of history to the "ark of Christianity". They live in ernest desire of completing what they partially possessed. This quest has put Africans in crisis. And moreover African religious minds live in complete confidence and trust in divine Providence.

At this juncture it may be interesting to point out that African religious tradition or community, past or present was and to some extent still remains unsystematic in thinking. African Church is not systematic in her activities. She mostly "re-acts" in the face of challenges, threats, etc.

---

50   Cf. Apo 145-6.

Most if not not all of the African Church's plans, steps, documents, declarations, are responses to particular situations. Some examples may suffice. African Traditional Religion and Culture were introduced into some Catholic Higher Institutions in response to the challenges posed by cultural revivalists.

Most of the pastoral priorities, options and strategies are reactions to threats from African Independent Churches, Islam, New religious Movements, and political turbulances. And particularly most of the biblical songs, associations and healing centres in circulation today within the radius of the African Church are reactions to "provocations" from many religious sects which abound in the continent. And even these "reactions" are largely unsystematic.

This is equally true at the level of African theological writings. Most African theological works lack a systematic approach. This is not only due to the fact that experience of God defies logical moulding and precise systematization. It has to some extent to do with African ontology which is more "natural, simple and spontaneous" rather than systematic.

3.3.2 THE SACRAMENTAL PRINCIPLE AND AFRICAN SYMBOLIC UNIVERSE

We have already pointed out that in African cosmology the world is not just an amorphous dumb object. It is rather like an orchestral group in which every instrument has a role. It is like a choir in which every voice is necessary for a harmonious performance. For an average African creation sings a melody.

The architectural structure of the cosmos portrays a quasi- sacramental order. Things are more than just ordinary objects; they transmit a message; everything says more than what is perceived. God is a mystery and a light which shines through and in all things. He is transparent in all things; all things are transparent because of him. Seen in this light everything changes into a "sign" of God. The words of Irenaeus confirm African experience and religious vision: "in God there is no emptiness, but everything is a sign".[51]

Consequently concrete reality in this world evokes another transcendental reality. What may appear simply as material, wears in the relig-

---

51   Irenaeus, Adv.haer.4,21; PG 7,437.

ious eyes of the African a quasi-sacramental garb; it remains for the African a vessel of mysterious forces; a sign through which something beyond is seen. This is what Tradition, Ancestors, Community, Rituals are in the African religious world. They signify more than their face value. Behind them is hidden a higher meaning. They bear some resemblance to the things whose symbols they are.

The African spirit reads the Permanent in the ephemeral, in the temporal the Eternal. In such a vision, the ephemeral is transfigured into the signal of the presence of the Permanent; the temporal into the symbol of the reality of the Eternal; the world into a great sacrament of God. Such a mentality is not far from Newman's Sacramental Principle. And it this point more than any other that makes Newman relevant to the African.

The African Sacramental Principle finds a purification and complementation in the light of Christian causality. The African Christian has to embark on an "Exodus" from the symbolic to sacramental vision, from seeing his world as full of God's presence to seeing him definitively present in Jesus of Nazareth.

The African believer has to shift from seeing signs of God in the rituals of the traditional religion to seeing God present in the particular elements, chosen and ordained by God as efficacious instruments and signs of what God realised in his Son. The African Christian has to move from symbol to Symbol, from natural to Christian symbolism, or rather from symbol to sacrament, and from sacrament to the God of Jesus Christ.

This means that the Creator is present and active in the world through the Spirit of Jesus. This Spirit operates among other things through some elements recommended and empowered by Christ as the signs and instruments of what he himself stands for. Encounter with God is therefore christological and because it is christological, it is sacramental. Thus God is in the world and away from it, present and absent, immanent and transcendent.

3.3.3 AFRICAN COMMUNITY VIS-A-VIS NEWMAN'S ECCLESIOLOGY

Africans believe that the universe is made up of a web of relationships of its component parts, and thus forms a cosmic family. Just as to be an African means to be religious so does to be religious in the African context mean to belong to the community. It is a community of unrestricted brotherhood.

In African traditional society to be human is to be with others, to be for others, and to be because of them. For outside the communal relationships is life meaningless. To be religious is to be so in and with the community.

Many African Christians are convinced that it is not by ourselves alone that we come to the Father, but in *community*, membered to him and to each other.[52] It is through the communitarian reality that we experience the religious reality and express it.

But it was a communal religious living marked by sin, tainted by unfaithfulness to the demands of a pure religion, and threatened by the sentiment of Cain. Consequently the mission of the Son of God is valid for the African reality. The Son of God came to redeem this community and to teach its members God's will on what a true community should be, where to find it and how to live in it.

It is in this sense that the Church, as an "Assembly", "Ecclesia", "Convocatio" is a new reality to the African. It is no longer by their initiative that the Africans come together or gather. Henceforth African believers gather because God the Father willed their coming together; they gather because God the Son called them to form a community, to live in community. They are directly called by God through Christ in the Spirit.

In this sense African community is no longer what it used to be. It is now a new community, a new "people of God", the "body of Christ", the "mystical body". In his own way God called African Christians together anew in a community endowed with innumerable gifts of grace.[53]

In the physical absence of Jesus Christ, this community the Church, remains the evidence of his continuous presence among men. Men receive and learn the codes of a new life from the Church through Word, and sacraments.

To the average African Christian, the Church is also a sign and anticipation of the next world. She is a «... a picture, a revelation of the next world ...»,[54] where there is no division, no sin, no sorrow. The external

---

52   Cf. B.C.,Butler, *The Church and Unity*, London, 1979, 9.
53   see PPS III, 221 (15.10.1835).
54   PPS II, 66 (28.12.1833). Also in this type of description of the Church one can see her as an anticipation of that cosmic family without barriers, where there is one language of love, one song of praise, one uniform of faith, one identity of common brotherhood.

forms of the Church are means which God uses to communicate his life to believers.

Henceforth to encounter the believeing community is to encounter the Lord and vice versa, and to be religious is to be so in, with and through the believing community.[55] Henceforth whoever seeks Christ must first find the believing community. She is Christ-bearer.

Just as an African who wished to find a fulfilling life normally resorted to the community[56] so does all average African believers resort to the Church community. For the African the Church is the new language of the Spirit, the "New village Square" where the members of today's society are called to gather. Africans are called to move from a reality which is human and to which they are used to another reality which is both human and divine, visible and invisible.

On this point African Anthropology is a good "stepping stone" for an African Ecclesiology. Just as for the average African person, it is unimmaginable to be religious without the community so, it is absurd for an average African to be a Christian without a Church. For Africans any individualistic religion is out of the question. For them religion is necessarily communitarian or ecclesial.

The Church in the Africa context is therefore a "New rallying Ground". Just as we were used to gathering in our village squares for important matters and events so do we now gather in the "New Square" called the Church for an important matter, namely, to hear the word of God. The former "town Crier" who used to convoke Africans in the village square has now been substituted. The "New Town Crier" is Jesus the Lord, who came from God, with a message from God, the message of salvation.

Just as Africans used to gather in the heat of the sun under the shade of their big and generous trees in the the village squares, so do they now gather in the "New Village Square", the Church under the shade of the Holy Spirit. In other words African Christians now gather under the Tree of Life; they are led to it by the Spirit, and remain under it in the Spirit of Life. In the reality of the Church, Africans who reflect on their faith, find a fulfilment of the good work God began long ago in us. To use the words of Schillebeeckx:

---

55 Cf. see Giovanni Velocci, *Newman al Concilio*, 45.
56 see Simon S.Maimela, 'Religion and Culture: Blessings or Curses?', *in Journal of Black Theology In south Africa*, vol.5,no.1, May 1991, 12.

The triumphant grace of Christ is visibly active everywhere in this world, which has therefore already become "Church" in the broad sense of the word. But the Church of Christ in the *full* sense of the word is the *concentration point* of this visible presence of Christ in grace. The fullness of the power of God dwells "bodily" in this Church as it does in Christ.[57]

It is pertinent to point out here that a major difference between Jesus the Lord and African town criers, is that while the town criers were only messengers, the "New Town Crier", Jesus is God. He came with a message which is his. Jesus is not only a Messenger, he is the Message as well. In the new community of Christians, human traditions are no longer the absolute norms. Jesus the Lord who, called this community into existence is the absolute norm, the "norma normans". After his ascension to the Father, the Lord continues to summon us and to deliver his message through the persons whom He appointed to speak in his name in the community.

God calls all and sundry through Christ and in the Spirit to form a new community and remain in it. Refusal to respond to this call and refusal to participate in the life of the new community or absenteeism means a self-deprival of the benefits that are lodged in this community.

It is our union with each other that gives us a part in the benefits of the bestowed on the community. Judging from this, an African can easily agree with Newman that it is only by being *taken* into the Church that the individual can become and remain a Christian:

It has been the great design of Christ to connect all His followers into one, and to secure this, he has lodged His blessings in the gatherings of this body to oblige them to meet *together* if they would gain grace each for himself. The body is not made up of individual Christians, but each Christian has been made such in his turn by being *taken into* the *body*.[58]

The Church is the community of those who are united by the Holy Spirit in Christ. This new community is the home and locus of God's glory on earth, the appointed way and means whereby His mysterious purposes are to be wrought out.[59]

The reality of the Church community as a part of the believers relationship to Christ, and which sees one linked to all and all linked to one,

---

57 E. Schillebeeckx, *World and Church, London*, 1971, 146.

58 MS Sermon 213, 7 (25.10.1829).

59 Cf. Keble,J., SOP,XXIX, 355 and 357.

means that certain religious practice or piety like working for one's personal salvation (in an individualistic sense) or perishing in hell fire are foreign to African religious spirit.

For Africans the salvation of one is a triumph for the others, the entire community; likewise the perdition of a member of the community is a loss to the community since it entails the diminishing of its life-force.[60]

The biblical expression of the joy of angels at the conversion of a sinner is the type of ecclesial piety that suits African religious outlook. The reality of the Church is thus an essential part of man's relationship to Christ.

However this ecclesial model cannot undermine the other aspect of faith as a personal relationship with and committment to God, which the community can enhance but not substitute. The act of faith in the Lord of the new community, is such that the believer is expected to encounter and to respond to the Lord, directly, in the first person.

The communitarian aspect should not overshadow or erase the other dimension of faith: Solus cum solo. While the validity of the communitarian dimension stands, the believer is called to a special "loneliness with God". This aspect of faith, this aspect of religion is little or not known at all to the traditional religion.

Following Newman the African can say of the Church: she is the safety dock that shields men from insecurity and despair.[61] She shields men from the uncertainties of life, from «the ... upheavals of life, from the burden of grief and sorrow, from the reign of death, the universal power of demons and the malefic astral deities, ... from the consciousness of guilt, the wasting of disease, from the taedium vitae, and from the ills that made humman life a hell»[62].

For the African mind the Church is a fortress, castle, and chamber[63] where the individual receives assurance that he or she is at the centre of the universe, not just destined to die but above all to live and worship God.

---

60 Elsewhere we have noted that one of the reasons for conversion to Christianity was the desire to remain together in life or in death whichever the new faith might eventually bring.

61 Cf. Diff.I, 217 (The Providential Course of the Movement of 1833 Not in the Direction of a sect); also Giovanni Velocci, *Newman al Concilio*, 49.

62 S.Angus, *The Mystery Religions and Christianity*, Edinburgh,n.d., 226.

63 Cf. WA 44,713.

In this sense the Church is the beacon of Christ's grace placed in the world. The Church is not only a means of salvation. She is a place of refuge or the refuge herself, and to some extent, salvation itself, that is, the bodily form of salvation, salvation as appearing in this world. That is why the Church is "full of" the reality that she signififies.

Another aspect of Newman's Ecclesiology which strikes the average African believer is the composition of the Church. According to Newman, the Church is not a mere assembly of the living; she is rather a mystical body, nourished by an interchange of relation between her visible and celestial members. In her pilgrimage, the Church is accompanied, protected, and aided by those of her members who have gone before their brothers and sisters marked with the sign of faith.

The prophets smile when the Church community reads their books; the apostles and Evangelists listen when their writings are proclaimed; the saints nod when they are invoked in litanies; angels, archangels, cherubims, seraphims, thrones, sovereignties and powers are moved when the Church joins them in praising the Lord of Hosts.

For Africans, whose world is characterised by communion between the living and the dead, this mysterious composition and sublimity of the Church is yet another evident truth which makes the Church attractive. To this sublime characteristic of the Church, the Nigerian Catholic Hierarchy was referring when she wrote:

Those members of our families who have lived according to God's will have gone to heaven and are our advocates there. (In Christian terminology, they are saints, our brothers and sisters, who having gone to God, offer for us the firm hope that where they are in God's presence, we one day will come through His mercy).

More surely than in times past do we know that those who belong to the realm of the just can by praying for them exercise an influence for good on their descendants. Let us insist at this stage on the social nature of the Church. All the saints - those who seek God still in this world and those who are happy with him in the other world - are in communion with one another. We ourselves can claim kinship with the great saints of all times and all places. The Christian Church is the greatest of all extended families, stretched out as it does to embrace the world and transcend the centuries.[64]

---

64 *Nigerian Episcopal Conference, now, Nigerian Catholic Bishops' Conference,* Pastoral Letter, 1960, "Christianity has come not to destroy but to fulfil", no.8.

For the African religious mind, this big and new community called the Church, provokes wonder and gratitude, and grace and power surround it.

Described with African categories, the Church is great family, far greater than any extended family. She is the greatest immaginable extended family, united around one family head, God himself,[65] and yet open to all irrespective of their status, race or language, in which hospitality is the norm, love the rule, truth the light.

She is the biggest possible community, with God himself as the community leader, the elders his collaborators, and in which all live as brothers, homo hominibus frater! Her membership is all-inclusive. This means the sum total of all the community members, who hear the voice of the Head, that is, all the believers.

This ecclesiological model depicts in a new light the African extended family system. For an average African believer, «the Church is a new community. It is a new spiritual family, whose members become one's brothers and sisters and elders, which constitute the believer's new "home"».[66]

In this new family of God, the Church, the African has got more brothers and sisters. This time from different peoples, cultures, races, languages. And for the African the presence of many brothers is a blessing. It is a privilege to belong to this community. In this sense, the African believer can say of the Church like Newman: she is «that *new language* which Christ has brought us».[67]

---

65 Expressing such a truth Newman, said: «with the circumstance or condition of unity in those who receive them; the image of Christ and token of their acceptance being stamped upon them then, at that moment, when they are considered as one; so that henceforth the whole multitude, no longer viewed as mere individual men, become portions or members of the indivisible Body of Christ Mystical, so knit together in Him by divine Grace, that all has what He has, and each has what all have» (PPS VIII, 232-33 - 8.11.1829).

66 Benjamin C.Ray, 'Aladura Christianity: A Yoruba Religion', in The Journal of Religion in Africa, vol.XXIII-Fasc.3, August 1993, 272.

67 PPS V, 44 (2.6.1839). The emphasis is mine.

3.3.4   THE ANCESTORS RE-VISITED IN THE LIGHT OF THE
FATHERS OF THE CHURCH

In as much as Africans define themselves first and foremost in relation to others,[68] they understand their lives, their world, their values, their religion, all they are and have as belonging to those generations which preceded them. Africans,

> ... encounter the world around them as a place which has been prepared and made ready. The contributions of others, of the generations which preceded them, are not fortuitous, but form an essential part of their identity.[69]

Thus the Ancestors are appealed to as source and garantors of whatever is fundamental to the life of the community. For through them the High God communicated his will to the human family. They themselves have lived by this divine will and have passed it on to later generations.

The fact of transmitting their religion and values to their descendants is an argument for the veracity of what is transmitted because were such not for the benefit of the community the ancestors would not have passed them on to their children.

By stressing the Incarnation as the central truth of the Gospel, Newman presents Jesus of Nazareth as the "Functional Code" with which to read the past, the present and the future. Consequently even for the African Jesus is the key for reading and understanding the values and traditions of the ancestors.

Being God whose will is supreme, Jesus of Nazareth transcends the category of ancestor. We have already indicated some of attributes of an ancestor. An ancestor must have been a historical person, he must have lived a pure moral life, he must have had some moral and spiritual authority, and must have left behind some moral and spiritual teachings. Jesus of Nazareth was all these and more than that and in a perfect way. There is therefore an argument in favour of continuity. He was not only a

---

68   These others implies the dead, the living and the unborn as we have already indicated. A famous case was reported of the dialogue between Bishop Shanahan Cssp, and a local Igbo chief whom the Bishop wanted to convert by the threat of the torments of hell fire for unbelievers and the reward of heaven for believers. The old chief is reported to have told Bishop Shanahan that the Christian heaven had no appeal for him - he preferred to join his fellow chiefs and townsmen in hell.

69   Jan Heijke, 'Belief in Reincarnation in Africa', in *Concilium* 5, October 1993, 47.

historical person, a member of the community; Jesus, as the Christ came from the Trinitarian family, and came to introduce us to the life of the Trinity. He is not only man but also true God. He is therefore, at once continuity and discontinuity.

Unlike the ancestors Jesus is the only meritorious mediator before God, and who revealed through his life what the will of God is and what man's faithfulness to God is.[70] In his life, actions and teachings are concentrated all the favours God has in stock for men.

Jesus is the supreme realisation of religion and the reference point for all religious minds. His life and teaching made him attractive and many realised that only in association with him is life in the new community of the Church possible.

Henceforth religion and fundamental values are valid on the authority of Jesus in whom God is present in a new and definitive manner (Heb.1,1-4). Now all that Jesus revealed to the human community has passed over into mysteries since his return to the Father's house.[71]

Such mysteries are Word, sacraments, and other ordinances of grace. Therefore, the sacramental life of the Church community is the commemoration of the Jesus-event, actualization of it in the present, and anticipation of the final goal of the Church's sacramental system.

Just as we accepted norms and teachings on the authority of the ancestors so have we done in the new dispensation. Our forefathers in faith namely, the Apostles, Fathers of the Church, Saints, martyrs, confessors believed on the authority of Jesus, and we believe on the authority of our forefathers in faith.

In the Christian era those of our community who believed first, dedicated their whole life from the time of their conversion to their death to the study, elaboration, defence, teaching of the Gospel and who bequeathed it to us urging us to do as they did and even to do more are our ancestors and Fathers. Such "ancestors" and "Fathers" include Tertullian, Cyprian, Athanasius, Augustine, etc.

---

70 Evidences abound in the Scriptures that "no one was wise like him"; "no one spoke like him"; "no one taught with such an authority like him"; "no one cured the sick or calmed the storms with simple words like him"; no one was found to be as original as him. And over and above these, he pre-existed before time; he is the Word through whom all things were made; he is the Maker an Redeemer of the African ancestors.

71 Cf.Leo the Great, *Tractatus* 63,6, CCL 138A

Just as the ancestors were in the traditional religion, representatives or vicars of the gods, so has Jesus delegated power to some men to teach and guide others in his name. In this rung of representation, the Apostles in their capacity as those who saw, heard, touched, and contemplated the historical Jesus come first.

They are therefore the first ancestors. Close to the Apostles come the Fathers of the Church, who defended and determined what constituted the Apostolic faith. For Africans such delegates are worthy pillars of religion.

Paradoxically just as some of our fathers and ancestors hesitated before accepting the Christian faith because it was unknown to their ancestors; so do most of the later generation adhere to Christianity for the sole reason that it was the way trodden by their fathers. Thus what was a reason for hesitation or refusal in the past is today a reason for choosing Christianity.

African ancestors are endowed with hallo and such a degree of sacredness which make their deeds, norms and utterances authoritative and almost unquestionable[72]. The ancestors constitute an authority and guide. In the African religious world, faithfulness to the legacy of the ancestors is considered a duty and achievement in life:

When the descendants remained faithful to their inheritance, and thus made the experience of the ancestors their own, they remained in living communion both with the ancestor and their own kin, continually reliving the history of their people and proclaiming the marvels which God had performed for them.[73]

Africans live and act on the authority of their Fathers. To them the biblical injuction: "ask your fathers and they will tell you, interrogate your elders and they will explain" strikes a strong note.

When therefore, Newman says, "Did St. Athanasius or St. Ambrose come suddenly to life, it cannot be doubted which communion he would take to be his own"[74], he expresses what is an eloquent African sentiment.

In the light of this evidence many African Christians are determined to worship the God of their fathers, ready to follow in the footsteps of their

---

72 see E.A.Ruch and K.C.Anyanwu, *African Philosophy*, 29.
73 Bénézet Bujo, *African Theology in Its Social Context*, 21.
74 Dev.97.

ancestors in matters of faith and morals and sincerely hope not to disappoint them whose offsprings they are:

The angels and the saints are the senior members of the great family of God. The communion of saints - the vast community of the just who are with God and the just who live in this world - embraces those African ancestors who have gone to heaven just as much as it does those who have been called the "holy pagans of the Old Testament".[75]

Many African believers realise that each and every one of them is called by the great king, the supreme being to repeat the melodies which our fathers and brothers sang before us, to dance that divine tune in God's honour which our fathers and ancestors enjoyed.[76]

It was the tune of the Word of God proclaimed by the Church that our Fathers in faith enjoyed. To this Church of the Fathers have Africans clung. From the great importance of music, singing and dancing in the African world, a christological model can be developed. It is a christological model that portrays Jesus as "Drummer". As a member of the Trinitarian family, Jesus of Nazareth knows the "tune" of the Word and Will of the Father. Jesus came to the world to call men together in order to teach them how to beat, sing and dance the "divine tune". While he beats the tune, he instructs all to sing and dance like him and around him. To sing or dance well is to follow the beat and the steps of Jesus the divine master. And to follow the steps of Jesus is to be pleasing to the Father.

According to one of these new ancestors, Irenaeus, Christ himself was the ultimate source of Christian doctrine, being the truth, the word by whom the Father had been revealed; but He had entrusted His revelation to His apostles, and it was through them alone that knowledge of it could be obtained.[77]

African Christians believe that their fathers in faith made them Christians. And so Athanasius, disputing with Arians, claimed that his own doctrine had been handed down from father to father, whereas they could not produce a single respectable witness to theirs.[78]

---

75   Nigerian Episcopal Conference, Ibid., no.8.
76   Cf. PPS VI, 230 (29.11.1840).
77   Cf. Ad.haer.3,preaf. 3,5,1; PG 7.437.
78   Cf.St. Athanasius, *Discourses against the Arians*, PG 26,467; *also De decret*.Nic.syn.27.

3.3.5   ANTIQUITY AND TRADITION: NEWMAN IN AN AFRICAN
PERSPECTIVE

In a world-setting such as that of the African, a major tendency is to appeal to the Tradition of the ancestors and fathers. In African traditional societies, Tradition is the pedagogue that indicates the direction of the society and the content of its norms and beliefs.

Irenaeus' words ring continuously to the ears of African Christians: «Through none other, than those by whom the gospel reached us have we learned the plan of our salvation»,[79] and what was believed and preached in the churches was absolutely authoritative because it was the selfsame revelation which they had received from the apostles, the Apostles received from Christ, and Christ from God.[80] Africans are convinced that,

Behind them - that is, in the direction of the past - there stretches a very important substratum of their being. They are carried forward by the living past. They constantly remembered those who produced them. They remain as it were deeply under the impact of the world which others have prepared for their coming.[81]

A direct consequence of this consciousness is to conduct a life of gratitude to the ancestors or fathers, not to betray or contradict[82] consciously their legacy and to transmit in turn to others what one has received.

What is transmitted is authoritative because it is antique and has been uninterrupted; it is antique because it dates back to the source, and uniterrupted because it has been always transmitted. They are things which by the force of their value have endured through the ages as fundamental values of life.

On this question, De Vere argued that while Newman lived in the nineteenth century his true home was in the Christian antiquity, especially the fourth and fifth centuries.[83] This observation of De Vere may be true to some extent because of Newman's admiration for the vibrant

---

79   Irenaeus, *Ad.haer.3,praef.*3,1,1.
80   Cf. Tertulian, De praescr.13; PL 2,12.
81   Jan Heijke, Op.cit.,47-8.
82   To buttress this point there is an African proverb that says "one does not bite the fingers that fed him".
83   Cf. Aubrey de Vere, *Recollections*, London, 1897,31, quoted in *Ward's Life of Newman*, I, 66.

faith of the early Christians and the theological insight of the Fathers of the Church.

In his Anglican days he once reminded his congregation of their great privilege to enjoy communion with one of those branches of the Apostolic Church, which follows the primitive model.[84] In the light of the above, one can say that if our fore-fathers who died before the light of Christianity were to appear suddenly today they would make the choice of Christianity and would blame those who did not.

Of course Tradition does not only mean ancient customs. Tradition is that complex which includes value-systems, beliefs, cosmovision, art, customs, social attitudes, reactions to particular situations, setting out the key-points of a culture and religion, and embodied in symbols.[85] In short, in general terms, Tradition is the expression of the continuing community, the way a particular social group lived and still does. African symbolic thinking is Africa's fundamental Tradition.

It is through Tradition that the Church reproduces and succeeds herself age after age. It is through Tradition that the African genius is preserved in the midst of change and cultural contact.

In the great extended family of the Church, Tradition means those things which Jesus did, taught, urged to be taught and lived; and how these things have been taught, understood and lived all this while.

Henceforth, it became possible to speak of «the root and source of tradition» or of «the fountain-head and source of the divine tradition»,[86] which has been inherited, expounded, conserved, and handed on by the "wisdom of the holy fathers".[87] One of the age-long values in "spirit and in truth" (Jn. 4:24),[88] which is a part of the Christian Tradition and of which African believers have become heirs is the "sacramental thinking".

---

84   MS Sermon 12f (15.8.1824).
85   see Edward B.Tylor, *Primitive Culture: Research into the Development of Mythology, Philosophy, Religion, Language, and Custom*, London, third Ed.,1891,1; also C.Geertz, *Interpretation of Culture*, New York, 1973,89; Ladislas Orsy, 'The Interpretation of Laws: New Variations on an Old Theme', in *Art of Interpretation. Selected Studies on the Interpretation of Canon Law*, Canon Law Society of America (CLSA), Washington D.C., 1982,70.
86   St. Cyprian, *Ep*.63,1;74,10; CSEL 3/1, 214.
87   Cyril Of Alexandria, *In Iohannem ev*.4,11; PG 74,216.
88   John Paul II, 'Ai partecipanti al Congresso Nazionale del Movimento Ecclesiale di Impegno Culturale', January 16, 1982, *Insegnamenti di Giovanni Paolo II*, vol.5, no.1, 1982, 131.

In the new dispensation, authentic Tradition is rooted in the Eschatological Word of God and in the community of yesterday. Each comunity's witness to the Word and profession of faith must, originate, like the community itself from the community of past times, from which that of today arose. It behoves every community not to conduct itself as though religion, the quest for truth, rites and sacramental thinking began today.[89] This consciousness of the past is an African trait.

For African Christians, to discard with Tradition is to dispense with the history and experience of faith, to reject the wisdom of the fathers, ancestors and elders as they reacted to the challenges of life and responded to those fundamental querries that prick the human heart in the light of God's Word. An aspect of Newman's understanding of Tradition as «the Church's dowry ... rich with the accumulated wealth of the ages»,[90] tallies with African spirit.

Africans attach great importance to Antiquity. For them the Church as an old institution is an object of admiration and respect. This is because they consider her to possesss in her bosom the experiences of her members: illustrious men and women, erudite and holy writers, and wise saints, who have walked the path of faith before us. No wonder Africans have chosen the Church of God. No wonder they are struggling to remain in her and with her.

3.3.6   AFRICAN CONCEPTION OF AUTHORITY IN RELATION TO NEWMAN'S SACRAMENTAL SYSTEM

A crucial element in African cosmology is its hierarchical ordering. The first and original outlay of this hierarchy is two, namely, God and the created order. In African cosmology it was after the so called "retreat of God" from the world that a mediatorial-hierarchical order became necessary. However, if correctly understood, the apparent remoteness of God from the daily and common life of men is only the consequence of the respect Africans nurture for authority.

In African traditional society no one may approach a chief directly to speak with him without an intermediary. If this is true of the created

---

89   see K.Barth, *Evangelical Theology: An Introduction*, London, 1963, 40-1.
90   Tract 38,9 (1834).

beings how much then with the most supreme being, God?[91] It is therefore, respect for God's authority that is accountable for what an outsider[92] may interprete as deus otiosus in the African religious world.

In the African logic at the moment of God's retreat into the sky the following rung was established: God, spirits, ancestors, elders, kings, priests, family-heads. The common belief is that each has received a function and authority from God and together they form one chain. These are not mere wielders of secular power. What they exercise is a typically priestly function whereby they act as mediators[93] between the family or community and the ancestors in the case of family heads, kings and priests or between God and the world in the case of the spirits.

Thus wielders of authority are cultic and sacred persons, and are expected to incarnate the qualities of the Divinity.[94] This is why they are normally surrounded by a number of taboos.[95]

Christian dispensation knows of a single mediator, Jesus Christ in whom are concentrated all religious offices and sacrifices. Other "sacred" persons are the delegates and instruments of the only mediator between God and men. Such persons have been appointed by Christ to act as his oracles. These are the ministers of the Church.

Even when the leaders of the community are elected by the community their authority is believed to come from God. Thus in African traditional societies, wielders of authority are symbols of the solidarity of the group. Ritual matters are indispensable parts of their function.

Eldership is synonymous with the exercise of this role. Actually a religious leader may be young but considered an elder because of his posi-

---

91 Cf. Peter K.Sarpong, 'Meno Etichette per favore', (Riflessione sull'Instrumentum Laboris, Sinodo dei Vescovi, Assemblea Speciale per l' Africa), in *Nigrizia*, Anno III, no.10, Ottobre 1993, 50f.

92 *Outsider* here does not mean non-African observers, scholars, who, in spite of their goodwill may be and are usually conditioned by their cultural lenses to understanding that which they are looking for instead of what is there. *Outsider* refers equally to those Africans who are strangers to their people's religious tradition and often have either not understood or have misunderstood the African religious tradition.

93 Cf. Paul VI, *Africae Terrarum, Message to the Sacred Hierarchy and All the Peoples of Africa*, 29 October 1967, AAS 59 (1967): 1073-1097.

94 Cf. Mercy Amba Odudoye, 'The Value of African Religious Beliefs and Practices for Christian Theology', 5.

95 Cf. C.N.Ubah, 'Changing Patterns of Leadership Among the Igbos 1900-1960', in *TransAfrican Journal of History*, vol.16, 1987, 170.

tion; because of his close association with the Divinity, he is considered the age-mate of the gods and knowing things beyond ordinary men. This is a major reason why in contemporary African societies ministers of the Christian Religion are accepted and respected even though they may sometimes be much younger than the members of the community entrusted to their care.

African Christians retain the ministers of the Church as chosen by God and treat them as such. Many African believers would agree with Newman that the commission and word of promise made to the first generation of ministers of the community of the faith is valid for their successors.[96]

And what binds men's conscience to accept the Church's faith as true is that it is "divinely guided" to teach the truth.[97] This is an affirmation that confirms African religious obeissance. In African traditional societies norms are accepted on the authority of the community; beliefs, rites, behavioural patterns are retained valid because they community teaches and sanctions them.

3.3.7   THE SEVEN SACRAMENTS IN THE LIGHT OF RITUAL CELEBRATIONS IN AFRICAN RELIGION

In the African religious world, ritual acts that re-enact God's deeds for men characterise religious practice. Through ritual practises Africans celebrate their encounter with the Sacred and communion with one another:

Through ritual man transcends himself and communicates directly with the divine. The coming of divinity to man and man to divinity happens repeatedly with equal validity on almost every ritual occasion. The experience of salvation is thus a present reality, not a future event. The passage from the profane to the sacred, from man to divinity, ... occurs Here and Now.[98]

Thus ceremonies and rituals of great import are common features among all African peoples after the birth of a child, such as the name-

---

96   Tract 8,2 (1833); see also Froude, *Remains* II:I,132.
97   VM.I, 190 (The Indefectibility of the Church Catholic).
98   Benjamin C. Ray, *African Religions. Symbol, Ritual, and Community*, New Jersey, 1976, 17.

giving ceremony, or congratulatory banquets, before graduation into adulthood, such as initiation rites, marriage, funeral rites, etc.

Such ceremonies could be called "sacraments" of the old religion. In themselves, they constitute as St. Thomas wrote, «a sign of a holy thing, in as much it makes men holy».[99] However, they are far below the Christian sacraments.[100] At the natural level, material things are purveyors of God's goodness. But at the Incarnation, this quasi-sacramental vocation of material phenomena was purified and elevated to a new altitude. The mirabilia Dei which Africans perceived in the created world, in sacred objects, in events and in history found concentration point in the person of Jesus of Nazareth. By assuming the sacramental vocation on himself, the Son of God redeemed, elevated and put a new seal and meaning on it. Henceforth rather than everything, certain elements and rites are by the express will of the Redeemer purveyors of divine life or sacraments.

The novelty is that Christian ordinances are condensations of the power of the Lord's life, acts and words. They infuse divine life in those who partake of them; and they are efficacious in virtue of the Spirit of Christ which operates in and through them.

Henceforth initiation is no longer solely participation in the life of the divinity and the secrets of the community, but an immersion in the life, death and resurrection of Jesus; Sacred banquet or common meal is no longer solely to commune with the divinity or with fellow partakers but to eat of the body and blood of Christ; marriage is no longer the celebration of the sacred origin of life but the union of God in Christ with the redeemed community, etc.

Christian sacraments differ from ordinances of the traditional religion, not in that it has no rites, but that those rites have superior power never known before, not that the Gospel has nothing outward, but that the traditional religion has nothing as inward as the Gospel gifts, not that the Gospel has no rites and ordinances; but that they convey great gifts, regeneration and justification.[101]

Such is the abyss of difference because the traditional religion knew little or nothing of the religion of the heart and of the reality of the Holy

---

99   S.T.q.60,a.2.
100 The requisites for a sacrament are articulated above.
101 see MS Sermon 26, 360 (16.11.1834).

Spirit who is the agent that transforms material things into the instruments of God.

In traditional religion, the signs of God are seen in nature, his voice is heard as well in nature but God is not seen. Christianity on the contrary is a "historical event". God was heard but above all seen in the person of Jesus, as God-with-us.

It is therefore Christ and him alone whom we receive through the medium of these ordinances. Through them believers experience the powers and wonders of his deeds.

Above all, they are integral parts of the true cult in spirit and truth. Though we are anchored bodily in this world, we are lifted spiritually, to become as it were sensible of the contact of something more than earthly, namely, that whose sacrament certain Christian rituals are.

African Christians see in religious rituals, the expressions of those truths that cannot be exhausted in words. Such religious rituals are deeply evocative and implicate the believer. And Africans like being involved. This is why participation in worship is a feature of African religiousity.

And it is only by being involved, by being implicated in the encounter that religion can affect the life of a believer. In ritual celebrations, particular communication is affected between the participant and the Divinity, a communication that carries the subject across a logical gap and thus can effect a conversion.[102]

Through the sacramental ordinances of the Church Christ communicates himself to men, and thus diffuses a new life for the renewal of mankind.[103] The reality of such a new life infused through the sacraments is manifested in the transformed life of the believers. Documented evidence of this is the joy, liveliness, massive participation and festive mood of African Christianity. In Newmanian terminology, sacramental ordinances bring about regeneration.

African religiousity is founded on the principle that religious rites are committed to the community. The sacraments, are social and public by their very nature. Baptism for example effects our incorporation into Christ's spiritual body, and still more the Communion as being a «joint partaking of the benefits of redemption».[104]

---

102   see Avery Dulles, *Models of Revelation*, Maryknoll, 1992, vii.
103   Cf. I.Wilberforce, Incarnation, 322.
104   MS Sermon 213, 11 (25.10.1829).

From the unity and the oneness of the Church follows «the duty of united worship; for thus the multitude of believers coming together, claims as one man the grace which is poured out upon the one undivided body of Christ mystical».[105] Divine providence has thus a wonderful way of feeding believers with the truth of the Gospel. African Christians are delighted to know that through her rituals, the Church speaks in different tones to her children of diverse temperaments:

The Catholic Church is the poet of her children, full of music to soothe the sad and control the wayward, wonderful in story for the imagination of the romantic; rich in symbol and imagery, so that gentle and delicate feelings, which will not bear words, may in silence intimate their presence or commune with themselves. Her very being is poetry[106].

Thus the African religious mind rich in symbols and imagination has much to gain by way of enrichment from the elaborate Church ritual-celebrations; for the heart is much more overcome, touched, more moved, by the sacramental embodiment of religious truth.[107] In the Christian religion rich in rituals, Africans recognise a reality which says something to them; a religion which draws them irresistibly.

3.4 CONCLUSION

The relevance of Newman's sacramental theological thinking to an average African believer can be found in the fact that Newman's doctrine can help Africans to enrich their symbolic or quasi-sacramental mentality with the Church's sacramental system.

This can be done by taking into consideration those pillars on which African religion are founded, namely, Antiquity, Ancestors, Tradition, Community, Religious rituals, etc. These are types, or images, and in their degree and place, representatives and organs of an unseen reality or world, truer and higher than themselves.[108] Africa's care for these in

---

105 PPS II, 91 (23.11.1834).
106 Newman, Ess.II, 442 (John Keble Fellow of Oriel).
107 Cf. Geoffrey Rowell, 'Cor ad Cor Loquitur. Newman's choice of his Cardinalate Motto as a pointer to the Understanding of Christian faith and its communication', in J.H.Newman:*Theologian and Cardinal*..., 63.
108 see. Ess.ii.193.

religious life is a bringing out in its own way of the sacramental Principle.

The equivalents of these in Newman's sacramental theologising, namely, Christian Antiquity, Fathers, Tradition, Church, Sacraments, etc. constitute good points of contact between Newman's thought and the average African believer.

In the light of the above, what Gottfried Söhngen said in comparing Newman's importance for German speaking Catholics with Shakespear's place in literary Germany, can be applied to Newman's relevance for African believers: Just as the Bible through perfect translations has become part of us, so has Newman become our religious thinker, a thinker who appeals to us, without diminishing his importance for Christians in England and throughout the world.[109]

---

109 Cf. G.Söhngen, *John Henry Kardinal Newman, Sein Gottesgedanke und Seine Denkergestalt*, Bonn, 1946, 9.

GENERAL CONCLUSION

The central message of African symbolic thinking is the fact that everything such as the pillars of the traditional society, comes from God, bears a superior meaning and points to God. This pointing to God, this yearning for completion on the part of symbols is a good basis for the doctrine of Incarnation, namely, the irruption of the Trinitarian life into history in the person of Jesus of Nazareth.

Inasmuch as Jesus is truly God and truly man, he is able to mediate efficaciously between two worlds. This type of mediation, African ancestors and spirit-gods could not do because even though they were believed to have something supernatural in them, they could not share the same nature with God as Jesus and therefore were not truly God. In the Jesus-event was therefore realised a meeting between nature and grace. And the life of grace concentrated on Jesus is offered to men through particular sacramental ordinances.

As a religion of grace, the Christian religion is a fulfilment of the traditional religion. The Incarnate Son of God is the authentic meaning of those symbols with which African culture is replete. What is at stake is that the "symbolic existence" of Antiquity, Ancestors, Tradition, Community and Rituals in African religion has now been overtaken by the sacramental presence of a higher reality.

In its place there arose a new existential reality, which is both a symbol but above all more than a symbol. Jesus is this new existential reality. Careful reading of African religious culture, would show that God had somehow prepared the way for the coming of Christ also through the history of Africa, which had reached its climax with his death and resurrection.

Thus is the goal of African universe of symbols. They are not simply fixed static signs, representative of something that is absent. Instead, they are "relational events"[110] and, as such they have to some extent led

---

110 see D. Zadra, 'Symbol und Sakrament', in *Christlicher Glaube in moderner Gesellschaft* 28, Freiburg, 1982, 94-95; also Herbert Vorgrimler, *Sacramental Theology*, 69.

adherents of traditonal religion to Christianity. In the wake of Christianity, rereading African religious world is a characteristic symbolic action from which African Christianity can benefit much.

Jesus is the meaning of Antiquity. And given that for Africans antiquity is a point of reference should this "I am before all Abraham" not become a focal point? To say the least, the religious values which African ancestors imparted on their descendants, they owed to the "I am before Abraham". He is also Tradition itself. He taught us the rule of life that governs the Trinitarian family; he bequeathed on believers the Trinitarian ways. And rightly do we say that his Spirit spoke through the prophets.

Those to whom Jesus addressed his words and taught the rule of the Trinity community constitute a different type of family, viz. the Church more open, more integrating, more fulfilling. To be part of this new family called into being by God himself and transcending all race and nationhood is to capture the symbolism behind African comunity spirit.

This community is completely new because it follows the paths of Jesus. Jesus leads the way; he looks behind now and then to watch the faces of those he leads; he feeds them with divine bounty. That path is sacramental. So is the path of Jesus. So is the Christian path.

On these grounds, the "per ipsum, cum ipso et in ipso" says much to an average African believer. The Christian sacraments with which Jesus nourishes the inmates of his community, are not just "touch and go", for through them God makes a claim on us; a claim that demands free assent. Sacramentality by its nature calls for this. Thus is the movement from sacraments to Christian sacraments. For many African Christians, Jesus is not only different from the ancestors; he *is* the difference. And to belong to Christ, to be a Christian means to be a sacrament of Jesus as Jesus is the Sacrament of God; to be a Christian is to live and act sacramentally. For an African, it entails among other things acquiring a sacramental mental configuration, a shift from the symbolic to sacramental mental mould.

Newman's Cardinalate motto, "Ex Umbris et Imaginibus in Veritatem", "From Shadows and Images to the Truth", can be used to describe the history of salvation as it touches African believers. The African itinerary has been from shadows and images to the truth, from types to archtype, from natural to Christian symbolic mentality, from Ancestors, Community, Tradition and Ritual, to Christ, the real Ancestor, the Church as the community of those who believe in him, the Faith Tradi-

188

tion of this community, Authority of Christ's ministers and sacraments. The Object of African worship is Jesus Christ in the place which Jesus himself indicated namely, the Church.

It is therefore befitting that the "ways" of this Object of African Christian worship, permeates through the rites of the African Church, and transforms African traditional associations, so that, at every turn, their lives might be penetrated by the mysterious force of the name of Christ.[111]

Even when they fall back to the shadows and images, even when they do not follow the kindly light or feel its warmth, African believers live in this consciousness

---

111 see St. Augustine, Conf.III,iv,8; PL 32,659; also Peter Brown, *Augustine of Hippo*, London, 1967, 246.

SELECTED BIBLIOGRAPHY

I. WORKS BY J.H. NEWMAN

A. UNPUBLISHED

N.B. The numbers indicate the sermon given by Newman, while the numbers between brackets refer to the shelfmark in the Birmingham Oratory Archives, e.g. A.17.1 indicates cupboard A, pigeonhole 17, position 1.
MSS. Sermons
nos. 2 (A.17.1); 5 (A.17.1); 6 (A.17.1); 8 (A.7.1); 9 (A.7.1); 12 (A.17.1); 14 (A.7.1 also A 17.1); 16 (A.17.1); 19 (A.7.1 also A.50.6); 22 (A.7.1); 23 (A.7.1); 29 (A.7.1); 54 (A.7.1); 150 (A.17.1); 156 (A.50.3); 157 (A.50.2); 360 (A.17.1); 449 (A.50.5).

B. PUBLISHED

N.B. In the case of letters and sermons the dates have been indicated in footnotes to the text. For other works, the present bibliography indicates between brackets the date of the first edition and also of the edition quoted, whenever we have used a reprint of the latter.
Apologia pro Vita Sua, (1864),3rd. ed. London 1887.
The Arians of the Fourth Century, (1832), 3rd. ed. London 1871.
Callista: a Tale of the Third Century, (1855), 4th. ed. London 1889.
Certain Difficulties felt by Anglicans in Catholic Teaching, 2 vols., London vol.i(1850), 1876.
'The Providential Course of the Movement of 1833 not in the Direction of a Branch Church' (1850), in Diff.I, 164-196.
'Letter Addressed to Rev. E.B. Pusey on the Occasion of his Eirenicon' (1850), 1867, in Diff.II, 1-170.
Discourses addressed to Mixed Congregations, (1849), New Impression, London 1871.
Discussions and Arguments on Various Subjects, (1872), New Impression, London 1873.

An Essay in aid of a Grammar of Assent, (1870), New ed. London 1891.
An Essay on the Development of Christian Doctrine, (1845), New ed. London (1878), 1897.
Essays Critical and Historical, 2 vols. 5th. ed.London 1890.
'Poetry, with Reference to Aristotle's Poetics' (1828), in Ess.I., 1-29.
'The Theology of St. Ignatius' (1839), in Ess.I., 222-261.
'Catholicity of the Anglican Church' (1840), in Ess.II., 2-73.
'Note on Essay X' (1868), in Ess.II., 74-111.
'The Protestant Idea of Antichrist' (1840), in Ess.II., 112-185.
'Milman's View of Christianity' (1841), in Ess.II., 186-248.
'John Keble Fellow of Oriel' (1846), in Ess.II., 421-453.
Historical Sketches, 3 vols. (1872) New ed. London.
Lectures on the Doctrine of Justification, (1838) 3rd. ed. London 1874.
Lectures on the Present Position of Catholics in England, 1851, London.
Lectures on The Prophetical Office of the Church Viewed Relatively to Romanism and Popular Protestantism, (1837) 3rd. ed. (1877) in Via Media I.
Loss and Gain: The Story of a Convert, London (1874) 6th ed. London 1891.
Meditations and Devotions, 1893, London.
Oxford University Sermons, 1871 3rd. ed. London.
Parochial and Plain Sermons, 8 vols. London 1868.
Selected Treatises of St. Athanasius, 2 vols. (1881), London New ed. 1890.
Sermons bearing on Subjects of the Day, (1843), New Impression, London 1869.
Sermons 1824-83, vol.1: Sermons on the Liturgy and Sacraments and on Christ the Mediator, P. Murray (ed.), Oxford 1991.
Tracts, Theological and Ecclesiastical, (1874), 2nd. ed. London 1895.
Tracts for the Times, 1833-1841
Tract 6: The Present Obligation of Primitive Practice (1833), 1840.
Tract 8: The Gospel a Law of Liberty (1833), 1845.
Tract 11: The Visible Church (1833), 1840.
Tract 34: Rites and Customs of the Church (1834), 1840.
Tract 71: On the Controversy with the Romanists (1836), 1841.
Tract 85: Lectures on the Scripture Proof of the Doctrines of the Church (1838), 1842.
The Idea of a University, defined and illustrated, London 1852.

The Via Media of the Anglican Church, illustrated in lectures and tracts, 2 vols London 1877.

* * *

Autobiographical Writings, ed. Henry Tristram, London, 1956.
Letters and Correspondence of John Henry Newman during his Life in the English Church, ed. Anne Mozley, 2 vols., London, 1891.
The Letters and Diaries of John Henry Newman, ed. Charles Stephen Dessain et al., vols. i-xxxi (1961-78).

II. OTHER BRITISH SOURCES 17th - 19th CENTURIES

Arnold, T. Chrisitian Life, its Hinderances, and its Helps. Sermons, 5th ed. London, 1849.
Bowden, J.E. The Life and Letters of Frederick William Faber, 5th ed. London, n.d.
Butler, C. The Life and Times of Bishop Ullathorne, vol.ii, London, Burns & Oates, 1962.
–: Church and Unity, London, 1979.
Butler, J. The Analogy of Religion Natural and Revealed to the Constitution and Course of Nature, (1736), ed. W.E. Gladstone, Oxford, 1897.
Church, R.W. The Oxford Movement. Twelve Years 1833-1845, 3rd ed.London, 1891.
Dalgairns, J.D. 'Dante and Catholic Philosophy', in British Critic, XXX, no.65, 1843, 110-143.
Faber, F.W. The Blessed Sacrament, London, 1855.
Fairweather, E.R. The Oxford Movement, New York, 1964.
Froude, R.H. Remains I-II, London, 1838-9.
Haweis, T. The Communicant's Spiritual Communion or an Evangelical Preparation for the Lord's Supper, 10th ed. London, 1818.
Hooker, R. The Laws of Ecclesiastical Polity, (1888), ed. R.Bayne, London, 1902. Keble, J. The Christian Year, London, 1878.
–: Lyra Innocentium, and Other poems, Oxford, 1914.
–: Sermons Academical and Occasional, Oxford, 1847.
–: Sermons Occasional and Parochial, Oxford, 1878.
Liddon, H.P. Life of Edward Bouverie Pusey, 4 vols., London, 1893.

Oakeley, F. 'Sacramental Confession', in British Critic, XXX, no.60, 1843, 295-347.

–: 'Rites and Ceremonies', in British Critic, XXX, no.60, 1841, 422-465.

Pusey, E.B. A Letter to the Bishop of London in Explanation of some Statements contained in a letter by W. Dodsworth, 4th ed. Oxford, 1851, 428-451.

Sandys, Works, London, 1844.

Scott, T. The Force of Truth, 11th ed. Edinburgh, 1818.

Stanley, A.P. The Life and Correspondence of Thomas Arnold, 2 vols., London, 1845.

Ward, W.G. 'Heurtley's four Sermons', in British Critic, XXXI, 1842, no.62, 428-   451.

Webster, A.B. Church order and Reunion in the Nineteenth Century, London, n.d.

Wilberforce, R.I. The Doctrine of the Incarnation, (1848), 3rd ed. 1850.

–: The Sacramental System. A Sermon preached at St. Mary's Church before the University of Oxford, London, 1850.

Williams, I. The Church Prayer-Book a Safe Guide. In Plain Sermons by Contributors to the 'Tracts for the Times', vol.ii, London 1840.

–: The Baptistery, or the way of Eternal Life, Oxford, 1842.

III. WORKS ON NEWMAN AND CHRISTIANITY IN GREAT BRITAIN

Allchin, A.M. 'The Theological Vision of the Oxford Movement', in The Rediscovery of Newman 50-57.

Beckam, J.F. 'Another View of Newman', in American Ecclesiastical Review, vol.138, no.1, 1958, 30-41.

Beek, W.J.A. John Keble's Literary and Religious Contribution to the Oxford Movement. Doctoral Dissertation, Nijmegen, 1958.

Biemer, G. Uberlieferung und Offenbarung. Die Lehre von der Tradition nach John Henry Newman, Freiburg, 1961.

Blehl, V.F. 'The Spiritual roots of Newman's Theology', in John Henry Newman. Theologian and Cardinal, Rome, Urbaniana University Press, 1981, 17-31.

Boekraad, J. 'Newman as Theologian. His Candour and Loyalty', in Newman Studien, vol.10, 47-59.

Bouyer, L. Newman's Vision of Faith. A Theology for Times of General Apostasy, San Francisco, Ignatius Press, 1986.

Bremond, H. The Mystery of Newman, London, Clarendon, 1907.

Carpenter, S.C. Church and People 1789-1889. A History of the Church of England from William Wilberforce to Lux Mundi, London, 1933.

Chadwick, O. Newman, Past Masters, Oxford, Oxford Unversity Press, 1983.

–: The Spirit of the Oxford Movement. Tractarian Essays, Cambridge, Cambridge University Press, 1990.

–: From Bossuett to Newman, 2nd edition, Cambridge, Cambridge University Press, 1987.

Chapman, R. Father Faber, London, 1961.

Coleridge, H.J. 'The Father of Souls', in The Month, no.70, 1890, 14-22.

Coulson, J. Newman and the Common Tradition, Oxford, Clarendon Press, 1970.

Cross, B.J.L. 'A Biographical Introduction' in Shadows and Images, 3-15.

Crumb, N.L. The Oxford Movement and Its Leaders. A Bibliography of Secondary and lesser primary Sources, New York, The American Theological Library Association and The Scarecrow Press, 1988.

Dessain, C.S. Newman's Spiritual Themes, Dublin, Veritas Publications, 1977.

–: 'The Biblical Basis of Newman's Ecumenical Theology', in The Rediscovery of Newman, 100-122.

Dick, K. 'Das Analogieprinzip bei John Henry Newman und seine Quelle in Joseph Butlers Analogy', in Newman Studien, vol.5, 21-69.

Dupuy, B.D. 'Newman's Influence in France', in Coulson and Allchin (eds.), The Rediscovery of Newman, 147-173.

Faber, G. Oxford Apostles. A Character Study of the Oxford Movement, London, Oxford University Press, 1933.

Härdelin, A. The Tractarian Understanding of the Eucharist, Uppsala, Almqvist and Wicksells, 1965.

Harrold, C.F. A Newman Treasury. Selections from the Prose Works of John Henry Cardinal Newman, New York, Arlington House, 1975.

Henkel, W. Die religiöse Situation der Heiden und Ihre Bekehrung nach John Henry Newman, Rome, Catholic Book Agency, 1961.

Holmes, J.D. 'Personal Influence and Religious Conviction. Newman and Controversy', in Newman Studien, vol.10, 26-46.

Honoré, J. Itinerario Spirituale di Newman, trans. Luigi Castiglione, Brescia, Editrice Morcelliana, 1991.

Janseens, Newman. Introduzione al suo spirito e alla sua opera, Città del Vaticano, Tipografia Poliglotta Vaticana, 1945.

John Henry Newman. Lover of Truth, Strolz and Binder (eds.), Roma, Urbaniana University Press, 1991.

Ker, I.T. The Achievements of John Henry Newman, Notre Dame, University of Notre Dame Press, 1991.

–: Newman on Being a Christian, Oxford, Oxford University Press, 1989.

Lash, N. 'Tides and Twilight. Newman since Vatican II', in Ker and Hill (eds.), Newman after a Hundred Years, Oxford, Clarendon Press, 1990, 447-464.

McKeating, C. Eschatology In the Anglican Sermons of J.H.Newman, Dissertatio ad Doctoratum, "Extract", Pontificia Universitas Gregoriana, 1992.

Moe, C. 'John Henry Newman and the Concept of the Church. A Contemporary Reflection', in Shadows and Images, 141-149.

Morrone, F. Cristo il Figlio di Dio fatto Uomo. L'Incarnazione del Verbo nel Pensiero Cristologico di J.H.Newman, Milano, Jaca Book, 1990.

–: 'L'Incarnazione nel Pensiero cristologico di Newman', in Rassegna di Teologia, XXXIII, no.3, 1992, 315-332.

Murray, P. Newman the Oratorian, Dublin, 1969.

Newman Studien, vol.i-xiv, eds. Fries and Becker, Nürnberg, Glock und Lutz, 1958-1990.

Newsome, D. 'The Evangelical Sources of Newman's Power, in The Rediscovery of Newman, 11-30.

Norris, J.T. Newman and His Theological Method. A Guide for the Theologian Today, Leiden, E.J. Brill, 1977.

Parker, T.M. 'The Rediscovery of the Fathers in the Seventeenth Century Anglican Tradition', in The Rediscovery of Newman, 31-49.

Powell, G. 'The Roots of Newman's Scriptural Holiness. Some Formative Influences on Newman's Spirituality', in Newman Studien, vol.10, 13-20.

Ratzinger, J. 'Newman gehört zu den grossen Lehrern der Kirche', in John Henry Newman. Lover of Truth, 141-146.

Raymond, M. Love Does Such Things, Milwaukee, The Bruce Publishing Co., 1955.

Rediscovery (The) of Newman, J. Coulson and A.M. Allchin (eds.), London, Sheed and Ward, 1967.

Richmond, G. Scenes from the Life of J.H.Cardinal Newman, London, CTS, 1945.

Rodriguez, P. Newman and the Oxford Movement, Trivandrum, All Saints' College Press, 1983.

Runcie, R. 'Newman's Journey and His Intellectual Example Should Encourage Us Never To Rest Complacent', in John Henry Newman. Lover of Truth, 157-158.

Sarolea, C. Cardinal Newman, Edingburgh, 1908.

Seynaeve, J. Cardinal Newman's Doctrine on Holy Scripture, Dissertation, Universitas Catholica Lovaniensis, 1953.

Shadows and Images, B.J.L. Cross (ed.), Melbourne, The Polding Press, 1981.

Sharkey, M. 'Newman and Revelation', in Stolz and Binder (eds.), John Henry Newman. Lover of Truth, 21-35.

Söhngen, G. John Henry Kardinal Newman, Sein Gottesgedanke und seine Denkergestalt, Bonn, 1946.

Stern J. Bible et Tradition chez Newman, Paris, Aubier-Montaigne, 1967.

–: 'The Institutional Church in Newman's Spirituality', in Newman Studien, vol.10, 80-87.

Tardivel, F. La Personalité littéraire de Newman, Paris, Cerf, 1937.

Trevor, M. Newman: The Pillar of the Cloud (vol.i); Newman: Light in Winter (vol.ii), London, Macmillan, 1962.

Velocci, G. Newman al Concilio, Alba, Edizioni Paolini, 1966.

Walgrave, J.H. Newman the Theologian, London, Geoffrey Chapman, 1960.

–: John Henry Newman. Growing Towards the Light, Roma, Centre of Newman Friends, 1980.

–: 'A Psychological Portrait of Newman', in John Henry Newman. Theologian and Cardinal, Rome, Urbaniana University Press, 1981, 155-171.

Ward, W. The Life of John Henry Newman, based on his Private Journals and Correspondence, 2 vols., London, 1912.

Weatherby, H.L. Cardinal Newman in His age. His Place in English Theology and Literature, Nashville, Vanderbilt University Press, 1973.

Withey, A. John Henry Newman: The Liturgy and the Breviary. Their Influence on his life as an Anglican, London, Sheed & Ward, 1992.

IV. WORKS ON AFRICA AND AFRICAN RELIGION

Achebe, C. Morning Yet On Creation. Day Essays, London, Heinemann, 1982.

Appiah, K.A. In My Father's House, New York, Alba House, 1965.

Arinze, F. Sacrifice in Ibo Religion, Ibadan, Ibadan University Press, 1970.

–: Answering God's Call, London, Geoffrey Chapman, 1983.

–: Living Our Faith. Lenten Pastorals 1971-1983, Onitsha, Tabansi Press, 1983.

Basden, G.T. Among the Ibos of Nigeria, London, Frank Crass, 1966.

Bastide, R. 'Religions africaines et Structures de civilisation', in Présence Africaine 66, 1968, 105-112.

Bujo, B. African Theology in its Social Context, Nairobi, St.Pauls, 1992.

–: 'Der afrikanische Ahnenkult und die christliche Verkündigung', in Zeitschrift für Missions und Religionswissenschaft 64, 1980, 293-306.

Busia, A.K. The Position of the Chief in the Modern Political System of Ashanti, Oxford, Oxford University Press, 1951.

Claridge, G.C. Wildbush Tribes of Tropical Africa, London, Longman, 1922.

Davidson, B. The African Genius, London, An Atlantic Monthly Press Book, 1969.

Ejizu, C.I. Igbo Ritual Symbol, Enugu, Fourth Dimension Publishers, 1986.

Ela, J.M. My Faith as an African, (trans. from French, Ma foi d'Africain, Edition Karthala, Paris, 1985), Pairman Brown and Susan Perry, Maryknoll, Orbis Books,   1988.

Frend, W.H.C. 'The Christian Period in Mediterranean Africa, c. AD 200 to 700', in The Cambridge History of Africa, vol.2. From c. 500 BC to AD 1050,   Cambridge, Cambridge University Press, 1978, 410-489.

Hastings, A. African Catholicism. Essays in Discovery, London, SCM, 1989.

Healey, J. A Fifth Gospel: In Search of Black African Values, London, SCM, 1981.

Heijke, J. 'Belief in Reincarnation in Africa', in Concilium 5, October 1993, 46-53.

Idowu, E.B. African Traditional Religion, London, SCM, 1970.

Kayode, J.O. and Dada, E.A., 'Religions in Nigeria', in Olaniyan, R., (ed.), Nigerian History and Culture, Ikeja, Longman, 1985, 233-252.

–: Olòdùmarè - God in Yoruba Belief, London, Longman, 1962.

Ikenga, R.O. Igbo Catholicism. Onitsha Connection 1967-1984, Onitsha, Africana-Fep Publishers, 1985.

Isichei, E. 'Ibo and Christian Beliefs: Some Aspects of theological Encounter', in African Affairs, vol.68, no.271, 1969, 121-134.

Jordan, J.P. Bishop Shanahan of Southern Nigeria, Dublin, Clonmore and Reynolds, 1949.

Meeting for African Collaboration (MAC), (a body acting within the Symposium of the Episcopal Conferences of African and Madagascar, SECAM), 'New Christian Movements in Africa and Madagascar', in Catholic International, vol.4, no.1, 1993, 28-36.

Maimela, S.S. 'Religion and Culture: Blessings or Curses?', in Journal of Black Theology in South Africa, vol.5, no.1, 1991, 1-15.

Mbiti, J.S. African Religions and Philosophy, London, Heinemann, 1976.

–: An Introduction to African Religion, London, Heinemann, 1975.

–: Bible and Theology in African Christianity, Nairobi, Oxford University Press, 1986.

–: Bible and Eschatology In An African Background. A Study of the Encounter between New Testament Theology and African Traditional Concepts, Nairobi, Oxford University Press, 1971.

–: (ed.), African and Asian Conrtibutions to Contemporary Theology, Switzerland, Celigny/Bossey, Ecumenical Institute/WCC, 1977.

Moila, M.P. 'The African Version of Christianity', in Journal of Black Theology in South Africa, vol.5, no.1, 1991, 33-39.

Nigerian Episcopal Conference, now Nigerian Catholic Bishops' Conference, Christianity has come not to destroy but to Fulfil, Pastoral Letter, 1960.

Nkrumah. K. Ghana, Edingburgh, T.Nelson and Sons, 1959.

Nyamiti, C. Christ as Our Ancestor, Gweru, Mambo Press, 1984.

–: 'African Tradition and the Christian God', Spearhead, no.49, n.d. 48-65.

Oduyoye, A.M. 'The Value of African Religious beliefs and Practices for Christian Theology', in Conférence Panafricaine des théologiens du Tiers-Monde, Accra, 17-23 December, 1977, 1-12.

Okafor, F.C. Africa at Crossroads, New York, Vantage Press, 1974.

Parrinder, G. West African Religion, London, Epworth Press, 1969.

Ray, C.B. 'Aladura Christianity: A Yoruba Religion', in the Journal of Religion in   Africa, vol.XXIII, Fasc.3, 1993, 266-291.
–: African Religions. Symbol, Ritual, and Community, New Jersey, Prentice-Hall, 1976.
Rattray, R.S. Ashanti Proverbs, Oxford, Oxford University Press, 1923.
Ravenscroft, A. 'Religious Language and Imagery in the Poetry of Okara, Soyinka, and Okigbo', in Journal of Religion in Africa, vol.XIX, Fasc.1, 1989, 15-29.
Ruch, E.A. and Anyanwu, K.C. African Philosophy, Rome, Catholic Book Agency, 1984.
Schebesta, P. Revisting my Pygmy Hosts, London, Longmans, 1936.
Smith, E.W. African Ideas of God, Edingburgh House, 1926.
Talbot, P.A. The Tribes of the Niger Delta, London, Oxford University Press, 1932.
Ubah, C.N. 'Religious change among the Igbos during the Colonial Period', Journal of Religion in Africa, vol.xviii, Fasc.1, 1988, 71-91.
Westermann, D. The African Today and Tomorrow, London, Longmans, 1949.
Zoa, J.B. 'Committed Christians Building a New Africa', in AFER, vol.8, no.2, 1966, 26-32.
Zuese, E.M. 'African Traditional Religion', in Abingdon Dictionary of Living Religions, 1981, 5-12.

V. OTHER SOURCES AND STUDIES

Allbery, C.R.C. Manichean Psalmbook, Part II (Manichean Manuscripts in the Chester Beatty Collection, vol.ii), 1938.
Althäus, P. The Theology of Martin Luther, Philadelphia, Fortress Press, 1966.
Angus, S. The Mystery Religions and Christianity, Edingburgh, n.d
Barth, K. Evangelical Theology. An Introduction, London, Collins, 1963.
–: Church Dogmatics, vol.I/1, Edingburgh, T & T Clark, 1956.
–: Church Dogmatics, II/1, Edingburgh, T & T Clark, 1957.
Baynes, N.H. 'The Hellenistic Civilization and East Rome', in Byzantine Studies and Other Essays, Boston, Faber and Faber, 1955, 447-501.
Bigg, C. The Christian Platonists of Alexandria, Oxford, Clarendon Press, 1968.

Boff, L. I Sacramenti della Vita, Roma, Edizioni Borla, 1985.

–: 'Sacrament of Marriage', in Michael Taylor (ed.), The Sacraments. Readings in Contemporary Sacramental Theology, New York, Alba House, 1981, 193-203.

Brown, P. Augustine of Hippo, London, Faber and Faber, 1967.

–: The Church and Unity, London, 1979.

Chauvet, L.M. Simbolo e Sacramento. Una rilettura sacramentale dell'Esistenza Cristiana, Torino, Elle Di Ci, 1990.

Congar, Y. The Revelation of God, New York, Herder & Herder, 1968.

–: La Liturgie après Vatican II, Paris, Cerf, 1967.

Crichton, J.D. Christian Celebration, The Mass, The Sacraments, The Prayer of the Church, London, Geoffrey Chapman, 1971.

Danneels, G. 'La Chiesa, Riconciliata e Riconciliatrice', in Commento All'Esortazione Apostolica, La Reconcilatio et Paenitentia, Città del Vaticano, Libreria Editirice Vaticana, 1985, 25-30.

Deferrari, R. Hugh of St.Victor on the Sacraments of the Christian Faith, Massachesetts, The Medieval Academy of America, 1951.

Der Meer, F.V. Augustine the Bishop, trans. Battershaw and Lamb, 1961.

Dulles, A. Models of Revelation, Maryknoll, Orbis Books, 1983.

–: 'Symbolism', in New Catholic Encyclopedia, vol.13, 861-863.

Geertz, C. Interpretation of Culture, New York, Basic Books, 1973.

Hughes, P.E. Theology of the English Reformers, London, Hodder and Stoughton, 1965.

Igwegbe, O.O.I. The Understanding of "Sacrament" in Contemporary Catholic and Protestant Theologies, Unpublished Licentiate Dissertation, Pontificia Università Urbaniana, 1992.

–: 'The Challenge of Religious Sects and the Future of Christianity', in NACATHS Journal of African Theology, vol.3, 1993, 65-74.

International Theological Commission, 'Some Current Questions in Eschatology', in The Irish Theological Quarterly (ITQ), vol.58, no.3, 1992, 209-243.

Lürker, M. Dizionario delle Immagini e dei Simboli Biblici, Milano, Edizioni Paoline, 1987.

Magnine, J.P. Pour une poétique de la foi: essai sur le mystere symbolique, Paris, Cerf, 1969.

Mitchell, N. 'Symbols are Actions, Not Objects', in Living Worship 13/2, 1977, 1-2.

Moltmann, J. Experiences of God, London, SCM, 1980.

Niebuhr, H.R. The Responsible Self, New York, Haper & Row, 1963.
Nolan, T.J. 'Do we still need the Sacraments?', in Michael Taylor (ed.), The Sacraments, 3-17.
Origen, In Rom. Comm.4,2.
Orsy, L. 'The Interpretation of Laws: New Variations on an Old Theme', in Art of Interpretation. Selected Studies on the Interpretation of Canon Law, Canon Law Society of America (CLSA), Washington D.C, 1982, 61-73.
Parente, P. Theologia Fundamentalis, Torino, Marietti, 1954.
Polanyi, M. and Prosch, H. Meaning, Chicago, University of Chicago Press, 1975.
Pourrat, P. Theology of the Sacraments, Freiburg, 1910
Ricoeur, P. Symbolism of Evil, Boston, Beacon, 1969.
Schillebeeckx, E. Interim Report on the Books Jesus and Christ, New York, Crossroad, 1981.
–: World and Church, London, Sheed & Ward, 1971.
Schineller, P. A Handbook on Inculturation, New York, Paulist Press, 1990.
Stein, M.R. 'Signs and Things: The Vita Heinrici IV Imperatoris And the Crisis of Interpretation in Twelfth Century History', in Traditio. Studies in Ancient and Medieval History, Thought and Religion, vol.xliii, 1987, 106-119.
Tillich, P. Dynamics of Faith, New York, Harper, 1957.
Tilloston, G. and K. Mid-Victorian Studies, London, 1965.
Thornton, L.S. The Common Life in the Body of Christ, 2nd edition, Westminster, Dacre Press, 1942.
Turner, W.V. The Ritual Process, U.S.A., Penguin, 1974.
Tylor, B.E. Primitive Culture: Research into the Development of Mythology, Philosophy, Religion, Language, and Custom, London, John Murray, 3rd edition, 1891.
Urban, W. Language and Reality, London, Allen & Unwin, 1939.
Vorgrimler, H. Sacramental Theology, Collegeville, The Liturgical Press, 1992.
Wicks, J. 'The Sacraments: A Catechism for Today', in Michael Taylor (ed.), The Sacraments, 19-29.
White, V. God and the Unconscious, Cleveland, Meridian Press, 1952.
Zadra, D. 'Symbol und Sakrament', in Christlicher Glaube inmoderner Gesellschaft 28, 1982, 88-121

TABLE OF CONTENTS

PART TWO: **NEWMAN'S SACRAMENTAL THEOLOGI-
           CAL THINKING
           POSITION AND EXPOSITION**

PART THREE: **EVALUATION OF NEWMAN'S SACRA-
MENTAL THEOLOGICAL THINKING
AND ITS RELEVANCE TO THE AFRICAN
CONTEXT**

Emmanuel Lartey / Daisy Nwachuku /
Kasonga wa Kasonga (Eds.)

The Church and Healing
Echoes from Africa

Frankfurt/M., Berlin, Bern, New York, Paris, Wien, 1994. 155 pp.
African Pastoral Studies. Edited by Daisy Nwachuku. Vol. 2
ISBN 3-631-47227-7   pb. DM 53.--*

Healing is central to any understanding of African Christianity. In this volume, the second in the *African Pastoral Studies* series offered by the African Association for Pastoral Studies and Counselling (AAPSC), African Christian theologians and health care professionals present studies of different aspects of the quest for health and wholeness in Africa today. Aspects of psychotherapy, traditional medicine, ritual and symbol systems as well as healing communities encountered within the sub-Saharan African sub-region are explored. Experiences from Francophone as well as Anglophone Africa inform the studies. Christian perspectives on spirituality and wholeness as perceived through African eyes are offered in response to and as a challenge for the Church in Africa.

Contents: Counselling and spirituality for healing and liberation · Communities and African Christian "palaver" · Rituals and symbols in healing infertility in Nigeria · Curses, offenses and mental health · Psychosocial approaches to HIV and AIDS · Pain, headache and humanitarian psychiatry in Zaire · African and Christian perspectives on wholeness

Peter Lang **Europäischer Verlag der Wissenschaften**
Frankfurt a.M. • Berlin • Bern • New York • Paris • Wien
Auslieferung: Verlag Peter Lang AG, Jupiterstr. 15, CH-3000 Bern 15
Telefon (004131) 9402121, Telefax (004131) 9402131
- Preisänderungen vorbehalten - *inklusive Mehrwertsteuer

DATE DUE